D0759471

International
Library of the
Philosophy of
Education

**Preface to the
philosophy of
education**

International
Library of the
Philosophy of
Education

General Editor

R. S. Peters
**Professor of Philosophy of Education
Institute of Education
University of London**

# Preface
# to the philosophy
# of education

John Wilson

Department of Educational Studies,
Oxford University

Routledge & Kegan Paul

London, Boston and Henley

First published in 1979
by Routledge & Kegan Paul Ltd
39 Store Street,
London WC1E 7DD,
Broadway House,
Newtown Road,
Henley-on-Thames,
Oxon RG9 1EN and
9 Park Street,
Boston, Mass. 02108, USA
Set in Baskerville
and printed and bound in Great Britain by
Unwin Bros. Old Woking, Surrey
© John Wilson, 1979
No part of this book may be reproduced in
any form without permission from the
publisher, except for the quotation of brief
passages in criticism

British Library Cataloguing in Publication Data

Wilson, John, b. 1928

Preface to the philosophy of education
—(International library of the philosophy
of education)
1. Education—Philosophy
I. Title II. Series
370.1      LB17        79-40329

ISBN 0 7100 0283 1

# Contents

# General editor's note

There is a growing interest in philosophy of education amongst students of philosophy as well as amongst those who are more specifically and practically concerned with educational problems. Philosophers, of course, from the time of Plato onwards, have taken an interest in education and have dealt with education in the context of wider concerns about knowledge and the good life. But it is only quite recently in this country that philosophy of education has come to be conceived of as a specific branch of philosophy like the philosophy of science or political philosophy.

To call philosophy of education a specific branch of philosophy is not, however, to suggest that it is a distinct branch in the sense that it could exist apart from established branches of philosophy such as epistemology, ethics, and philosophy of mind. It would be more appropriate to conceive of it as drawing on established branches of philosophy and bringing them together in ways which are relevant to educational issues. In this respect the analogy with political philosophy would be a good one. Thus use can often be made of work that already exists in philosophy. In tackling, for instance, issues such as the rights of parents and children, punishment in schools, and the authority of the teacher, it is possible to draw on and develop work already done by philosophers on 'rights', 'punishment', and 'authority'. In other cases, however, no systematic work exists in the relevant branches of philosophy – e.g. on concepts such as 'education', 'teaching', 'learning', 'indoctrination'. So philosophers of education have had to break new ground – in these cases in the philosophy of mind. Work on educational issues can also bring to life and throw new light on long-standing problems in philosophy. Concentration, for instance, on the particular predicament of children can throw new light on problems of punishment and responsibility. G. E. Moore's old worries about what sorts of things are good in themselves can be brought to life by urgent questions about the justification of the curriculum in schools.

There is a danger in philosophy of education, as in any other applied field, of polarization to one of two extremes. The work could be practically relevant but philosophically feeble; or it could be philosophically sophisticated but remote from practical problems. The aim of the new International Library of the Philosophy of Education is to build up a body of fundamental work in this area which is both practically relevant and philosophically competent. For unless it achieves both types of objective it will fail to satisfy those for whom it is intended and fall short of the conception of philosophy of education which the International Library is meant to embody.

Mr Wilson calls his book *Preface to the Philosophy of Education*, but it is in fact a sizeable and controversial contribution to it. The concept of 'education' has always presented a problem to philosophers of education. Some have implicitly written their ideology into it; others have more or less equated it with upbringing; others have held that it is an 'essentially contested' concept which will always reflect the ideology of the society or group using it. Mr Wilson, by contrast, thinks it possible to derive many important principles from conceptual arguments to do with the form that the enterprise of education must have.

He also claims to show that, despite the particular demands of time and place, certain sorts of educational content – certain things that ought to be learned – have permanent and universal applicability to man as such. Some of these are connected with his analysis of what it is to learn something; and towards the end of the book this point is related to certain general and inexpellable features of the human condition, which suggest the supreme importance of seriousness and learning to love for any non-trivial and well-considered educational system.

This is an interesting book which combines readability with detailed argumentation. If Mr Wilson's thesis is tenable it should prove an important contribution to the philosophy of education.

R.S.P.

# Preface

The nature of this book, and the need for it, are both explained in the Introduction which follows; here I wish only to make one or two brief explanations and apologies.

The first concerns audience and style. The book is intended as a preface or introduction to the philosophy of education; but if one believes, as I do, that we do not yet have a clear idea of how to pursue this subject, there can be no question of trying to simplify an existing corpus of philosophical knowledge for the benefit of beginners. There is no such corpus, and we are all beginners. I have therefore tried to write simply and clearly enough for those who do not have much philosophical sophistication, without being tedious to those who do. This procedure obviously involves a good deal of compromise, and some may find certain passages either difficult or laborious.

An apology is also owed to those philosophers who have done so much for the subject over the last decade or so. I have in mind particularly Professor Peters, Professor Hirst and some others, whose work has at least given us something serious and worth debating, and continues to exercise a vast influence in the UK and many other countries. I have in fact quoted and criticized certain passages in the course of my argument without filling out the background of what they believe (or then believed), and without trying to keep completely up to date on their revised opinions. This must create at least the appearance of some injustice, and I can only plead that to analyse their views in full detail would require a whole book in itself, and a different sort of book.

Finally, in acknowledging with gratitude the help and advice received from many critics (too many to mention individually), I must apologize to at least some of them if I seem not to have incorporated their remarks into the text of this book. Part of the difficulty is that, in this field, different pieces of advice tend to be diametrically opposite: another symptom of the confused state of the subject. I must, however, express my particular indebtedness to Richard Peters for his most helpful comments; if I have failed to do justice to them all, it is partly because this would have unduly extended a book that is already long enough. I also owe thanks to the Philosophy of Education Society of the USA for permission to reprint, in a revised form, some of the material which now appears in chapter 1.

J.B.W.

# Introduction
# Philosophy and
# education

'Philosophy of education' is a name for nothing clear; but despite this there seem already to be two bodies of opinion, or at least general attitudes, one or the other of which the phrase can be relied on to evoke. The first is roughly to the effect that we should not pretend to a genuine subject with this title: that any such supposed subject is a non-starter: and that, though no doubt there are ways in which philosophy and education can and should be related to each other, we ought rather to speak of 'philosophy in education', or 'philosophy for educators', or something along those lines. The second view may rather be induced from existing institutions connected with the subject than from any very clear and accurate account of its nature; the fact that there are professors and students of it, degrees and diplomas in it, and well-attended societies for its promotion, might be taken to suggest that many people regard the subject as satisfactorily established already.

I reject both of these views, ultimately for the same reason. Both assume that we are clear enough about what education is and what it involves either to know that 'the philosophy of education' is a non-subject, or to know that the subject as now institutionalized is reasonably satisfactory. This assumption seems to me demonstrably false; and I take the opposing views that there is, in principle, a *sui generis* subject or area of philosophical enquiry properly to be entitled 'the philosophy of education', which can and ought to be pursued: and that, despite a good deal of useful work by philosophers of education, we have not yet come very near even to identifying that subject, let alone pursuing it effectively.

This is not to deny the importance of relating philosophy to education in other ways; indeed I have myself often tried to do so elsewhere. But as the multiplicity of rubrics ('philosophy in education', 'philosophy for educators', etc.) may suggest, there are a number of very *different* tasks to which this idea may lead us; and in trying to sort these out, we find it difficult or impossible to specify any of them properly without *some* clearer notion of what is to count as 'education' ('an educational problem', 'an educator', etc.).

Consider three different areas which can at least be mentioned both as being reasonably distinct from each other, and as calling for a good deal more detailed work:

1 There is first the question of what philosophy is needed by individuals who are intending to do practical jobs in education: teachers, administrators, educational psychologists, and so on. But (a) these jobs are very various, so that we can expect no single answer to the question; and, more radically, (b) without some prior concept of education we should not know what people to include. Arguably, for instance, not only parents but also parsons, policemen, psychotherapists, social workers and many others are engaged in educating as much as (or even, given some schools as they are today, more than) many teachers.

One might still say 'Yes, but as teachers (administrators, etc.) they are in fact going to meet certain kinds of practical situations and not others, and we should prepare them for these'; but there are difficulties even here. First, it is not conceptually or even empirically obvious that the best way of preparing somebody for dealing with certain problems is specifically to rehearse *those* problems with him beforehand. It might be (as I should myself claim) that by far the most important job for philosophy here was a very general one; that student-teachers should learn to express themselves clearly and precisely, be able (and willing, an obvious but in practice much-neglected point) to detect nonsense, employ linguistic clarity as a defence against their own and other people's fantasies, grasp what a conceptual question was and what sort of treatment it required, identify such questions in practice, and so on; and that, while obviously their educational interests *might* offer good material for this sort of training, it was an open question what actual topics would be best for the purpose. Perhaps the selection of topics is not very important; we might do better if we aimed more generally at asking them to criticize various passages, discuss intelligently, take an interest in words and meanings for their own sake, and use the English language properly. Or perhaps the most stimulating topics – if 'stimulating' suggests the most important criterion of selection, which is doubtful – might not be to do with education at all, but rather with some of their own personal beliefs and problems. In other words, their chief need might be for something far too general to be called anything except 'philosophy'.

Second, many of the situations they meet will not be, or could certainly be argued not to be, *educational* situations in any reasonable sense of the word, but might rather fall under the headings of politics, or economics, or public relations. If we are somewhat less naive in talking about the 'practical situations' that students are 'likely to meet', we may remind ourselves that a good deal of the preparation of teachers is bound to be a matter of getting them to *perceive* certain 'situations' in the first place: to use certain descriptions and grasp certain problems when these are not always forced upon them. If this is so, a question arises about what situations *ought* to be thus perceived: what they should, as rational beings, attend to (rather than what they need to attend to merely for survival and progress in their jobs, or for giving service within an uncritically accepted institutional structure). Conversely, many 'situations' which we took for granted as in some sense 'forced' upon teachers ought perhaps *not* to be, or ought *not* to form part of a teacher's job; and we might not wish to endorse existing practices by preparing teachers to meet them uncritically – particularly if such practices may shortly disappear. There are reasons, as I have argued elsewhere[1], for hanging on fairly tightly to what is *necessarily* (rather than contingently) part of 'being a teacher' as the core of our preparation. But, clearly, all this raises the question of what things are of real importance – if not *sub specie aeternitatis*, at least not wholly in terms of some particular society in the late twentieth century: and of what descriptions to use for these things. 'Education' is clearly a strong candidate for one such description, and it is difficult to see how one could seriously consider this problem without reaching some conclusions about education – and hence about 'philosophy of education'. Those conclusions might bear very strongly on the importance we had earlier attached to the general idea of philosophical training which was going to be of actual use to intending teachers.

2 Again, philosophy is obviously much needed in two other areas, which may overlap with what is needed by practical educators but which are certainly not co-extensive with it: the areas of (a) the study of education, and (b) educational research; 'philosophy in education' (*sc.* the study of education) might be a fair title for this. But it is surely clear that any philosopher who took either of these areas seriously – I mean, who wanted to do rather more than make an occasional conceptual point about whatever was under discussion – would need at some stage (and surely, at an early stage) to be clear about what was to *count as* 'the study of education' or 'educational research'; and this might lead to some rather radical conclusions, or at least conclusions which cast doubt upon a good deal of current practice.

The same point emerges when the philosopher has to consider just *what* problems, or areas, or concepts he should pay attention to in the study of education. Thus some candidates crop up frequently and specifically (sometimes uniquely) in educational literature: for instance, 'autonomy', 'creativity', 'integration', 'comprehensive',

3

'divergent thinking', and so on. But as this (admittedly preselected) set of examples shows, one might have grave doubts about whether many of these notions were *worth* serious philosophical examination. Many might be thrown up by mere fashion; it might be, for instance, that in a few years' time 'creativity' will have passed out of use, and educators will be content to talk only of 'imagination' or 'originality'. Other candidates might have a more permanent appearance – 'equality', 'punishment', 'discipline', etc.; but at once the thought arises that many of these do not seem very good candidates for philosophy in any sort of specific relationship to *education*: these examples, for instance, might be thought more naturally to come under political or moral philosophy, just as others might more naturally count as part of the philosophy of mind or epistemology.

3 The task just described would thus lead the philosopher to another connected but rather different task, which one might initially be tempted to describe as the *methodology* of education. 'Education' in this context again entitles a subject of study: the task is to determine how this subject may be effectively studied, or how the study should be viewed and organized. Some plausible parallels here might be 'social welfare', 'mental health', 'youth work' and 'town planning' (or 'the environment'). All these name practical enterprises, aiming at rather general and ill-defined goods; and the study of each, plainly required because we want the practical enterprises themselves to be more effective, involves putting together a number of very different considerations, many of them directly philosophical.

'Methodology' is not a very good word for the task I am talking about; for in many contexts it is used to refer to down-to-earth (though important) procedures within a single discipline: to highly particularized 'research techniques' and so on. But in 'interdisciplinary' enterprises, of which the study of education is certainly one, there are a great many problems at a more fundamental level. How much of the work is conceptual and how much empirical? What sort of psychology do we need for it? How do theory and practice relate to each other? In a word, how are we to *do* this subject? Just what *is* the study of 'education' ('mental health', etc.) and how are we to engage in it? These questions are clearly more general than questions about particular topics *in* (the study of) education and educational research, of the kind described in (2) above; and initially, at least, they usually involve philosophical questions of one kind or another.[2]

Might we not call this 'philosophy of education' ('education', we remember, being here the title of a theoretical enquiry), on the analogy with 'philosophy of science', 'mathematics', 'history', and so on? I think not, because of two difficulties. First, 'education' can also entitle – indeed, more usually entitles – a *practical* enterprise, and we might prefer to use 'philosophy of education' for the philosophy of this enterprise, more on the analogy with 'philosophy of law' or 'philosophy of religion'. Secondly, theoretical enquiries such as science, mathematics and history are today reasonably clear intellectual enterprises, consisting (to put it roughly) of a single discipline with a respectable history of solid results tucked under its belt. Hence we know, more or less, what 'the philosophy of' any of these is in fact philosophy *of*; the subjects are on the intellectual map, reputable in themselves and coherent at least in their broad outlines. This is not true of education as a subject of study, just as it is not true of 'social welfare', 'mental health' and others. When one tries in practice to make sense of 'education' as a subject, it becomes clear that very general questions of procedure have to be raised right at the start: questions which might just as well be classified under 'common sense' as under 'philosophy'. We have to ask, in the broadest possible way, how we are to *make sense* of education as a subject: what sort of people, under what sort of conditions, we need to pursue it: what kind of results we can look for: and so forth. If and when we achieve some clarity at this level, an enormous amount will still remain to be done, more easily to be chopped up under 'philosophy', 'sociology', and so on. But at the present time 'philosophy' is too specific – one might say, too misleadingly high-minded – a term to use for this task: just as 'methodology' is too misleadingly pedestrian for it.

This does not, of course, imply that philosophers who are interested in education should not see this task to be important: as important, in its own way, as those described under (1) and (2) above. 'Philosophy for education' (*sc.* the study of education) might perhaps be a not too misleading title for it. But it is clear, in any case, that until we know what education *is* – what the practical enterprise is *about* – we shall not make much progress.

Can anything more positive be said about what 'philosophy of education' could be? It seems initially plausible to say that, if we are prepared to take the phrase seriously at all, we might fairly regard it as parallel to 'philosophy of law', 'religion', 'art', and perhaps some other cases. At least it is clear that we should not want to take it as wholly parallel to (1) 'the philosophy of Rousseau' ('the nineteenth century', 'classical Greece', etc.), or (2) 'the philosophy of the Labour movement' ('comprehensive schooling', 'the Montessori system', etc.). In these (heterogeneous) examples, we are surely right to feel that the 'of', or the 'philosophy', or

5

perhaps the conjoined 'philosophy of', has the wrong sort of sense. In (1), we might translate along the lines of 'the philosophical work produced by', or 'opinions held in': in (2), 'the general or most important values and beliefs lying behind', or 'inherent in'. In rejecting these parallels we would not, of course, want to be interpreted as claiming that (1) what Rousseau said about education, or (2) what ideas lay behind 'comprehensive schooling', were either unworthy of philosophical attention or had nothing to do with education. We should rather be claiming, at the very least, that 'philosophy of education' meant more than this: just as more would be meant by 'philosophy of religion' than (1) the philosophy of Aquinas, Hume and others, and (2) the philosophy of the oecumenical movement, 'worker priests', etc.; and more by 'the philosophy of art' (or 'aesthetics') than (1) the philosophy of Lessing and Coleridge, and (2) the philosophy of impressionist or neo-vorticist painting.

If we now ask 'But *what* more should "philosophy of education" be?' we should cling to the parallel with 'philosophy of law' ('religion', etc.) by claiming that 'the philosophy of X' should involve at least some *general* or *overall* consideration of X. We want to know what is, or what should count as, or what is the general nature of, 'law', 'science', 'art', and so forth. To say this does not commit us to some specific philosophical doctrine or procedure: it commits us simply to the idea that 'the philosophy of religion', for instance, should at least in part consist of an attempt to get clear, and say something both general and important (as well as 'philosophical'), about whatever we are to mark by 'religion'. We might feel all the more confident in suggesting this because, in practice, many 'philosophers of' X (law, religion, art, etc.) do spend quite a lot of time on it.

Somebody might say: 'This is all very well, but are there to be "philosophies of" *every* human enterprise? What about enterprises devoted to whatever goods may be sought under the headings of "mental health", or "social welfare", or "economics"? What about more down-to-earth cases like vine-pruning or fishmongering or being an air hostess? Or hopelessly vague cases like "personal relationships", or "the environment"? There are already courses, in some universities hitherto thought respectable, entitled "philosophy of feminism", "philosophy of Black Achievement", "philosophy of salesmanship" and so on – aren't we just opening the door to the usual pressures of fashion and politics?'

This is difficult to answer briefly, because the reasons which disqualify many of the examples are different. There is, first, the point that some enterprises in themselves simply do not give rise to many or any philosophical problems. Vine-pruning, fishmongering and being an air hostess have their problems, but not philosophical ones. The point is not well put here by saying that these activities are essentially practical; morality and politics are practical activities if anything is, but also give rise to philosophical problems if anything does. We should say rather that, while one can imagine philosophical problems arising for, say, a teetotal vine-pruner, a vegetarian fishmonger, or a puritanical air hostess, the problems are not uniquely connected to the enterprises. We see vine-pruning as just one situation in which teetotallers might want to stop and think (others being bar-tending, or hop-picking, or perhaps even bottle-making); and even these we might want to put together with, say, fox-hunting or joining the army and count as one class of cases ('associating with a practice contrary to one's moral principles', or whatever) which needs philosophical inspection in general. Education, however (like science, religion, art and other enterprises which it is strategically sensible to count as *sui generis*), is not in this position. I shall argue that it is sufficiently general, sufficiently disconnected from other human enterprises, and sufficiently permanent to have a philosophical problem of its own.

Second, there are undoubtedly cases where philosophical problems of a fairly recognizable kind would stem from a title without too much forcing or distortion, and where (for quite pragmatic reasons) one might still want to keep the title as a focus of interest. For instance, it is not absurd to start with 'feminism' or 'the position of women' as an area of interest, from which one might be led to philosophize about the concept of a person, or of equality, or of a social role; or about how, if at all, one could make sense of the supposed evidence produced by Freudian psychoanalysts, and distinguish this from evidence of 'social conditioning' (whatever that may mean). All this would still enable us to say that we were interested in the original title ('the position of women', or whatever) in a way that we should not, after some initial discussion, be able to say that we were still interested in *vine-pruning* as such. Nevertheless, it is at least still conceivable that we should stop being worried about the position of women, or about the blacks, or about air hostesses, because our worries clearly depend to some extent on (different kinds of) contingent facts. Aeroplanes may become obsolete; human beings may all take on a uniform colour or become colour-blind; one may even cease to *mind* very much about whether one is a woman or not. But this again is not, in my submission, true of education.

Third, it is far from absurd to suggest that some enterprises *may* need 'philosophies of' them, where none now exist. To make such a suggestion is really only to say that a proper categorization of certain rather general human enterprises is largely lacking at the present time (if it ever was not), and obviously important. We have the *words* – 'mental health', 'social welfare', 'penal reform', 'environmental problems', and so on – and we also have large sums of money and powerful institutions attached to these titles. What we do not have is an adequate taxonomy which distinguishes goods, goods which at present (one might guess) often overlap or are overlooked. One might start by asking questions like 'What is it to be "mentally healthy"?', 'What specific aims does the social welfare worker have in mind?', 'What are we going to count as an "environmental" problem?', and so on, hoping eventually to get a bit clearer about the different sorts of things we are trying to do. Now one might think, that rather as with 'the position of women', these and other cases would reduce themselves to the status of 'areas of interest': that is, areas which 'drew on established branches of philosophy' (see below) (as usual, moral philosophy, political philosophy, epistemology and philosophy of mind)'. But I do not think that we can regard this as certain: an enterprise might emerge as something genuinely *new*, or at least as something seen for the first time to have the importance – philosophical as well as practical – which it does have. What we now call 'science' would be a fair example.

It may still be said 'Even if we had a rather firmer and more specific picture of "education", surely all the problems that "philosophers of education" will actually want to discuss cannot help but lead them back (and pretty quickly too) to traditional areas of "pure" philosophy. So "philosophy of education" will still be something derived or *ad hoc*.' This seems to be the view even of philosophers who have done a great deal to put the subject on the map. Thus Peters writes:

> To claim, however, that philosophy of education is and should be a branch of philosophy is not to suggest that it is a distinct branch in the same [?] sense that it could exist apart from established branches of philosophy such as epistemology, ethics, and philosophy of mind. Rather it draws on such established branches of philosophy and brings them together in ways which are relevant to educational issues. In this respect it is very much like political philosophy.[3]

But there are a number of reasons why this might be challenged. First, it is parochial: what is to count as an 'established branch of philosophy'? If we use the criterion of what is, so to speak, institutionally established, then we have to grant that this varies from one

8

culture to another. Plato's and Aristotle's classification was different from ours, as Peters' example of 'political philosophy' glaringly shows; and if someone were to argue that this was *just* a matter of their meaning something different by *politikē* from what we mean by 'politics', the obvious reply is that such differences themselves represent a different classification – it is *not* that we stress the same differences as Plato but just use different verbal markers for them. In any case, 'philosophy of education' might itself be regarded as in *that* sense 'established': that is, there are plenty of institutions (syllabuses, lecturers, examination papers, etc.) which have been operating for some time, and likely to go on operating, a 'branch of philosophy' with that title.

Of course we may (and should) be dissatisfied with using this criterion and seek for a better one; but this is equally true of other branches. It is hardly possible to think that we know, or are even agreed, what 'moral philosophy' or 'political philosophy' should be *about*; though it is (I suppose) possible to think that this does not matter much, at least for some purposes. These and other 'established' branches are not (yet) established by the application of purely logical demarcations or some obviously sensible taxonomic principles. Some even seem to think that this is in principle impossible, roughly on the grounds that such categorizations themselves must depend in some degree on one's 'value-judgments' or 'ultimate positions'. I do not myself think this to be a clear or coherent position, let alone a proven one, in the case either of education or other areas. But even if it were granted, it would provide no *more* of an argument against philosophy of education than against these 'established' branches.

Second, it is in fact very difficult to understand what is *meant* by 'distinct branches' of philosophy, or by the 'branch' of philosophy of education 'drawing on' them: as perhaps the confused metaphors suggest. Philosophers have always been concerned with a number of very general problems or problem-areas, in themselves difficult to classify, and a great deal of philosophizing tends to lead back to one or more of these; this is no doubt true of philosophy of education, but not only of it. There is a sense in which one might say (or, more likely, have said a few decades ago) that many problems 'led back to' or even could be 'reduced to' questions about language, or meaning, or methodology, or logic, or something along those lines; rather as it has sometimes been said that various branches of science could be 'reduced to' physics or a combination of physics and mathematics. But even if these ideas could be made clear, and then shown to be true, it is hard to see how they could have a unique application to philosophy of education.

9

In so far as these brief and scattered points yield any conclusions, they are negative but important. In short:

1 We are *not* clear what may properly fall under the heading of 'education'; and

2 We are *not* clear what would properly count as an 'established' or respectably *sui generis* branch of philosophy.

Either of these truths would, in my judgment, make it unwise to claim that philosophy of education (in the required sense) is a non-starter; in conjunction, they make any such claim absurd, if only because largely unintelligible. Naturally this goes no way to show that there is, or even perhaps that there could be, a respectable subject with that title; or to show what such a subject would consist of. That can only be done by trying, not just to make *some* sort of philosophical contribution to education, but to explore the possibilities of such a subject, and at least to identify the subject-matter and some of the central problems.

Some may suppose that the answers to this enquiry must already be obvious; others that there are different answers, none of which have any special claim to priority (perhaps on the grounds that 'the concept' of education is 'contestable', whatever that may mean (see p. 34)). These views seem to me mistaken: I shall try to show that there is an enterprise marked by the term which is of permanent and inalienable importance to all rational creatures. It may then become clearer, partly at that point and partly as we proceed in later chapters, in what way and to what extent the 'philosophy of' this enterprise is either possible or necessary. My suggestion is that the ground which ought to be covered by 'philosophy of education' has nearly always been misunderstood; and this misunderstanding is, in turn, due to certain systematic errors in thinking about education, errors which are as characteristic of first-rate philosophers from Plato to Russell as of anybody else.

This situation can only be put right by trying to be clear about a few basic concepts, principles, categories and questions which form the skeleton of the subject. Even this initial task is very onerous, and it would be absurd to attempt more than a preface or prolegomenon: hence my title. The business of delimiting the outline and identifying the main questions in the philosophy of education may not appeal to those who are anxious to get down to what are often called 'substantive' issues in education, or matters of 'content' rather than of 'form'; but it seems to me an essential first step, and one which has not yet been properly taken. Philosophers hitherto have characteristically adopted partisan positions of a moral, political or ideological kind, and distorted the area of education to fit these positions. In other words, there has been insufficient incentive to investigate education in its own right. This fault appears first in Plato; and it is a matter of deep regret that much of what Aristotle wrote on education is lost to us. (Perhaps, if it had not been, the subsequent history of the subject would have been less depressing.)

In the first two chapters of this book I shall try to give a correct and fairly detailed delimitation of the enterprise marked by 'education', 'educate', etc. (chapter 1), together with some account of the common mistakes made in relation to this enterprise, and the kind of philosophical ground that may be gained by a more just consideration of it (chapter 2). I shall then try to say something about some of the central or major questions which seem to follow from the delimitation. There are, as I see it, four main areas where these questions are to be located. I do not claim, though I feel fairly confident, that these represent *the*, rather than just some, major or central issues; and I do not feel at all confident that they should all be tackled in the order in which I give them (or, indeed, that there is one right order). But they do seem to form the core, or part of the core, of anything seriously to be described as 'philosophy of education', at least in that (1) they arise fairly obviously and immediately from the delimitation of education given already, and (2) they are very general questions, such that it would not be possible to maintain that they are primarily empirical. They are, briefly, as follows:

1 First (chapters 3 and 4), and this must surely come first, there are questions about learning, which figures prominently in the delimitation of the enterprise. What is it to learn something, and what sorts of things are there to learn? This seems an essential preliminary to any questions about what *ought* to be learned, questions about which the philosopher may have something to say, but which may in any case look very different (and, one might hope, very much easier to tackle) if we can establish some conceptual clarity, and some effective sets of categories, in regard to what *can* be learned.

2 Second (chapter 5), what is the enterprise *worth*? Can anything be said generally about the sort of goods it aims at, and how these goods compare with other goods in life? Can we establish some criterion by which to judge *how much* education a man needs, or to what extent we should devote time, money and effort to this enterprise as against others?

3 Third (chapter 6), since the enterprise is concerned with serious and coherent learning, is there some *general* or overall virtue (or quality, or state of mind) which is particularly relevant here? What is it to be a *serious* learner? What are the obstacles to serious learning? How (again very generally) do we get people to be *good at* the enterprise?

4 Finally (chapter 7), in the light of (1), (2) and (3) immediately above, can anything general be said about *what* people should learn, and what sort of background (context, methods, techniques) we need in order to get them to learn it? Are there some things, or is there some one thing, which can reasonably be given priority?

These brief specifications are perhaps sufficient to show something of the natural, if largely unformulated, interest that a serious student of the subject might have. A fair parallel, obviously inexact at some points, may be found in the domains of religion, law, art, and other human enterprises. Thus if we reached some such rough delimitation of religion as 'institutionalized or endorsed awe and worship', it would seem natural to regard our major enquiries as including (1) what it was to worship something, and what sorts of things there were (gods) that could in principle be worshipped: (2) what the particular importance of religion was, in comparison with other enterprises: (3) whether there was some virtue or state of mind especially relevant to the enterprise: and (4) whether there were some things, at least, which formed necessary or appropriate objects of worship.

It seems fair to say that modern philosophers of education have not, on the whole, advanced our understanding very much in these areas (and the same holds, incidentally, of their parallels in the case of religion). A certain amount has been said (1) about the nature of learning, though in most institutions concerned with the study of education the topic is usually made over to the psychologists; and various attempts, more or less plausible, have been made to categorize some of the things that can be learned. So far as (2) the worth or justification of learning is concerned, I cannot see that we have made much advance on what Plato and Aristotle have said; equally (3) not much has been done, since Plato and Aristotle, on the question of what constitutes a good or serious learner. Finally, (4) while plenty of philosophers and others have advertised a particular content for education, it is (to say the least) far from clear that their arguments for doing so are irrefutable.

Whatever the reasons for this (I suspect, as before, some premature attachment to a particular educational content), it seems important to make some kind of attempt on these areas; and I shall be more than happy if what I have to say inspires other philosophers to consider them more carefully. My main hope, however, is to demarcate the subject properly: and that must depend on an adequate account of education itself, to which we shall now turn.

# Education       part I

# The words and the enterprise

We shall start by being clear about the way in which the terms 'education', 'educate', 'educated', etc., are used in contemporary English: how else can we, as English-speakers, be sure that we know what we are talking about? This procedure has been demonstrated and explained by many philosophers from Socrates onwards, and I shall not argue for it at length here; partly because it is not clear what the status or value of any argument could be, if the participants were not already committed to the idea of mutual intelligibility. We need, at the least, an insurance policy against muddle or vagueness.

We may also gain rather more than this. If there is a single and coherent concept marked by these terms, then this concept may have what we might grandly call translinguistic or transcultural importance: that is, the terms may represent a general human interest, not just the interests of contemporary English-speakers. If that were so, we might expect to find similar demarcations in other natural languages: in those languages, at least, spoken by societies whose members had developed similar interests to our own. The importance of the concept would not, however, rest on this; even though linguistic demarcations of it might be lacking in some – or even all – languages, nevertheless they might still be needed. There might *be* a universal human interest which needed such markers, even though men had not *recognized* it and hence not marked it. I shall argue, later, that the terms are in fact marked in at least some other natural languages, and do in fact represent such an interest; but that is a separate enquiry, which must wait upon an adequate analysis of the terms themselves.

We should not be deterred from this task by *a priori* notions about the virtues and vices of 'linguistic analysis'. A certain impatience with this (for some) pedestrian business, coupled with fashionable (or recently fashionable) ideas going under such banners as 'family resemblances', 'multiple usage', or 'contestable concepts', tempts some to say, in advance, that consideration of how certain terms are used is unfruitful. The thought often seems to be that, once we have rid ourselves of the false idea that there is 'one true meaning' for the term – that there is some essence which it marks – then we can dispense with the obligation to sketch its limits of intelligibility. But that is a back-firing argument: it is particularly when such terms are ambiguous, or used in widely different ways, that we need to make such sketches and make them more carefully. Only somebody who believed that 'education' (or whatever term we have in mind) could be used in just *any way at all* could have reason for avoiding the task: but nobody believes this. So there are limits, and we have to find out what they are.[1]

Equally one does not have to believe in essences or single meanings to believe, what is quite different, that a great many terms at least can be seen to have more or less central or paradigmatic uses on the one hand, and more or less eccentric, peripheral, parasitic or metaphorical uses on the other. There are central uses of 'religion', despite the semi-metaphorical use of the adverb 'religiously': nor do such phrases as 'natural law', 'the law of the jungle', and 'a law unto himself' persuade us that there is no reasonably distinct phenomenon or set of phenomena which is represented by the way in which 'law' is normally or centrally used. Even the (by no means easy) question of determining by what criterion we are to distinguish between central and eccentric uses could hardly arise if we did not believe that some such distinction was possible.

Again, the idea (which perhaps underlies much of the contemporary opposition to this task) that 'nothing substantive' is gained by mapping out usage could only commend itself either to those who thought that the 'substantive' issues were already clearly expressed, or to those who thought that such clarity was unimportant. When 'substantive' pronouncements are made about education, it is, for instance, important to know whether the speaker has in mind (1) some transcendental enterprise whose criteria of identity are time-free, culture-free and value-free, (2) some particular educational ideal of his own or other people's, or (3) some particular educational system or set of practices – and these categories are not exhaustive. How could one proceed sensibly in any discussion without getting this much, at least, clear beforehand? It may be, indeed, that *some* issues in education can be discussed without undertaking this task at length, just because those discussing might tacitly share the same concept or range of meaning marked by 'education'; but can we even be sure *which* these are unless we ourselves are consciously clear?[2]

Loose talk about 'concepts' ('views', 'ideas', 'pictures', 'analyses', etc.) 'of education' makes it necessary to stress that we are concerned solely with how we – that is, contemporary English-speakers – normally use certain terms. The accuracy or inaccuracy of our account is tested only by what we would, or would not, normally say; and whatever else may properly be meant by 'we' or 'normally', I intend here at least to exclude contexts in which some word may have become a semi-technical term or a term of art. People who have axes to grind may do all sorts of things with words like 'education', as they have clearly done with the term 'curriculum';[3] and if there are a lot of such people, or if what they say is widely influential, it may appear that these words no longer have a normal use at all: as if they had abandoned any fixed abode and become irretrievably nomadic. But this appearance, at least with 'education' ('educate', etc.), is deceptive; these terms are in everyday use, outside the encampments of educational theorists and philosophers. It is this everyday use with which we are about to deal. One could, in fact, do a good deal worse than start with the *Oxford English Dictionary*, which speaks of 'systematic instruction, schooling or training' as a primary sense of 'education'; and for 'educate' gives 'to bring up (young persons) from childhood so as to form (their) habits, manners, intellectual and physical aptitudes: to instruct, provide schooling for.' This is substantially correct, though there are not a few implications to be elucidated and additions to be made.

1 'Education' and 'educate', in what I take to be their primary senses, mark a particular kind of human enterprise, a certain mode of activity directed towards producing certain kinds of results or goods: roughly, those goods gained in or by learning. In practice, this enterprise takes on visible forms: it is realized or institutionalized in some way or other, cast into particular moulds by particular men. This gives us a secondary sense, or senses, dependent upon the first but distinct from it, whereby 'education' and (though less commonly) 'educate' refer not to the timeless enterprise, but to one or another of the particular realizations or institutionalizations of it. Thus we may talk of 'an education', 'his (my, your, etc.) education', or 'a classical (liberal, etc.) education', in this second sense: whereas for the primary sense the addition of articles or possessive pronouns would be nonsensical – rather as 'his (my, etc.) philosophy' will only make sense if 'philosophy' is not the name of a general enterprise, or discipline, or subject. Even without these additions, however, we may say such things as 'Education is in an awful mess (very expensive, a political issue, etc.) nowadays'; we refer to a particular educational system, an instantiation of the enterprise.

I describe this second, 'institutional' sense as *dependent* on the first for the obvious reason that what institutions or instantiations are or should be called derives from what enterprises they pursue or are supposed to pursue. 'My education', 'a classical education', 'education in ancient Greece', etc., are particulars which partake in a general enterprise, the enterprise of education. If they did not, we should have no reason for talking of 'my education' rather than, say, 'my time at school'. This sort of secondary sense is tolerably well known in philosophy (some philosophers have described it as 'sociological'). There is justice, and British justice: morality, and Polynesian morality: religion, and the Christian religion: 'restoration', the art of restoring buildings, and 'a restoration'. These and other instantiations or practical cases do not all stand in the same relationship to their enterprises, and for this reason it is dangerous to rely on some one word for such relationships. No doubt this merits more philosophical attention. For our purposes, however, it will be sufficient to make the broad distinction, and in particular to distinguish these secondary senses from the primary sense with which we shall henceforth be (at least for the most part) concerned.

In their primary sense, 'educational' and 'educate' mark a rather general activity or *praxis*, not a specific performance or *poiesis*. There is no single fixed state which brings educating or being educated to an end, in the way that knowing one's tables brings to an end the performance of learning one's tables. Education stands to teaching or learning X rather as looking after a person's health stands to curing a particular disease: once X is taught or learned, or the disease cured, there is an end of it; but education and medical attention may continue. Again, one may teach or learn something quickly or slowly; but not educate quickly or slowly. When we speak of people as 'educated', 'uneducated', 'not having had much education', etc., we do not refer to an end-state reached in a certain time. A person's education may go on indefinitely. In the secondary sense, however, we may talk of completing one's education, of it taking a long time, and so on. Compare (a) the general idea of medical treatment or curing, (b) a particular course of treatment ('the treatment') and a particular 'cure' (e.g. at some spa): 'treatment' and 'cure' could be used in either sense.[4]

A third sense of use of 'education' needs to be added, connected with the first two and dependent on them: that is, roughly, its use as a *subject-title*, equivalent to 'the study of education'. One can, nowadays, take a degree or 'major in' education just as one can in mathematics or philosophy. With this sense also we shall not be very much concerned; it is, though, relevant to the question of what 'philosophy of education' might be, which has been discussed already.

2 The *kind* of things we do to children (and by extension, as the *OED* allows, to adults) under the title of 'education' are more

limited than those we can do under such titles as 'bringing up' or 'rearing'. Feeding a child may be part of the child's nurture, and ensuring his safety part of bringing him up; but neither is part of his education. The limit is set by the idea of the child's being, or becoming, a person with a mind: more specifically, by the idea of the child as a *learner*. Cases in which we 'form habits, manners, intellectual and physical aptitudes' by methods which did not involve learning would not be cases of education: for instance, surgical operations or chemicals might 'form', or at least help in forming, a child's physical or even mental abilities; but anyone who said that when operating on the child or giving him drugs we were educating him would not know much English. Hence the *OED* rightly uses such terms as 'instruct'. A further point, the implications of which carry a good deal of weight, is that education is tied to the notion of *human* learning: that is, the learning of those entities which we may here briefly describe as 'creatures with minds', 'rational creatures', or 'people'. These two points eliminate two swathes of phenomena: first, those not conceptually connected with the idea of learning at all – a child may develop, or change, or grow, or be improved in all sorts of ways without learning anything; and second, those which come under the concept of learning but not of human learning – we can teach animals, and they can learn: but they cannot be educated.[5]

3 To count as education, the learning must satisfy a condition difficult to describe with exactitude, but perhaps clarified to some extent by such phrases as 'above the level of nature', 'sophisticated', 'serious', or 'coherent'. What a child or adult picks up naturally for himself fails to satisfy this condition, even if what he picks up is very important – for instance, the learning of his mother-tongue at an early age. Clearly what is naturally picked up will vary from child to child, and society to society; and it may seem odd that the same content – for instance, learning to speak French – may form part of an English child's education, but would not count as part of the education of a French child who learns it informally. But that is how we speak: we reserve 'educate' and 'education' for learning above the level of nature. I do not deny that there are plenty of border-line cases where the criterion is difficult to apply with any certainty; but that does not make it invalid.

If the content of education has to satisfy this condition, it would not be surprising if the enterprise of educating had also a condition to satisfy: roughly, that it should be something undertaken intentionally or deliberately – for how else could people ensure that the content would be sufficiently above the level of nature? This involves some discussion of the links between education and (a) a certain kind of intention, (b) a certain kind of result; each could be regarded as either (i) a necessary or (ii) a sufficient condition for the application of the term. Questions of this kind have received a good deal of general discussion, but 'educate' and 'education' do not seem to fit very comfortably into most of the distinctions and categories which philosophers have set up.

One point at least seems fairly clear: that the intention alone is not sufficient. We talk, quite normally, of intending or trying to educate somebody but failing: that is, we may make the attempt of encouraging him to learn whatever it may be, but the attempt does not succeed because he does not in fact learn it. By the same token, *some* kind of result is necessary: that is, the person must engage successfully in some sort of serious learning. For, though the general enterprise of education does not move towards a final goal or definitive end-state, it nevertheless moves in a certain direction; we have to be assured that there *is* this movement – that some *progress* is being made – if we are to be assured that the enterprise is actually proceeding, that it is not just going on in the educator's head. We may say, then, that (a.ii) the intention is not sufficient, and (b.i) some kind of result is necessary.

Rather more difficult is the other linked pair (a.i) and (b.ii). It might be held that the result is sufficient, and hence that the intention is not necessary. This would take 'educate' as analogous to 'cure' rather than, say, 'treat' or 'give medical attention to'. A man can be cured by the operations of nature, or a sudden shock, or a miracle: why can we not say that he can be educated without any intention on anyone's part (even his own) to educate him? This suggestion does not depend on the fact that 'cure', unlike 'educate', looks to a specific end-state: for a man can be *being* cured by nature. In the same way, a man can be aesthetically improved ('beautified') by the work of a beautician; but this may also happen without any human intention – he changes climate and gets a sun-tan, or his digestion improves and his spots clear up, or whatever. Can we not use 'educate' in the same way? It will not do to say simply that 'educate' is a transitive verb; for this suggestion would still allow as genuine subjects of the verb such things as 'nature', 'life', 'the environment', and so on. Nor is it enough to say that, in practice, only human intentions would suffice to generate the serious and sophisticated learning – above the level of nature – that is required for education; for the fact is that children in certain favoured circumstances (e.g. in intellectual families) do learn a great deal without the benefit of human intention – without, at least, any intention to *educate* them. Is this not to be counted as part of their education?

Whatever the temptations to do so, I think we do not in fact count it. Consider again the case where child A naturally picks up, from a sophisticated family background, a good command of spoken English. Child B, just arrived from abroad, has to attend remedial English classes in order to obtain even a working knowledge of the language. It seems clear that, in fact, we do not say that A is being educated, and do say that B is. This conclusion is reinforced by the border-line case of an English-speaking child C, who goes abroad and lives with a French family for some years, thereby picking up the French language; whether or not we would count this as part of his education would, surely, depend on the background intentions. If his parents or tutors deliberately sent him there to learn French because they thought this important to him as a person, we should use 'educate': if the Foreign Office sent him there because French is useful for the role of diplomat, we should probably say that it was part of his training: if he just happened to be there without any background intention that he should learn, we might well say neither.

The result by itself, then, is not sufficient (b.ii); and the intention is necessary (a.i). It will be obvious that 'intention' here means 'intention to educate', not just any intention. The parents who speak English and play games with the child act intentionally; but this only counts as education when, and insofar as, the parents view what they do as contributing to the child's serious learning, and intend it as such. The viewing alone is not sufficient: it must be *meant as* so contributing – and however this phrase is to be explicated, one crucial test of whether they so meant it would be whether they were willing to modify it in the light of educational criteria. For instance, parents may enjoy talking and playing cricket: for this to count as education, they would not only (i) have to see it as a serious contribution to their child's learning, but also (ii) have to be willing to modify their conversation and cricket-playing so as to improve this learning.

I do not deny, of course, that there are uses which disregard the criterion of intentionality: particularly, perhaps, uses of the adjective 'educational'. The term has rather a contrived look about it, and is often used to mean not much more than 'promoting learning', without any implication that the learning is deliberately promoted; people talk nowadays about 'educational experiences', meaning only that they learned something from the situation. In the same sort of way there are remarks, often of an overtly daring or semi-paradoxical kind, such as 'To love her was a liberal education', which reflects the same move made with 'education' and 'educate'. But this move can fairly be described as an extension or development of the central usage. The difference between, say, an educational cruise and an ordinary cruise is that the former is specifically designed to promote learning; similarly, though a boy may learn more in the streets than at school, schools and not streets are educational institutions. The move is the same as, though less obviously dramatic than, saying that one was educated 'in the University of Life': nobody really thinks that life is a university, however much one may learn from it.

4 So far we have the picture of an enterprise concerned to promote human learning above the level of nature, deliberately conducted as such, and at least to some degree successful in its effects. What other conditions, if any, apply to this learning if it is to count as education? This is not at all an easy question: there is, I believe, a fairly clear answer to it, but to arrive at this answer depends upon following up a number of different clues.

One clue may perhaps lie in the *OED*'s insistence that the instruction be 'systematic', and its (admittedly rather odd) talk of bringing up children 'in preparation for the work of life'. The implication is that educating is a more *general* or *comprehensive* enterprise than what might be marked by such terms as 'teaching', 'instructing' or 'training'. Certainly there is something odd in saying that one was being educated from 10 to 10.30, if not in saying that one was educated for four years at Oxford; perhaps the enterprise is normally conceived as too general to operate effectively in a short time. Again, we should normally regard educating someone as a matter of teaching him a number of *different* things: perhaps as a matter of taking some overall view of what he needs to learn as a person, rather than merely to do some particular job or fill some particular social role.

This is reinforced by a second clue which has more obvious linguistic markers. So far from being tied to particular tasks or to a particular content, the grammar of 'educate' specifically rejects any such tie. It may seem a fine, but is certainly an important, point that we do not normally say 'educated *to*' (do or be such-and-such).[6] The ancient Persians were brought up to, and taught to, shoot straight and speak the truth: not educated to do these things. Nor, despite certain aberrant or loose uses ('education for twentieth-century man', and so on), can one educate a person *for* anything: 'What are you educating him for?' can only mean 'What are your reasons for educating him?', not 'For what particular job (task, role, etc.) are you educating him?' Again, one can bring somebody up as a gentleman (Catholic, etc.), and the 'as' here may have the force of 'to be'; but 'educated as a gentleman' more naturally means 'educated in the way befitting a gentleman'.

What lies behind these points of grammar? Of course the content of a man's education may be more or less suitable to his station in life, so that we should naturally choose such content with an eye on that station; nevertheless, when we educate a man we are not concentrating on just *one* good or set of goods in the way that, by training or upbringing, we may be trying to *make him into* a good teacher, or a good Catholic, or whatever. In the case of moral or political education, for instance, we should naturally have an eye on what sort of society the man will be a member of; and part of such education might reasonably involve giving him whatever facts and other mental equipment were necessary for surviving and playing a satisfactory part in that society. But if we are really going to *educate* him, even if we insist on using some such phrase as 'educate him as a citizen', we have to attend to some distinction between the need that the man should fill a particular role on the one hand, and some more general goods on the other.

One suggestion arising from this might be that, if a piece of learning is to count as education, it must be thought of as for the good of the learner, the person being educated, rather than for other goods – for instance, the desirability that social roles should be filled. If we have to educate people *qua* people, does this not indeed follow? No: there is a difference between saying that what is educated is always a person, and saying that the person must always be educated for his own good. Indeed in some areas of education – for instance, teaching a person to disregard his own interests in favour of other people's – the opposite seems to be true. The difference between, say, a trained teacher and an educated teacher is not to be explicated by saying that what the former learns is for the benefit of his pupils – so that the role of teacher can be better performed – whereas the latter learns things that benefit *him*; both sorts of learning may benefit him *and* his pupils. The difference, or one difference, is rather that the notion of education covers more ground, or takes more things into consideration, than the notion of training.[7] We have our eye on a wider range of goods: but not on the goods of anybody in particular.

Another suggestion is that it is a matter of what we take as our 'ultimate values', or of particular 'importance' (particularly 'worth while', 'valuable', etc.). This alleged connection of education with what is valued will need more discussion below (see p. 27). But even at this stage, it might plausibly be argued that the criterion of importance is more or less vacuous; does not the fact that certain kinds of learning *are* systematically and formally promoted by those responsible – that they are in the curriculum, for instance, or on the time-table – itself show that this learning *is* thought to be important? Certainly there is some fairly close conceptual tie between what a person thinks important and what, under normal circumstances, and if given the chance, he chooses to devote time and energy to: hence, on this interpretation, the suggestion is tantamount to saying that *any* kind of learning which educators concentrate on will count as education; and that, in turn, amounts to the view that there is *no* other criterion which we apply. As long as the learning is deliberately promoted and above the level of nature, that learning is part of a man's education.

But this account does not quite fit the linguistic facts. Those responsible – the school, or the parents, or the government, or whoever – may indeed say something like 'It is important that you should learn a trade, so we will make this *part of* your education', but they may also say 'It is important that you should learn a trade, so we will arrange this *as well as* educating you.' Not all those who send their daughters to secretarial colleges think that they are forwarding their education, however important they may think it that their daughters should learn secretarial skills. Still more obviously, in time of war it may be extremely important that our young men should learn to fly Spitfires; but we could, and in fact did, say that their education was being interrupted rather than extended or altered: though one could imagine a situation, as in ancient Sparta, in which some form of military training *was* counted as part of a young man's education.

What makes us say one thing rather than the other? Nothing is gained, and much obfuscated, by saying simply that it turns on what is 'valued', or what 'options' or 'ideologies' we choose to take up: as if the ancient Spartans cared a lot about survival but Britons in 1939 only a little. Different people do indeed take up different options; but our problem is to determine what it is to take up an option here. Certainly it is not just to 'value' some piece of learning and link it with the word 'education'. To count something as part of a man's education is not just to assign 'importance' to it; indeed, there could be certain elements in his education which were *not* regarded as particularly important – though that could not be generally or characteristically the case, for obvious reasons (roughly, because the enterprise would lack point). We may say, if we like, that it is to assign a certain *kind* of importance to it; but this still leaves us with the problem of what kind.

We have to say, I think, that we normally speak in the light of a *policy* (not 'ideology') which, as educators or people responsible for learning in general, we have already taken up. In order to form a policy at all, we usually survey the scene: we consider the needs and qualities of those we are going to educate, the demands of society, the particular pressures which apply to both individuals and society at the time, and so forth. Having surveyed it (and I do not deny that our own 'values' will affect both how we survey it and what policy we form), we reach some general if provisional conclusions about what people ought to, and can, be brought to learn. These conclusions cannot, on the one hand, be too disconnected from prevailing circumstances, otherwise they would be of little practical use; there would be no point in the Spartans saying that, ideally, the most important things for their citizens to learn were rhetoric and poetry, if in fact they would not survive to learn these things unless they first learned the martial arts. But, on the other hand, the conclusions cannot be too particularized or *ad hoc*, because this might not produce any policy at all: we cannot normally form a policy just for next Tuesday afternoon, and the enterprise of education requires some sort of semi-permanent content to be established.

We rely, in fact, on some idea of 'normal conditions' prevailing for a reasonably long stretch of time (perhaps in particular the life-times of those we educate), and form our policy in that light. Naturally these 'normal conditions' vary from one society and historical period to another, which is why the content of educational policies will not, and ought not to, be wholly constant; though we may expect that some things to be learned will remain more or less unchangeable. The border-line cases are often cases where we are not sure about changes in the conditions. If slide-rules and pocket computers are going to form part of our everyday lives, then perhaps knowledge of how to use this hardware should be viewed as a necessary part of everyone's education, and mental arithmetic as no more than a party trick. If we envisage ourselves as more or less permanently at war, like the Spartans, then military training will be counted as part of education: if not, as an interruption to it. In other words, we no doubt ascribe some sort of permanent or semi-permanent importance to the learning, if we are to incorporate it in our educational policy; but it is the actual incorporation which determines whether or not we count it as education.

Even to say this much may be going too far. In adult education we do not normally have the same scope, or amount of time, or power over the students that we have with children; so that, though we might still be said to have some kind of 'policy' about what the adults should learn (or have the chance of learning), the policy would not be formulated in such an overall or blue-print kind of way as our earlier remarks might be thought to imply. Nevertheless, what distinguishes the formal or semi-formal enterprise of adult *education* – and the usage is neither aberrant nor parasitic – from the mere teaching of a few tricks or skills or bits of knowledge to some adults is still the adoption of some general view, scheme, or policy in the light of which the educators would, at least, offer some courses rather than others.

Nothing, however, directly follows from this about the *content* of education. One might take all aspects of a person under consideration, but decide that some were of such importance as to merit spending all our time on them, and others so unimportant as to be reasonably dismissed. From the necessity of taking a comprehensive or overall viewpoint nothing follows about a 'general', 'liberal', or 'comprehensive' *content*; the idea of the 'all-round' man, of pupils needing some familiarity with all or most kinds of available knowledge (one of the sciences, at least one foreign language, and so forth) represents only *one* educational ideal. If the slogan 'Education is of the whole man' contains any truth, it lies in the point that we have to educate people *qua* people rather than *qua* role-fillers or just *ad hoc*: not in the idea that we have somehow to cater equally for every aspect of a person.

In other words, the fact that we educate people *qua* people is logically connected with the fact that to educate somebody is to arrange learning for him from a fairly comprehensive or overall point of view. If we are seriously considering a person's education, we take seriously the task of deciding what it is important for him to learn. The notion of 'what is important' is broad; we do not necessarily have to decide according to our 'ultimate values', or anything of that kind – it may be that the current problems of society, or the type of individual we are dealing with, or the availability of good teachers, or many other things, play a very large part in our decision. But we should at least entertain some such thought as 'Here is this particular person, placed as he is in this society; now, taking this overall view and before we start listing particular skills and bits of knowledge in an *ad hoc* way, what ought he to learn?'

If we did not have some such perspective, I do not think we could be regarded as seriously concerned with *educating that person*. Suppose, for instance, that parents or schools paid no attention to moral education or the education of character. They might, indeed, defend this in various ways; they might say, though implausibly, that morality was not important: or that it was not the sort of thing that could be learned: or that, though important, they simply had no time for it in view of some prevailing crisis of greater importance: or that, though in principle learnable, they had no idea at all about how it could be learned. What they could not say, I think, is that they were seriously trying to educate children, but did not need even to *consider* what, if anything, should be done about their moral education. This is why we would not normally regard the arranging for *ad hoc* or fragmentary bits of learning as enough for education; for the implication of such arrangements is that the arranger has not seriously considered the problem of what the person ought to learn in a sufficiently comprehensive way – that there are aspects of the person, *prima facie* of some importance, which have simply not been thought about.

5 Contrary to much current belief, 'education' and 'educate' are usually (to use one terminology) 'descriptive' and not 'prescriptive' terms, or (to use another) 'factual' rather than 'evaluative'. Whatever may be meant by saying this, we are at least able to disapprove of, or criticize, or even express horror and disgust at, various cases which are certainly cases of education, without any appearance of paradox or contradiction. There seem in fact to be at least three general ways in which we can criticize a person's being educated, or in which we might say that there was something bad or wrong about his education. Most obviously, we might say (a) that it had been conducted inefficiently or incompetently: that is, we might accept the general aims or content of what the man had to learn, but think that the methods or techniques by which he was taught it left a lot to be desired. But we might also think (b) that the man had learned the wrong things: that some of these things were not worth learning, being a waste of time or positively pernicious (learning to be a good torturer, for instance), or that there were other things which he ought to have had to learn but did not. Both (a) and (b) are criticisms within the enterprise of education, so to speak: the former on grounds of efficiency, the latter on the grounds that the content of the enterprise was wrongly specified. But there is also the criticism (c) that too much, or too little, scope had been given to the enterprise as a whole: that the man had been over- or under-educated. It is perhaps worth noting that we might say this (i) with only the man's individual good in mind (because he could not stand so much, or was badly deprived by getting so little, education), (ii) with an eye on the general good of our society or some wider group (*he* might profit from more education, but there is a more urgent need to spend the money on defence or medicine or whatever).

The term 'educated' requires a special mention, if only because it is used as a term of art by not a few philosophers. It should cause no trouble, being simply the past participle passive of the active verb 'to educate'; just as 'doctus' in Latin is the past participle of 'docere' ('to teach'), and can mean simply 'having been taught'. Unfortunately such participles tend to acquire extra accretions of meaning, different in different contexts; just as the Latin 'doctus' may alternatively, or additionally, bear the force of 'cultured', 'learned', or 'well read'. Because 'educate' marks a very broad notion – that is, the notion of *some* serious and coherent learning, but not specifying any particular content or result – the extra meaning packed into 'educated' is usually some additional specification of content or result: again, like 'doctus'.

The reason for singling out an additional specification is often, though not always, to commend it; hence 'educated' (in this use) is often, though not always, a term of commendation or praise. Terms do not, of course, commend *per se*: commendation is something that *men* do by (or in) their speech-acts and by other means (for instance, clapping). Jack Cade would have used 'educated' as a term of abuse (*Henry VI, Part 2*, IV, 2). Most people, however, particularly those who write books or whose voices are heard in society, prefer to commend either some current additional specification or some new specification of their own, and hence use 'educated' with laudatory intent or force.

6 Just as 'educate' and 'education' do not imply that what is learned is necessarily of particular value or importance, so also they do not imply any particular kind of learning. Whether or not a piece of teaching and learning counts as part of a man's education, or part of the enterprise of educating, depends on whether or not it satisfies the criteria already laid down in (2)–(4) above. It has to be (2) above the level of nature, (3) intended and successful, and (4) part of some general policy or overall plan for the learning of persons *qua* persons.

We are likely to dispute the application of this last criterion more than, or at least as much as, the application of the others; and it is important to be clear about what sort of dispute this is. If a piece of learning, having satisfied the first two criteria, is in fact part of an overall policy (formulated by the tutor, or the school, or whoever), then it is part of the student's education – however much anyone else may disagree with that policy; equally, if it is not part of such a policy, then it is not part of his education – however much importance anyone else may attach to it (however much one may think that it *ought* to be, or to have been, part of a policy). In this sense, the content of education is entirely open. We can, of course, argue about what policy we ought to have (what sort of content, or things to be learned, we ought to include); but this is an argument about what *sort* of education we *ought* to have, not an argument about whether something counts as part of a man's education or not. At most one could say that it may be, in some sort of indirect way, and in certain contexts, an argument about whether something *is going to* count or whether we are *going to make it* count: that is, whether we are going to formulate a policy which includes ABC and excludes XYZ. But, again, what actually *makes* it count is our (or anyone else's) actual formulation, and practical realization, of a policy. The *concept* is not disputable or 'contestable'. To take a parallel, we can of course argue about what a particular task of interior decoration (which we ourselves are going to undertake) should *consist of* – whether to paint over the tiles or leave them as they are, and so on; but this is not an argument about what, in general, *counts as* 'interior decoration'.

It is natural to put this by saying, as I have said, that there are limits on the *form* of the enterprise, but not on its *content*; these are terms characteristically used in attempting some sort of distinction with regard to such enterprises, for instance in defining morality. But they are not very precise. Thus there is clearly a sense in which education is limited in regard to content: that is, the learning has to be above the level of nature, intended, and so on. These are limits of what sort of learning is allowable, in a certain sense of 'what sort of'; just as to say that moral principles must be over-riding, prescriptive, etc., is to say what sort of principles they must be. It is some improvement to say that there is no limit on what people being educated have to learn *about*, or what the *subject-matter* of the learning has to be, though even this is not wholly free from ambiguity. A bit better still, perhaps, is to say that, if we consider those expressions of what is learned, of the form 'learning X', 'learning to X', 'learning that X', 'learning how to X', etc., we cannot determine whether this learning counts as education *simply* by what X is.

Some might argue, as has in fact been argued in the (at this point) analogous case of morality, that to allow *just any* learning is to open the door too wide. Those who hold that not just anything can be thought important, or be counted as a human interest, must presumably also hold this; for if X cannot be thought important, it is hard to see how it could be thought important to make people learn X – which is a necessary (though not sufficient) condition for X being part of a man's education. They might claim, then, that there *is* some limit on the content of learning; just as, and perhaps just because, there are limits on the content of human interests.

I do not find this line of argument at all clear, and it raises very complex philosophical problems which cannot be properly tackled here (see, however, p. 150).[8] But it can, I think, at least be shown – and it is important for our purposes to show – that it cannot be used to rule out certain Xs *a priori* on grounds of unintelligibility or logical incoherence. For suppose that, as philosophers have done, we imagine some very odd or 'way-out' Xs – learning to eschew eating the cormorant,[9] or to clap one's hands three times an hour, or whatever – and ask whether anyone could regard these Xs as important. Then this is to ask either (a) whether there is some logical contradiction or incoherence in *saying*, e.g. 'It is important, and part of our policy, that our children should learn to eschew eating the cormorant', to which the answer is plainly 'No'; or (b) whether there could be some background which would enable us to understand what reasons he might have for saying this, to which the answer is plainly 'Yes'.

Of course not just anything counts as a *reason* for anything else; if someone said 'Children should learn X because of Y', then 'because of' has to make sense to us if we are to understand him. No doubt there is something incoherent in the idea of something making sense for, or being a reason for, just one person – that is, devoid of any kind of publicly intelligible background or set of interests; and no doubt many of our interests, so long as we remain human beings, are best seen as given rather than chosen. But what happens in practice, and what must always happen (since human action involves reasoning and the pursuit of ends seen as desirable), is that if anyone *were* to say – in ordinary life, not just as a philosophical example – 'Children should learn X', there *would* be some sort of background or reasons: if there were not, he would not say it, or at least would not mean it. The fact that it is (sincerely) said itself implies a background; hence we cannot eliminate *a priori* anything that anyone might actually claim. Nor, in view of (a) the wide variety of human desire, and (b) the almost infinite human capacity for misperception and other kinds of unreason, can we maintain that there are certain things that would, in fact, never be claimed.

A much more plausible idea, and one which we shall pursue later (p. 112), is that there may be conceptual reasons not for excluding but for including certain Xs. Just as (it might be thought) there are certain logically inalienable features of human existence and society which make it inconceivable that we could do without some kind of rules about decision-making, truth-telling, property and so forth, though this would not set any limit upon what *other* rules, principles or ideals might be promoted: so there may be certain other features – or perhaps partly the same ones – which make it conceptually necessary that we should learn, or have learned, certain Xs if we are to engage at all in any form of existence which could be seriously described or recognized as human. (One obvious candidate here is the learning of some kind of language.) But this is quite a different sort of claim; I mention it at this stage simply to point the difference between saying (a) that some Xs may be excluded from the title of education simply because of what the Xs consist of, which is a mistake: and (b) that there may be reasons why, given certain conceptual parameters (here vaguely referred to as 'human existence'), we are logically bound to include some Xs, which – I shall argue later – may be correct.

Other human enterprises offer reasonable parallels to education, in respect of the points made above: for example, the enterprise normally marked by 'interior decoration'. This phrase (a) may be used timelessly, to mark a general activity; or more specifically to mark a particular realization of the activity – '*the* interior decoration', or 'the décor'. Then (b) not just any kind of improvement to, or alteration in, a house or other building will come under this enterprise; it is specifically concerned with a certain swathe of goods – roughly, those concerned with improving the *appearance* of the inside of the building. (c) To justify using the rather grand phrase 'interior decoration', as against (say) 'just touching up the paintwork', or 'having the curtains cleaned', we should want to be assured that the appearance was being improved 'above the level of nature': that is, above what ordinary occupants might naturally do to it. There would have to be an *intention* to engage in the enterprise, and also some *result* or successful achievement. (If, by a strange fluke, the appearance of the house was comprehensively improved by an earthquake, or a sandstorm, or by insects nibbling away the horrible wallpaper, interior decoration has not taken place; neither has it taken place if what human decorators do is removed, as soon as they do it, by fairies – that is, if there are no concrete results: here they tried to decorate, but failed.) For much the same reasons (d), 'interior decoration' implies something more comprehensive or over-all than mere *ad hoc* improvements of appearance (however important for particular purposes): something like a plan, design, or general policy about the appearance. (e) We reserve the right, without any difficulty, to disapprove both of the way in which the interior decoration is done and of the extent to which it is done: even, in some cases, of doing it at all. (f) Within the broad limits set by the idea of improving appearance, 'interior decoration' does not specify any particular operations; there is nothing an interior decorator must, logically, do with regard to the walls, ceilings, furniture and so on: the enterprise has no given content.

How far (we may now want to ask) is or was this particular concept marked, in various societies, by some particular word? That is, how far is or was this particular range of meaning recognized and correlated with some linguistic marker? Obviously a full answer to this question would involve a lengthy guided tour, requiring conductors with linguistic and historical as well as philosophical expertise; but in default of this, the following points may at least partially illuminate the scene:

1 It seems on *a priori* grounds inevitable, and therefore unsurprisingly true in point of fact, that all societies will mark out two
areas with reasonable clarity. First, there are the (comparatively)
straightforward ideas of learning and teaching, for which non-
controversial terms are found in all languages – *disco, enseigner,
didasko*, and so on. Second, there is the very general idea of bringing
some creature (often a child) into a more satisfactory or well-
developed state of being. The mode or style in which this general
enterprise is conceived – the sort of operation it is – may be viewed
differently; and the root-meanings of various words suggest different
metaphors corresponding to these different views. Thus the idea of
forming or shaping emerges in the modern Greek *morphosis* or the
German *Bildung*: the idea of encouraging height or growth in the
French *élever*, or in our own 'bringing up' or 'rearing' (trans-
atlantically, 'raising', used indifferently of corn or cattle or children):
the idea of feeding in our 'nurture' or the classical Greek *trophē*: the
idea of setting in order, in the Latin *institutio*.

2 All these latter terms meet some of the criteria for our 'education', in that they suggest deliberate enterprises in which 'nature' is
at least assisted, if not transcended, and for which some sort of
general policy is adopted. But they are not, or certainly were not,
always used by every society in accordance with the further criterion
that the enterprise should promote human *learning*, or the learning
of people *qua* people, criteria which we have seen as also forming a
necessary part of the concept we now mark by 'education'; hence,
in these cases, the language-users in these societies may not have
entertained this concept. This is, of course a very different thing
from saying that they did not in fact educate their children, for
people can do things for which they have no clearly differentiated
linguistic markers – just as works of art can be created by men who
see them primarily as religious rather than aesthetic objects, or who
at least do not have the concept *we* mark by 'a work of art'. There
are, as we shall see, good reasons for supposing that virtually every
society must take seriously the question of what its children are to
learn. But not every society has to distinguish this, in overt terms,
from a more general question about what its children need to be able
to do and be (whether or not as a result of learning); just as, though
every society uses and marks some concept of what it is important
to do and believe, not every society distinguishes sharply between
(say) morality, law, etiquette and religious commandment. Equally,
to say that these societies did not have our concept of education is
not to say that they did not have what we may call the constituents
of this concept. They had available, as it were, all the constituent
criteria – human learning, deliberate enterprises, the making of a

general policy, and so on; but they did not put them together into a single range of meaning marked by a single term.

3 What seems to happen is that most societies do, at some time or other, come to acquire the concept and mark it; as with our own 'education', which marks something different and less broad than was marked by the eighteenth-century use of the word, or as the classical Greek *paideia* can be said either to have taken over part of the range of meaning marked by the broader *trophē* ('rearing') or to have developed this narrower range alongside of it. The fact is, so far as my advice goes, that the vast majority of societies in the modern world do mark this particular concept in some way – often if not always by a word whose root-meaning might be thought to suggest something broader, not specifically connected with learning – again, like the root-meaning of our own 'education'. *Bildung*, *l'éducation* and so on would normally be understood, at least in certain contexts, as covering the same range as our modern 'education'.

Why this should come about is, I suppose, a sociological question; but my guess would be that the phenomenon at least tends to correlate with an increase in the wealth, communications, economic complexity and 'pluralism' of societies, the time spent in general reflection about life and learning, and the possibility of putting different educational options into practice. As soon as the question 'What, in fact, ought our children to learn?' is raised in a more open way (because alternatives are now available), there is need for a differentiated concept; we become interested in children's physical needs under one heading (health, dietetics, or whatever), specific and *ad hoc* social needs under another (training, conditioning), and general policies about learning under yet another (education). When there is no time or money for, or even perhaps much scope for reflection about, general policies of learning – since, perhaps, what children have to learn and be is more or less *given* by the harsh pressures of the environment – the need for the differentiated concept is clearly less.

This, then, seems to be how the words are actually used. The positive criteria in (2), (3) and (4) (pp. 18–27) – that is, briefly, whether human learning above the natural level is being deliberately promoted in accordance with some general or overall policy – are sufficiently sharp to enable us, in the vast majority of cases, to say whether education is going on or not. Naturally there will be borderline cases: we may argue whether the learning is sufficiently above the natural level, or its promotion sufficiently deliberate, or the policy sufficiently general, to count. But to take one side or another in such an argument is a very different thing from abandoning the rules in use.

What about 'the concept'? I have used, and shall continue to use, 'concept' in the sense (roughly) of 'range of meaning'. Thus there is one concept marked by the words 'dog', '*chien*', '*Hund*', etc., and at least two concepts marked by the single word 'bank' (river banks and money banks). In this sense, 'the concept of education' will mean something like 'the range of meaning, or rules governing the use, of the term "education"'. Naturally this implies a background of speakers, usually taken as contemporary; for eighteenth-century English-speakers 'education' marked a different range of meaning – that is, a different concept.

I had taken this use of 'concept' to be standard and traditional, at least in British philosophy over the last few decades; but it is fairly clear that the use is not universal. Since other uses are seldom clarified, it is extremely hard to do justice to what some contemporary philosophers say about 'the concept of education'. Thus in one book[10] the authors say that 'Different individuals and social groups may use concepts differently' (not, 'use different concepts'): that some concepts may not 'occupy more or less fixed positions': and that

> in discussions about the nature of education, the concept will
> frequently be defined and used programmatically, and the
> adequacy of the definitions and uses will be defended not merely
> by what people say, but also by substantial normative arguments
> about what should go on in schools, colleges, and universities.

I do not at all understand what they mean by 'concept' in these and other passages. Sometimes they appear to use it as equivalent to 'word', as in 'Do all concepts have uses which can be indisputably identified? "Pencil" might, but does "education"?'; more often as equivalent to 'picture', 'idea', or 'view'. (Of course people have different pictures of, ideas about, and views on education: whether they use the word according to different rules is another matter.)

I find similar, though greater, difficulties in understanding what is supposed to be meant by saying that 'the concept of education' is '(essentially) contestable'.[11] Fortunately, however, we can for our purposes take a fairly short way with this view. For one (perhaps the most important) of the criteria which have to be satisfied if a concept is to be 'contestable', it appears, is that the concept must be '*appraisive* in the sense that it signifies or accredits some kind of valued achievement':[12] but I hope to have shown already (though we shall discuss it further, pp. 49 ff.) that 'education' is a descriptive (factual, 'non-appraisive' (?)) term; and in my sense of 'concept', at least, that would seem to be sufficient to show that the concept is not 'contestable'. It is, indeed, hard to see how any *range of meaning* can be 'contestable'. Of course there might be contests about what words we *ought* to attach to what ranges of meaning; but it is not obvious that there is any other plausible criterion for settling such disputes than mere clarity – that is, so long as we all know what means what, it doesn't much matter.

However, what may (legitimately) be in the minds of those who talk about 'different concepts of education' is the point already mentioned at the beginning of this chapter. It is one thing to ask what the ground covered by our 'education' is, and whether the same ground is covered by other terms in other languages; another to ask whether this demarcation is useful or necessary. Why should we categorize or mark out *this* area? Our first thought here might be that it would be odd to the point of unintelligibility if the demarcation served *no* useful purpose, appearing as it does in so many different cultures. To say this is not to assume some natural wisdom or unchallengeable set of demarcations built into 'ordinary language' or 'normal usage'; it is simply to say that, since men do not invent terms or demarcate areas arbitrarily, we need at least to understand and inspect these demarcations before we can feel confident about revising or improving them. This is, in fact, only one application of the general point that it is wise to understand how things are before altering or destroying those things: a point which applies as much to our language as to our other possessions.

In any case, there are fairly clear reasons why this particular demarcation is not only useful but virtually inevitable for human beings. The idea marked by 'learning', at least, is conceptually connected with the idea of being a person. The connection is not just (though this is important enough) that human infants could not grow up to be rational people unless they did some learning and had been taught some things (most obviously, the use of language); it is also that having a conscious and rational mind implies some degree of willingness and ability to be open to new experiences and to structure such experiences – that is, very roughly, to learn. Learning is one of the things that human beings inalienably do: both in order to become people, and *qua* people.

Two other points, of a rather different kind, can be added. First any social group concerned that its own members (or any other men) should continue to exist as people will necessarily thereby be concerned with learning. I do not mean by this only that, for instance, a tribe dependent on the skills of hunting or agriculture must be concerned to retain and pass on these skills in order to survive. That may also be true; but if the members of the tribe are given machines to do this work for them, or are effortlessly fed by other means, they still have to decide whether they and their children are to continue as people. This does not imply that they would have to have some specific ideal about 'what made life worth living' above the level of physical survival or the necessary appetites – an ideal inspired perhaps by such notions as culture, or religion, or intellectual achievement, or refinement of pleasure. They would need, of course, to feel that there was *something* about human life which made it worth living; for this would be part of what was meant by saying that they had some concern for its continuance. But such feelings might be extremely vague, and not necessarily attached to disputable ideals or valuations of this kind.

Second, insofar as members of the group reflect at all about the point and forms of such continuance – that is, about why they want their infants to become people, and what sort of people they want them to be – to that extent they will inevitably reflect about what they are to learn and why. That they would reflect to *some* degree about this seems to follow from the fact that they are themselves rational creatures, who actually have this concern. No doubt it is true, as one might generally grasp even without the benefit of sociological studies, that in certain kinds ('mass', 'pluralistic') of societies there is more opportunity and incentive for such reflection, or for wider reflection, than in societies whose individual members spend most of their lives in filling some particular role, perhaps dictated by economic necessity or rigid social forms. But if members of such a ('folk') society saw themselves and each other *solely* as fulfillers of tasks that could, in principle and without loss, be done by machines, they would have none of the concern we are speaking of; and in practice, as well as in principle, they will clearly see themselves to some extent as men rather than wholly replaceable role-fillers.

It seems, then, to be inevitable that the members of any group will have some conception of their own learning, and more particularly their children's learning, as an enterprise in its own right, to be taken with as much seriousness as their concern for the continuance of people is serious. There are, of course, *other* enterprises which they will also take seriously, following from other aspects of what is involved in being a person. For instance, some degree of health or, more generally, freedom from physical danger is required for personal survival; so that enterprises which might come to be labelled 'medicine' or 'defence' or 'food-production' inevitably arise. Similarly the existence of anything plausibly to be described as a 'society', without which (arguably) individual infants would not be able to grow into or function as rational creatures, suggests that some attention must be paid to social order and expectations: this might be classified as 'politics' or 'government'.

It does not, indeed, follow with absolute conceptual strictness that the members of the group are bound to take *education* seriously. They are, indeed, bound to consider whether education might not be one way, or the best way, or the only way, of ensuring that whatever learning they think necessary does actually take place; but it is logically possible that they might reject such ideas. Thus they might think that no learning above the level of nature (whatever that level was, in that society) was really necessary or important; or that no especially intentional or deliberate effort needed to be made by parents, tutors, schools and so forth; or that, though occasional efforts might be needed, nevertheless nothing like a general policy or overall plan for children's learning was necessary. In other words, they might reject any enterprise which had to satisfy all the criteria of education mentioned earlier.

But though such rejection is logically possible, it seems clearly unreasonable; nor, in fact, would we expect to find many societies which did not make some sort of effort, of at least a semi-formal kind, to teach their children in accordance with some kind of general policy. Even at primitive levels, survival depends on a grasp of technological and social rules which could not be picked up in a casual or fragmentary way; and if, as is almost invariably the case, we add the desire to initiate children into some kind of religious, or aesthetic, or moral, or other sort of ideal, the need for some structure and policy becomes even more obvious. Utilitarian pressures from disease, war, starvation, hostile climates and other sources on the one hand, and the non-utilitarian expansion of awareness in the arts and sciences on the other, both unite to render the enterprise of education more and more obviously necessary. *How* important (and for what reasons) the enterprise may be, for particular people under particular conditions, remains an open question: *that* it is important could hardly be denied by anyone who seriously valued either the utilitarian or the non-utilitarian goods just mentioned.

There is a connection here with the criterion of a general policy. Anyone who reflected about life at all (one is tempted to say) would have some appreciation of the *variety* of goods to be gained, directly or indirectly, by learning; and if he is concerned that his children should enjoy these goods, then a general policy is forced upon him just because of that variety. If his reflection were so minimal, or he were so attached to one kind of good only, that he failed to have anything recognizable as a general policy, we might well say that he was not educating his children (but only teaching them certain things, or training them for certain tasks). If his reflection were wider, but still not wide enough – if, for instance, he had simply not taken some whole area, such as moral education, under consideration at all – we might wish to say that his policy was sufficiently general for what he did to count as education, but that he had not reflected sufficiently about the different kinds of goods that can accrue to people by learning. Clearly there will be many borderline cases here. But in practice, as we have said, nearly all social groups will at least set out to educate: with good reason.

Finally, can anything useful be said about the relationship between the enterprise of education and other human enterprises? In particular, can anything be made of the idea (nowadays very popular) that education depends on, or can be reduced to, or somehow swallowed up by, other enterprises? Almost everything turns here on preserving a clear distinction between what we called the primary and secondary senses of the term. In its primary sense, whereby it entitles a time-free and culture-free enterprise, the only possible relationships are logical ones. Thus if, in this sense, 'mathematics' and 'medicine' are related to each other, this will not be because mathematicians sometimes fall sick or because doctors need to be able to count their change: it will be because mathematical knowledge may be relevant to, or a part of, medical science. In the secondary sense, whereby the term refers to particular practical realizations of the enterprise, empirical relationships are of course possible. But these will then be the relationships whereby one institutionalized enterprise facilitates or impedes another; as, for instance, an economics-oriented institution such as the Treasury or the Exchequer may facilitate or impede the operation of education-oriented institutions such as schools and universities, by giving them more or less money.

So long as we are fairly clear about what the delimitations of these enterprises actually are, and what goods they pursue, most of our difficulties can at least be negotiated. A more alarming situation arises when one enterprise seems to be capable of limitless expansion. This tends to happen when the enterprise is ill-defined and for one reason or another catches the popular imagination or exercises a dominant position in society; as, perhaps, 'religion' used to do in the past, and as 'politics' certainly does today. The difficulty of dealing with such cases lies precisely there; not much is to be gained by arguing with someone who says that all educational issues are ultimately political unless he can first be persuaded to say what counts as 'political' and (just as important) what does not. Even then, of course, he may say that there can be no correct or determinate answer to what counts as 'political' ('the concept is contestable').

But if he cannot or will not say even what the limits of the term are as *he* uses it, there is no arguing with him.

To continue with this example, it nevertheless seems fairly plain that whatever may be meant by 'political', the term can only represent some (not all) of the aspects under which the world may be viewed. Other aspects are equally legitimate. Just as the Chinese might object to Watteau because he was a bourgeois artist, so Watteau might object to the Chinese because their clothes were ugly; and just as Nazis might object to Einstein's scientific efforts because he was a Jew, so Einstein might object to Nazi government or political philosophy because it was unscientific. An economist might naturally view all enterprises in terms of their cost, a professional humorist in terms of the opportunities they afforded for wit. But nobody seriously supposes that this abolishes the distinctions between enterprises; for example, that philosophy as practised by Socrates or tragedy by Euripides are no more than humorous or attempts at humour, just because they are funny in certain aspects which Aristophanes chose to satirise in the *Clouds* and the *Frogs*.

The aspects (or *species*, or descriptions) under which a man chooses to view and assess something depends partly on his particular interests: that is, on the particular kinds of goods with which he is concerned. If the term 'political' is not to become vacuous, it must relate to some particular type of enterprise, with particular goods and reasons of its own; otherwise 'politics' would mean simply 'what men did', and 'for political reasons' would mean 'for some (any) reasons'. In normal speech, and in normal practice, we contrast 'politics' with other enterprises, and 'political reasons' with other kinds of reasons. Very often the kind of contrast is fairly clear; there may be obvious political (social, diplomatic) reasons for not wearing green in modern Ireland or ancient Byzantium, even though there may be aesthetic reasons why green suits my particular complexion. It may be politically desirable to include someone in a chess or football team because that person is, say, black or female or Catholic, even though the demands of chess or football might make us prefer another person who was none of these.

That there must be *some* possibility of contrast is clear; just what the contrast is will turn on how we propose to use such terms as 'politics'. The latitude we have here is not, in my judgment, best described by saying that 'the concept is contestable'; though it is clear, for instance, that some such notion as 'the welfare of the state (*polis*)' is only loosely specified – not only because we might argue about what is to count as 'welfare', but also because we might argue about who is to be included within the state or the body politic. Again, by giving some simple description in advance, we cannot disqualify certain features of the world as 'non-political', if by that we mean that they could not conceivably figure in somebody's 'political theory'; as the example of wearing green may suggest, almost anything could at least be *seen* (reasonably or unreasonably) as relevant to, or a constituent of, the welfare of the *polis* – if only because it is difficult to set bounds to human irrationality.

Because anything can, apparently, be seen as 'political', there is a temptation to suppose that everything can be thus seen without any loss of meaning. There are parallels here with other notions: some people feel inclined to say, for instance, not that their religion governs some part of their lives, but that it governs all their lives – that everything that they do is done 'for religious reasons'. Similarly, one might at least imagine someone with a very powerful aesthetic ideal regarding all his own and other people's actions under that *species*; the rightness and wrongness of what they did would, for him, be found entirely in the grace, charm, style, etc., of the actions. But such people, if seriously imaginable at all, would at least have some understanding of other *species*: there would be some possibility of contrast with *other* kinds of reasons relating to other kinds of ends. In fact, for a person of this kind, 'reason' is likely to approximate more to 'motivation' than to 'justification'; it is not that there are, or ever could be, religious (aesthetic, political, etc.) justifications for putting down 4 as the arithmetically correct answer to 2 plus 2, or using bicarbonate of soda as the best medical antidote to excess acidity, but rather that the person might see himself as inspired to engage in and perform well in arithmetic and medicine by his god (political party, ideal, etc.) – or see them as, in some sense, existing and being pursued by or in accordance with the will of his god. Similarly a Chinese table-tennis player may see himself as engaging in the game for political reasons, or as inspired by the spirit of Chairman Mao in some overall way; but if he decides at a particular point in the game to play a drop-shot rather than a smash, this will be for reasons internal to the game itself.

There is thus a certain incoherence in the idea that particular human enterprises – law, science, education and so on – can be totally 'politicized'. Suppose that *all* the ordinances and administrative decisions in a society stemmed solely from the will of a single tyrant; or that our beliefs about genetics and other scientific matters were *wholly* governed by their orthodoxy in terms of Communist political doctrines. Then the concepts that we now possess marked by 'law' and 'science' would have no application; these enterprises or *technai* would simply have disappeared. Even the idea that they can be partly 'politicized' – without loss, as it were – is a confused one; to the extent that political or other reasons take the place of reasons inherent in the *technai*, to that extent the *technai* are in practice diminished. We distinguish political trials from ordinary trials, and political inroads on science (art, music, religion, etc.) from the proper practice of science, precisely by the introduction of improper reasons: improper, that is, from the point of view of the *techne* in question. Whether or not these reasons ought, in this case or that, to be introduced and taken as overriding will naturally be always debatable. But the debate could not take place without the distinction between the two types of reasons being applied at some point.

The point at which it is in fact applied depends, of course, on the current beliefs and organization of the particular society; and the term 'politics' *may* be used to entitle the 'architectonic' enterprise of allocating priorities and arranging for the practice of other enterprises. But there neither is nor could be a society which did not have *some* understanding of, and give *some* weight to, certain *technai* in their own right. Without a minimal practice of basic arts and crafts – the production of food and the means of self-defence, for instance – and without a minimal amount of learning and 'socialization' on the part of its young, a society could not survive. In practice nearly all societies have under modern conditions to acknowledge the independent structures of medicine, science, applied technology, some kind of education, and some kind of coherent social structure involving laws and rules of various kinds; and in practice they do acknowledge, even if they do not for any obvious utilitarian reason have to acknowledge, such enterprises as art, music, literature, and many others. These become established in practice (one is tempted to say, the more effectively established the better the society's politics); so that, again in practice but to some degree necessarily or in principle, inroads upon them take the form of saying '*Although* the principles of science (law, medicine, art, chess, etc.) naturally point us in this direction, on this particular occasion there are political reasons which must override them.' To put this another way: if these activities really do pursue genuine goods (as medicine pursues health, for instance), then there will be at least a *prima facie* case for so arranging society that the activities can be pursued. Most of the day-to-day arguments here will be about priorities: that is, about the comparative importance of various goods. Some, perhaps less important or peculiarly difficult to arrange for, may have to disappear altogether in certain contexts: for instance, in time of war, plague or famine. But in general it will, necessarily, be right to *try* to cater for the activities; which means acknowledging the existence of the various goods, and – a point of great practical importance – understanding just what they are.

We have not yet reached the stage in our discussion at which we can pronounce with any certainty, or even clarity, about what the particular goods of education actually are; I shall say something more about this at the end of the next chapter (p. 63), and they will emerge more fully in the course of this book as a whole. Even at this early stage, however, it should be clear that the *form* of the enterprise, as here roughly delimited, carries certain conceptual obligations with it; and that there are various ways in which societies may lose their grip, as it were, on what education involves: in which, more by a process of self-deception or some other kind of mental confusion than by an overt rejection, they come to pay (at least) less attention to the enterprise. Perhaps the most obvious way is followed when a society becomes obsessed with a particular kind of desired result or end-product, and tries to insert this product into the content of education without observing that it violates the form of the enterprise. For instance, suppose we desire an end-product roughly described as 'believing what Chairman Mao (Jesus, Hitler, Marx, etc.) says', together with the suppressed thought 'at all costs'. Then we may find ourselves not minding *how* our children come to believe this (if believe is the right word: see pp. 170 ff.), or whether what Mao says is *true* (rather than just politically convenient); and this is likely to conflict with criteria implied by the notion of learning. For, as we shall show in more detail later, it is (to say the least) not clear that one can learn what is false, nor that all ways of *coming* to some belief or behaviour-pattern are also ways of *learning* it. So it may be that these particular goods or end-products, whether truly desirable or not, are anyway not educational goods, and that those who wish to promote them are, *pro tanto*, not – because they logically cannot be – interested in education.

This particular way of distorting or abandoning the enterprise has (unsurprisingly) received a good deal of attention and criticism from liberal-minded philosophers in liberal societies, under headings like 'indoctrination', 'brainwashing', 'conditioning', and so forth. Slightly less obvious, perhaps, at least to members of such societies, is a second type of distortion. Loosely to be associated with an out-look sometimes called 'relativist', its starting-point is a failure of nerve and intelligence in the task of identifying and allocating *some* sufficient content to the enterprise, a failure that makes much of its form pointless. As we have seen, the enterprise has to be systematic, reasonably comprehensive, and to some degree formal in the sense that it aims at instructing people well above the level of nature or of what they might pick up for themselves. To undertake it, we have to accept (at least provisionally) a set of tolerably clear and comprehensive objectives – things to be learned – which, we feel, are sufficiently important and well-grounded for us to put our money on; and we have also to accept a good many things which are logically connected with the idea of serious learning – for example, a clear grasp of and adherence to the standards of success and failure which constitute whatever is being learned, a structure of authority, discipline and obedience to rules, some effective procedures for examining or assessing progress in what is learned, and the necessity of a certain mental attitude on the part of the learner. It will be clear, particularly to anyone at all familiar with the history of so-called 'progressive' education in some countries over the last few decades, that to lose grip on these features involves a loss of grip on education. This second distortion equally involves the abandonment of what is demanded by the concept of serious learning: not, as in the first case, by over-insistence on particular end-products which do not fit the concept, but rather by progressively diluting the structures and objectives without which the concept is vacuous – that is, incapable of being put into practice. Some considerations in the next chapter may help us to avoid both these mistakes.

# 2 Mistakes and methodology

If what we said in the last chapter is more or less on the right lines, it is an extremely striking fact that these lines are (as I shall show) rarely followed. There should be, after all, no insuperable intellectual difficulty about grasping what we mean by 'education', seeing the necessity of the enterprise for human beings, and proceeding to investigate what it involves. The chances are, not that we have failed in being clever enough to set the subject on a sound footing, but rather that we have been driven by various temptations or *idées fixes* into making elementary mistakes: and that these temptations will continue to exercise their baleful influence until we can see them clearly for what they are. In this chapter, therefore, I propose to take a look at some of these mistakes (and show that they *are* mistakes), so that we can proceed on firmer methodological ground.

There are some predictable difficulties of procedure here: not only are there a number of different kinds of mistakes, but also most of them operate at different levels. By this latter I mean that a certain kind of mistake is likely to infect not only (1) philosophical accounts of what is meant by 'education' and (2) the methodological assumptions which philosophers bring to problems in the philosophy of education, but also (3) the study of education and educational research in general, and (4) – last but not least – the practice of education itself. A full and properly organized account would need more than one book; and though we shall ourselves be primarily concerned with (1) and (2), I cannot claim to have categorized the mistakes (or the temptations from which they flow) in any very precise or well-ordered manner. I hope only to show, in a fairly general way, at least some of the sorts of things that characteristically go wrong.

There is, however, one basic idea or way of looking at things which lies behind most, perhaps all, of these errors, and which it may help to describe (however baldly) in advance. It is the idea that the only way of setting definite limits on certain enterprises – that marked by 'education' is one case, but those marked by 'morality', 'religion', 'politics' and others offer reasonably good parallels – is by giving them a certain kind of *content*. Such content may be 'descriptive' or 'evaluative' (if I may employ these terms without further explanation): for instance, what some individual or society actually does, or what some educator or educational theorist approves of. But (so the idea goes) some content there must be if we are to set any definite limits at all. Either 'education' must mean (roughly) some set of institutional practices – or perhaps any set – that actually go on under our noses; or it must mean some particular type or style of teaching and learning which ought to be going on. What is lacking here is the notion of an enterprise which is indeed concerned with a certain area or department of life, but limited by its own nature and logic rather than by any set of prevailing 'facts' or 'values'.

1 We may begin with some examples of 'descriptive' content. O'Connor says: 'In one sense of "education", we all know very well what it means. The word refers to the sort of training that goes on in schools and universities and so on.'[1] Here we immediately think of the sorts of 'training' that we might well *not* want to count as education, and of the difficulties in identifying something as a school or university (rather than as, say, an indoctrination centre or a monastery or a prison) without some prior concept of a particular kind of enterprise which the institution was supposed, at least some of the time, to conduct: that is, without some concept of what it was to *educate*. Similarly Frankena allows himself to say that 'education is the process by which society makes of its members what it is desirable that they should become, either in general or in so far as this may be carried on by what are called "schools" ':[2] but, of course, 'society' can make its members richer, or better fed, or plenty of other desirable things without doing anything to them which could fairly be described as *educating* them.

In one way, of course, these accounts err in not setting *sufficient* limits on the sense of 'education' (essentially, by omitting the criterion of learning); but they are also instances of the opposite mistake – that is, of tying 'education' down *too* tightly, to a particular descriptive content: a content which adds up to something appallingly if only roughly like 'what society does under the heading of "education" '. This incorporates at least three errors. First, it reduces an enterprise which is, in one clear sense, time-free and culture-free to its specific social forms (as if the concept of religion could be cashed out without loss in terms of the actual religions we have). Secondly, it assumes that only 'society' (whatever, indeed, this may mean) can conduct the enterprise, whereas it is plain that individuals can also do so (as if the only religions in England were

45

those which 'society' sponsored). Thirdly, it assumes that what societies *call* 'education' or 'an educational institution' is always rightly called (as if anything *called* 'a house of prayer' *was* a house of prayer, even if in other respects it was indistinguishable from a den of thieves).

What is the attraction of bringing 'society' into the business at all? What do those who make this (extremely popular) move have in mind? No doubt there is a lot to be said about this; but part of the story, at least, may be that they are misled by misinterpreting the force of two or three harmless (if important) truths, which are worth mentioning here:

(a) The first, already briefly noted in the previous chapter (p. 17), is that most if not all that men do is carried on with the help or against the resistance of, or at any rate in some relationship to, other men; so that, since men are rational creatures and not just physical objects, what they do will be partly governed or influenced by 'society'. Certainly what goes on in art, or science, or religion, or vine-pruning will depend a great deal on 'society' (in the sense, perhaps, of the particular sovereign state, or the Western democratic world, or whatever); and it is also true that the enterprises themselves, being often practised by men in collaboration, are clothed in particular social forms: there will be particular social groups who go in collectively for art (science, religion, vine-pruning) – whether or not they are institutionalized as, for example, the Church of England or the Royal Society of Vine-Pruners. This too will affect their practice. But all this we know already: to say of particular educational policies and practices (particular realizations of the enterprise) that they go on in 'society', or are influenced by 'society', is to say virtually nothing: where else could they go on, and how could they not be so influenced?

(b) Second, it is often said (sometimes with an air of triumph) that these enterprises are 'social products'; and this too seems harmless, if it just means that the enterprises would not have seen the light of day, and would not now be conducted, were there not societies sufficiently favourable to their birth and continued practice. In that sense, all or almost all human activities are 'social products': including, of course, the awareness and practice of logic itself. If social conditions among apes or Neanderthalers had not been such as to promote the practice of language, we should not now be able to recognize the law of non-contradiction. But a person who wanted to remind us of this truism would not, presumably, wish thereby to cast any doubt on the validity of various enterprises as (more or less successful) attempts to extend knowledge and acquire truth. If someone tried to claim – I have heard it done – that, because the law of non-contradiction was 'a social product', it had no claim on language-users in general, it would be difficult to understand him or to accept his sincerity (particularly if, as one might fairly expect, he contradicted himself later on).

(c) Third, one may wish to stress the point that what men *take* to be these enterprises, or how the enterprises are *perceived*, may depend very much upon the society in which they live. That is of course true; though one would wish to add that it would depend on other factors also – not only the 'brute' factors of genetic endowment and basic psychological make-up (neither of which can fairly be described as 'social'), but also on how far the individuals in any society are sufficiently determined and clear-headed to think properly for themselves, whatever may be the prevailing social attitudes and pressures. Thrasymachus' main point,[3] I take it, was that what is in fact *called* 'just' or 'right' tends to be what serves the interest of the ruling classes; rather as one might say today that, in some totalitarian societies, what is *called* 'mental illness' tends to be whatever makes for political deviance. This is an important point; but its importance lies precisely in our *not* accepting that what some society calls X actually is X.

There is, I suppose, a standing temptation to construe enterprises in too particular terms: to identify education, religion, science, morality, politics and so on with what goes on in institutions under one's nose. A number of different reasons contribute to this, which it would take a (philosophically well-informed) sociologist or psychologist to tell us about, perhaps roughly summed up in the difficulty of emerging from what Plato calls 'the world of sights and sounds'. The man who is supposed to have said 'When I say religion of course I mean the Christian religion, and when I say the Christian religion of course I mean the Church of England' is supposed to have said something funny; yet, in fact, 'religious education' even in the most 'liberal' or 'pluralistic' societies has (at least until recently) been construed in something like this way. Strong resistances exist against the whole idea of time-free and culture-free enterprises and *technai*.

That this is not merely a 'linguistic point' may be seen if we go back to the example of politics. Nobody wants to deny that there is a use of 'politics', perhaps the most common among contemporary English-speakers, which refers (roughly) to the particular brand of practical politics conducted in contemporary English-speaking countries: 'I'm going into politics' means, I suppose, that the speaker wants to be an MP or a senator, or perhaps a trade-unionist or student leader or a local councillor, or something of that kind. It would be a great deal more odd for someone to say 'I'm going into

47

education' and mean that he wanted to be a school janitor or a civil servant dealing with the cost of school buildings: or 'I'm going into science' and mean that he wanted to run the canteen at an atomic power station: or 'into religion', to sell waders for Baptist ministers. This is because the terms in these latter examples are more tightly tied to enterprises rather than institutions (particularly in the cases of science and religion). But even if it were perfectly 'normal' to say and mean such things, that would go no way to show that there were not, in fact, such general or transcendental enterprises as politics, education, science and religion.

Other writers avoid the mistake of tying 'education' down to what 'society' does; but only at the cost of even wilder definitions. Consider a statement made collectively by members of the Philosophy of Education Society of the USA, a body containing many reputable philosophers. They say: 'the term "education" may refer to any deliberate effort to nurture, modify, change, and/or develop human conduct or behavior'.[4] *Any* effort? *Any* change? *Any* kind of behaviour? I can change a man's behaviour by terrorizing him, making him drunk, or administering a slow poison. And what about human *beliefs*, surely distinguishable from 'conduct' and 'behavior'? Can I not, indeed do I not centrally, educate a person by improving his beliefs and understanding? This is not far from (to catch one extremely reputable philosopher in an off-moment) Bertrand Russell's 'The essence of education is that it is a change (other than death) effected in an organism to satisfy the desires of the operator.'

These examples, however, at least appear to be shots at giving some kind of *definition* of 'education', even if rather bad shots. A good deal more alarming is the suggestion that there is no real target to shoot at. Consider, for instance, what one reviewer says about certain philosophers of education:

> For they hold that the decision to teach, say, Latin or Shakespeare or biology is a decision to pass on a culture in which society has a stake . . . Now if one is tempted to say that . . . when we speak of education we quite simply *mean* teaching people to understand and to contribute to the culture which they inherit and that this is nothing to do with politics, the answer is that such a definition of education is conservative, and thus political.

And earlier:

> But if, as I believe, the conservative conclusion is right, should one not, nevertheless, admit that it is based upon value-choices, choices about what is worth conserving, still more about what the point of education is, and what features of society, of

knowledge, art and manners one wants to see loved and understood? Even if such value-choices are not political in a narrow sense, they are surely moral.[5]

It is not clear here (nor, at least to me, either from the full text of the review or from the book itself) whether the authors are allocating a descriptive content to 'education', either of the form 'what society does' or of the form 'what society thinks it ought to do': or prefer an evaluative content of the form 'what it is actually right (for society) to do'. Perhaps the question is hardly worth asking, since we are in a world where definitions seem to be of interest only *qua* 'conservative' ('progressive', etc.); whereas normally we are chiefly concerned with whether they are good or bad definitions[6] – and definitions are not good or bad by being 'conservative' or 'progressive', any more than by being uttered in soft or loud voices. The quotation illustrates the result of yielding to the Thrasy-machean temptation; the mistake of reducing enterprises to their social forms rapidly involves the mistake of reducing philosophy to sociology – or we may, indeed, see the latter as one instance of the former. The immediate effect of this, as the last part of the quotation clearly shows, is to plunge us at once into some kind of ideological (political, moral) battle. There is, indeed, not much scope for other options, so soon as we lose faith in being able to achieve anything by linguistic clarity and conceptual argument generally.

2 Rather more commonly, perhaps, the content is 'evaluative', or 'prescriptive'. We need some such general term here, to avoid the mistake of specifying it too tightly under headings like 'ideological', 'political', 'moral', and so on. All these terms are obscure in their meaning, but it is at least clear that not *every* 'evaluative' position or pressure can sensibly be called by any one of such names. If we could agree on their delimitations, we might make some progress in the general area of 'evaluation'; as things are, the best we can do is to take note of the very wide variety of 'evaluative' pressures.

One of the earliest and clearest examples is from Plato:

When we abuse or commend the upbringing of individual people and say that one of us is educated and the other uneducated, we sometimes use this latter term of men who have in fact had a thorough education – one directed towards petty trade or the merchant-shipping business, or something like that. But I take it that for the purpose of the present discussion we are not going to treat this sort of thing as 'education'; what we have in mind is education from childhood in *virtue*, which produces a keen desire to become a perfect citizen who knows how to rule and be ruled as justice demands. I suppose we should want to mark off this sort of upbringing (*trophē*) from others and reserve the title 'education' for it alone. An upbringing directed to acquiring money or a robust physique, or even to some intellectual facility not guided by reason and justice, we should want to call coarse and illiberal, and say that it had no claim whatever to be called education. Still, let's not quibble over a name; let's stick to the proposition we agreed on just now: as a rule, men with a correct education become good.[7]

Here Plato overtly steals the word *paideia* (more or less equivalent to our 'education') to reinforce his view that education ought to consist primarily of a certain (political or moral) content. It is fair to say that Plato in general, along with many or most other educational writers, is concerned with a particular end-product: in his case, the *production of good men* by any methods or enterprises that are available (breeding, selection, 'noble fairy-stories',[8] censorship, training, education, etc.), not with the distinctions between different kinds of enterprises.[9]

More or less detailed specifications of 'evaluative' content, masquerading as definitions, can be found in a great many educational philosophers after Plato; but with the arrival of 'conceptual analysis' the masks become rather harder to remove. One problem is that it is not always clear exactly what thesis is being put forward, since the supposed link between education and 'value' can be of various kinds. In its most naive form, the idea seems to be (a) that nothing actually *is* a case of education unless it actually *does* 'transmit what is of ultimate value':[10] which might be thought to imply that, until we actually know 'what is of ultimate value', we cannot know what is education and what is not. Somewhat less demanding are the ideas (b) that to *call* something 'education' implies that the *speaker thinks* it to be valuable, and the very different idea (c) that a proper use of the term implies only that *someone* (perhaps the educator) thinks it valuable.

We have seen earlier that these views are false, at least in relation to the specific instances of the general enterprise (we can talk of 'bad education' in various ways); and also that we can object to the general enterprise itself being too strongly or too weakly deployed (of someone having had too much, or too little, education). Can we also disapprove of the enterprise as a whole? Well, of course, we *can* – in the sense that it would not be *nonsensical* to say that education was, in this general sort of way, a bad thing: just as we could *say* that interior decoration, or medical treatment, or any other enterprise was a bad thing or perhaps a waste of time. But those who undertake enterprises, or (more generally) act intentionally and deliberately to achieve ends, could not characteristically see themselves as attempting nothing worth while. They see themselves as trying to attain some good; indeed we may, as perhaps Aristotle did, construe 'good' roughly as 'what is aimed at' or 'desired objective', and make this an analytic truth. But this necessitates a distinction elsewhere, between 'apparent' goods and 'real' goods, or between the agent's view of his goal as worth while, and our own judgment about whether it actually is worth while. In other words, there is indeed a sense in which 'a commitment to what is thought valuable' is conceptually connected to intentional or purposive action (and not only in the business of education); but the connection does not have much more specific relevance to education than that.

To see the weakness of the connection, consider the case of a man whose outlook is atheistic and anti-clerical, and whose dying Christian neighbour makes him responsible for educating his orphaned children. Suppose he brings them up as good Christians, sends them to Sunday school, makes them learn the Bible by heart, and so forth. He may do this for various reasons; for instance, because he promised his dying neighbour to do it, or even because he cherishes such hate for his neighbour that he wants to take revenge by giving his children the wrong sort of education (as he sees it). We may offer the analytic remark that any of these reasons incorporates some *species boni* – keeping one's promises, or the pleasure of revenge – which makes the man's actions intelligible. But this will apply equally to any activity: including, for instance, torture or genocide. There is no doubt (a) that he, and those whom he empowers, are educating the children, and (b) that (in his judgment) this education will do them harm.

It is also sometimes difficult to know whether certain demands characteristically made on education are to be stigmatized as essentially mistaken on the one hand, or misplaced or exaggerated on the other. Consider the demands (a) that education is logically restricted to certain *methods*, and (b) that it is restricted to a specifically 'intellectual' or 'cognitive' *content*. One might prefer to describe these as misplaced, because the truths they contain are best seen in relation to the concept of learning rather than that of education: or as exaggerated, because they tend to be cast in too strong a form (often, either overtly or covertly, in the form of some kind of ideology or 'moral ideal'). Thus when Peters says (a) that ' "Education" at least rules out some procedures of transmission, on the grounds that they lack wittingness and voluntariness',[11] one can disagree only on the tactical or stylistic grounds that this is really a point about learning (that education rules these out only because learning rules them out). But when he says that ' "Education" . . . encapsulates criteria to which a family of processes must conform. The first is that something valuable should be transmitted in a morally unobjectionable manner',[12] we feel that philosophy has yielded to moralizing; clearly one can be educated, perhaps even well educated, by methods which oneself or others may regard as morally objectionable (for instance, corporal punishment). It is one thing to insist on the logical point that, say, electric shocks alone cannot make anyone learn anything, and another to raise moral objections to such methods – objections whose relevance seems, anyway, to depend on the view that the methods *could* result in learning.[13] Similarly (b) it would be hard to dissociate the idea of learning from *some* kind of understanding, knowing, or 'cognitive content': hard, because even the learning of simple skills or be-haviour-patterns – to keep one's temper or shrug one's shoulders – involves, at least for human beings, the operation of consciousness and some attention paid to the world. It is, as it were, essentially 'cognitive' from the start. But the demands which contemporary philosophers of education have made are a good deal stiffer. Thus on Peters' very stringent criteria, expressed in phrases like 'cognitive perspective', 'knowledge which is not inert', 'being on the inside of' activities which are 'worth while', and so on, very few people could be counted as educated at all.[14]

In Peters' major work it is, in fact, extremely hard to know (even in the light of his later writings) when he supposes himself to be (a) explaining how 'education' and 'educate' are used by contempo-rary English-speakers, (b) giving an account of some concept (range of meaning) which may or may not be marked by these terms, or (c) describing and advocating some particular view about what ought to be taught and learned. This makes criticism difficult; but in any case some of these claims are dropped in his later work. The kinds of confusions which occur at this stage are interesting and important, and worth a larger discussion. In what is probably the most widely read book in this field, Peters and his co-author cheer-fully allow for what they call 'the older and undifferentiated concept which refers just to any process of bringing up or rearing', but hang on tightly to 'the more recent and more specific concept', which (as they see it) is tied to the notion of 'the educated man'; and 'It will be with the implications of this more specific concept that we shall be concerned in this book.'[15] They go on to say:

We suggested, in our analysis, that insofar as we are concerned about education in what we called its specific sense, we are

committed to processes which assist the development of
desirable states in a person involving knowledge and
understanding. But how do we determine which states are
desirable? And why should knowledge and understanding be
so favoured as a necessary feature of them? Autonomy was
mentioned. . . . But on what grounds is autonomy singled out
as a desirable state? Why, similarly, should we put science
and poetry on the curriculum and not astrology and shove-
halfpenny? It is no good saying that we do this because we are
concerned about educating people; for what is at stake is the
justification of education. Conceptual analysis has enabled us
to get clearer about what is implicit in this commitment to
education. But it cannot, of itself, provide answers to the
ethical issues which it helps to make explicit.[16]

And on the next page: 'They [the authors] are conscious that a
definite moral point of view is implicit in their approach, but it is
not part of the intention of this book to attempt any explicit justification of it.'

What seems to be happening is that the authors, aware that the
word 'education' cannot do all the work they want done, deliberately retreat to a position in which they can be seen to be selling a
particular 'ideal' (to which, in a rather muddling way, they still
attach the term 'education'). 'Conceptual analysis', they say, will
explicate this particular 'ideal'; and the rest is a matter of 'ethical
valuation'. All this is extremely obscure; but taking this particular
passage as it stands, we should surely want to handle various parts
of these claims in very different ways:

(a) If we had already agreed to discuss something under the title
of 'education' and someone wanted to know why 'knowledge and
understanding' should 'be so favoured' or regarded as 'a necessary
feature', we should say that he did not seem to grasp what it was
that he was discussing. It is not *prima facie* intelligible to say 'I am
interested in education, but not a bit interested in anybody coming
to know or understand anything.' 'Education' just is not used like
that, because of its connection with learning; and learning has a
very close, if not absolutely unbreakable, connection with knowing
(see p. 72 ff.). So we should give some kind of *conceptual* answer to the
authors' first question, 'Why should knowledge and understanding
be so favoured?' This would also, I think, apply to almost any title-
word likely to be chosen here (*Bildung, paideusis, institutio*, child-
rearing, and so on); simply because it is hardly possible when
considering the upbringing of people or rational creatures *not* to be
concerned with learning and the objectives of learning.

(b) 'Autonomy', as I have tried to make plain elsewhere,[17] might or might not require conceptual argument. If it is taken to mean, roughly, 'enough freedom of mind to think for oneself, appreciate reasons for beliefs etc.', then this is logically required by the notions of learning and being educated. If it is taken to mark a specific disposition or cast of mind ('independent', the opposite of 'servile', perhaps sometimes 'stiff-necked' or 'bloody-minded') then the position is more complicated. (Either the word is taken to mark a disposition which is *ex hypothesi* a virtue, in which case we are back to conceptual arguments; or else a neutral disposition, in which case it will *not* always be justifiable.)

(c) We do not '*similarly*' ask why we teach science and not shove-halfpenny, because this is not obviously to be dealt with by conceptual argument.

Hence it becomes extremely hard to know just what the authors *do* put within their (or anyone else's) specification of 'education'. If all three ingredients – (a) knowledge and understanding, (b) autonomy, and (c) certain specific subjects (science, poetry) – are to go in the pot, then indeed 'a definite . . . point of view is implicit in their approach'; it is not necessarily right to call this a 'moral' point of view, but certainly they are trying to promote or sell some things which – as *they*, at least, maintain – are not or not obviously justified by conceptual necessity.

This is connected with the authors' methodology, which is worth briefly illustrating here. They draw a very sharp distinction between what they call 'conceptual analysis' and 'questions of value' (often using, again, the adjective 'moral' to point to these). Two examples are given:

'Our analysis of the concept of "need" has illustrated this point very well. It has been shown to be an inescapably valuative concept.'[18] Their earlier analysis included:

> If we say that a child needs something . . . we are suggesting
> (i) that he lacks something – love, a bath (ii) that what he
> lacks is desirable in some way. It is necessary *for* some
> desirable condition, the determination of which is a matter of
> ethical valuation.[19]

Now burglars (even child-burglars) need jemmies, chess-players need to castle early, and so on. Whence comes the temptation to describe this as anything to do with 'ethical valuation'? If anything is a matter of fact, it is often a matter of fact that X needs Y; and if we want to add that jemmies and early castling are needed only for the purposes of the individual in question (or some such remark), this itself shows that what is valuable is often a matter of fact. *This is how the words are used.*

> Surely, too . . . the operation of punishment as a deterrent presupposes a very important assumption about human beings, namely that they are responsible for their actions in the sense that they can be deterred by a consideration of foreseen consequences. And is this assumption justified? Is it not an assumption of great moral significance?[20]

What could it mean to say that some remark like 'Human beings can foresee consequences and because of this they (sometimes) stop what they're doing' involved an *assumption*? Well, perhaps Martians from outer space might observe terrestrial life and say 'We'll assume provisionally that *homo sapiens* does this, and to a lesser extent some other species too, but we need more observation to confirm this assumption', and so on; but this is scraping the bottom of the barrel. What would it be like for us *not* to believe this of human beings? How would one make sense of people playing games, or doing business, or almost anything? This is something we *know*; it is even rather odd to say that we have ways of 'justifying' this knowledge, because we are inextricably mixed up in a kind of life – human life, or the life of rational creatures – which makes it difficult or impossible to state any coherent alternative to such an 'assumption'; the knowledge is written into (among other things) the use of language itself. Certainly it has 'significance' – and not specifically 'moral' significance.

One part of the trouble here is the failure to distinguish 'assumptions' from conceptual necessities; but the major cause is a deep-rooted fear, common in a good deal of recent philosophy, of seeming to take up 'substantive' positions, or positions involving 'value-judgments' – a fear which, nevertheless, does not save many authors from whatever disadvantages (no doubt there are also advantages) are inherent in doing just that. This happens even when the authors are at pains to make the fear explicit. Thus, like Peters and many others, Downie, Telfer and Loudfoot are concerned with 'educatedness', or the specific state of 'being educated'; but Caledonian caution prompts them to take out an insurance policy against appearing to establish 'values' by purely conceptual arguments:

> While the term 'education' can be used in a very wide evaluative way such that whatever education is it is necessarily worth pursuing, it can also be used more narrowly and descriptively, in a way which leaves open the question of whether education in this sense is a good thing.[21]

55

Later, in a disarming postscript, their

> narrow view is based on certain traditional conceptions of
> education and of the teacher, although of course our description
> of the educated man has a large element of stipulation in it.
> Our narrow conception, however, is only *conceptually* normative.
> In adopting this conception, that is, we are recommending only
> that educatedness be seen in a certain way and not that it be
> preferred to other end-states.[22]

The stipulation, however, does not emerge as any the less arbitrary
for being declared 'only *conceptually* normative'. Thus the authors are
concerned, *ex hypothesi* (i.e. under the rubric of what they are going
to mean by 'educated'), with a man's having knowledge which is
'important' and 'relevant'. 'Important' for them means 'general' or
'wide-ranging':

> a man is not uneducated if he does not know whether the
> platypus lays eggs or not; but he is uneducated if he does not
> know that mammals are the most highly developed branch of
> the animal kingdom and that they feed their young on milk.[23]

By contrast, 'relevant' seems to mean 'relevant to one's own society':
'In history we would not call a man educated who knew nothing of
Greek and Roman civilization, but we might do so even if he knew
nothing of Indian or Chinese civilization.'[24] Hackles may be raised
by this, hardly to be lowered when we are told that 'we are making
it necessary in virtue of the meaning we are attaching to the term
"educated" that the knowledge . . . of the educated man has these
features'.[25] In other words, the stipulation has still to be defended
against the charge of being arbitrary.

The authors' conceptual manoeuvres begin with a curious logical
exercise in their first chapter, which results in the conclusion:

> Insofar as teaching is a skill-job we can characterize it only in
> very general terms, for the skills of the teacher are manifold.
> But the nature of the skills is necessarily linked with the concept
> of educatedness itself. Insofar as teaching is an aim-job we can
> depict its intrinsic aim as the creation of the educated man. . . .
> The point of characterizing teaching in this narrow way is to
> bring into sharp focus what we see as the essence, the bare
> bones or the Platonic Form of teaching.[26]

In this way the beginnings of a self-contained system are set up,
concepts marked by 'teaching', 'aim', etc., being now drawn in
under the magnetic influence of 'educatedness', which it is the
authors' prime concern to exhibit and justify. They 'accept the

traditional assumption' that 'basic to the distinctive endowment of a human being is his reason'[27] and advance a 'self-realization' argument which (after some pages of discussion) shows us, un-surprisingly, that 'Educatedness can be redescribed in terms of the realization of the theoretical reason, or what we have called the "intellectual self" '.[28]

They are clear-headed enough to see that this attempt at justification 'is successful only within certain very narrow limits'.[29] This is because they start from a notion of 'being educated' which is narrow enough for them to say that 'A person can be described as highly educated who is at the same time hopelessly bad at personal relations, incapable of planning his life, morally underdeveloped and lacking the capacity for strong feelings'.[30] A less stipulated notion of education might allow us to say, at least, that lack of education might be *one reason for* the deficiencies of such a person. If he is 'bad at personal relations', perhaps this is because he has not learned enough about people: if 'morally underdeveloped', because he has not learned enough about morality or about himself: if lacking in 'strong feelings', because he has not learned enough about the appropriate objects for such feelings. We might naturally say here that such a person's education had been incomplete or one-sided. But this is not what the authors allow themselves to say:

> To translate moral knowledge into action requires various
> qualities of character, depending on the circumstances; courage,
> self-control, perseverance, concern for others, love of justice,
> strength of will and so on. Nothing we have said gives us any
> reason to suppose that education, *as we have described it*, promotes
> these qualities at all (my italics)[31]

and similarly elsewhere, in other passages, where sharp distinctions are drawn between 'intellectual inclination within the moral sphere' and 'moral inclination proper', 'education' and 'inspiration', and so on.

The objection here is not just (a) that this delimitation of 'education' is artificial, contrary to normal usage, and unproductive – that, as an unbiased observer might fairly say, such consequences as these amount to something like a *reductio ad absurdum* of the delimitation. It is also (b) that – either because of, or following from, but anyway correlative with the delimitation – the authors cling to a view which severs 'morality' far too sharply from reason in general. It is as if they were insisting that large numbers of things clearly of great importance to men – personal relationships, courage, concern for others and so on – were not subject to reason and *could not be*

57

*learned at all* (for if they could, it would be entirely natural to include them within the aims of education, as did Plato and practically every subsequent philosopher of education). This also makes them miss the rather obvious point that 'morality' is not in a unique position as regards the (admittedly very obscure) connections between truth and action; qualities like self-control, strength of will and so forth are clearly required by a man in order to cope with areas we label 'science', 'history', 'mathematics', and so on – let alone whatever qualities we may need for the appreciation of art, or for doing philosophy.

As will be clear from this last example, the reason why so many authors suffer the disadvantages of a position which is 'substantive' or involves 'value-judgments', despite their fear of doing so, is basically that they are obsessed with the idea of 'educatedness'. This emerges clearly in their picture of what it is to 'justify education', the central feature of which is some notion of 'being educated' or 'the educated man' construed as the end-result of the process of educating. The process (*docere*) is to produce the educated person (*doctus*, often with the smuggled sense noticed earlier, p. 27); and what we have to justify, it is believed, is the latter. 'Educatedness' or 'the educated man' may be given various kinds of content; but in all cases there will be a distinction between the educated man and the uneducated man, even if this distinction is marked by some kind of cut-off point on a scale (being taken as a matter of degree rather than of kind). Different kinds of 'justifications' are then produced for this state of being – 'intrinsic' and 'extrinsic' justifications, 'transcendental' and 'redescription' arguments, and so forth. It is rather as if we were back with Aristotle trying to justify a particular kind of *life* – in this case, I suppose, something like the theoretic life: a particular *option* which some people took up and others ('the common herd') did not.

In trying to 'justify education', most contemporary philosophers have been dissatisfied with contingent and 'extrinsic' arguments of an 'instrumental' kind (roughly, to the effect that one needs to be educated as a means towards some external end – getting a better job, or whatever); but they then usually turn, either to justifying education as fulfilling some particular *part* of being a man, or to arguments which purport to show that what 'the educated man' *does* is somehow in itself superior. It is as if we were to believe that the only ways of justifying health consisted either in showing that health was the 'fulfilment' or 'realization' of the 'bodily part' of man, or in suggesting that what the healthy man did and the unhealthy could not do – perhaps climb mountains or participate in pentathla – was of superior quality.

This second line of argument has been popular in the philosophy of education from Plato to Peters, and resulted in a great many attempts to show (putting it briefly) why it is better to be Socrates dissatisfied than a pig satisfied, or to engage in poetry rather than push-pin. Peters' attempt, the details which I discuss below (p. 136), is in this context interesting in itself. In his most influential work, he seems early to dismiss the idea of 'justifying education' *per se*, since ' "education" implies the transmission of what is of ultimate value.'[32] Those who might reasonably be dissatisfied with this linguistic move, however, may fasten on what may fairly be called the central chapter of the book, 'Worth-while Activities'. This chapter begins with the words 'Education, it has been argued, involves the initiation of others into worth-while activities': we are then reminded that 'the curriculum of a school or university' encourages some activities and not others ('science, mathematics, history . . . not bingo, bridge and billiards') : and the paragraph ends with the question 'How then can the pursuit of such activities be justified?'[33] The rest of the chapter is an attempt to answer this question: that is, to solve the Socrates/pig or the poetry/push-pin problem.

What is important here is the absence of any attempt at justification other than (a) the early linguistic *fiat*, 'education'='the transmission of what is valuable', and/or (b) the justification of a particular content for education, a particular *specification* of 'the educated man' – roughly, one who has been initiated into and continues to care for certain specific 'worth-while' activities (which, rather surprisingly, seem to be more or less co-extensive with what we find in the curriculum of schools and universities in certain parts of the globe in the twentieth century). The point is not that the linguistic equation is wrong, or not consonant with 'normal usage'; nor that the particular content and specification are mistaken or not shown to be justified – even though both these objections can be sustained. The point is that, in a sense *between* the linguistic move of (a) and the specific-content move of (b), lies a whole area central to the philosophy of education. We have somehow to become clearer about what sort of thing it is – what sort of good, perhaps – to 'be educated' without any tighter linguistic specification than is absolutely necessary, and equally without any unnecessary or disputable specification of content.

3 I have already suggested that behind these typical errors lies a more general methodological doctrine about philosophy and – to use the most common but perhaps also the least helpful term – 'values'. Even to try to state this doctrine clearly, let alone criticize it, would take us too far from our particular topic of education. But

that it has dominated the philosophy of education for some decades is obvious enough; and at least we should be on our guard. Perhaps the most striking part of the doctrine, and one which (if taken literally) might well have the effect of nullifying most of the philosopher's efforts in this field, is the idea that, when it comes to 'values', philosophers have no business to 'lay down the law' for other people. Thus Peters tells us in the opening words of his major work[34] that

> There was a time when it was taken for granted that the philosophy of education consisted in the formulation of high-level directives which would guide educational practice. . . . Professional philosophers, however, are embarrassed by such expectations. . . . Few professional philosophers would now think[35] that it is their function to provide such high-level directives for education or for life; indeed one of their main preoccupations has been to lay bare such aristocratic pronouncements under the analytic guillotine.

Similarly, Woods, employing a distinction apparently still fashionable, writes: 'the philosopher *as a man* has a perfect right to say in what he thinks the good life consists, but his philosophical expertise will not enable him to pronounce authoritatively.'[36] This (easily recognizable) line is followed by innumerable other writers on the philosophy of education who have been brought up on what is still called 'the fact–value distinction'.

If we pay remarks of this kind the compliment of supposing that they mean what they say, we may consider cases of the following kind. As a 'professional philosopher', working in the field of education, I am called upon to advise a body of teachers about school rules. Many members of this body vigorously utter the words 'Schools ought not to have any rules', and in fact take practical action in their schools which seems to them to flow from this utterance and/or be consonant with it. I construct an argument – let the reader be kind enough to assume, a valid argument[37] – showing that there are conceptual connections between certain kinds of institutions and rules, and end up by saying 'Schools must have rules.' Is this not to 'pronounce authoritatively', and does it not count as the 'formulation of high-level directive which would guide educational practice'?

Someone will now say 'No, that's not a *directive*: the "must" in "Schools must have rules" summarizes a point of logic, it doesn't direct anyone towards practical action as "You must be a good boy today" does. Conceptual points by themselves don't prove anything "substantive"': or 'You can't deduce imperatives except from other imperatives: of course *if* they want schools, they can be brought to see that this necessarily involves them in having rules. But philosophers can't *make* them want schools in the first place.' But whatever may be believed about the logic and language of 'value-judgments', we have to decide what to do in various educational situations. Now one of two things: either (a) our decisions may be more or less reasonable, or (b) not. Nobody, I think, seriously believes (b): and if he did, there would be no clear basis for arguing about it, if only because what counts as a reasonable argument is itself something we must decide on.[38] If (a), then things may be said which have some weight by virtue of whatever principles of reason apply. Facts may be quoted, insights bestowed, parallels adduced, and conceptual connections established, all of which are at least *relevant* to the decision.

These things, as uttered in particular contexts, can certainly have action-guiding force because they can change the hearer's perception of and attitude to the situation. We may refuse to count them as 'directives', because they are not cast in a particular grammatical form.[39] But, when properly attended to, they certainly direct. We may say 'No, proper directives are of the form "Do X", "Adopt policy Y", and so on.' But what now can be meant by saying that 'philosophers cannot issue directives'? If 'issuing a directive' means just (a) uttering sentences in an imperative or modified imperative form – 'Do X', 'It's best to avoid Y', 'You ought to pursue Z' – then anyone, philosophers included, can do this. If it means (b) saying something, in whatever form, which supports, or vitiates, or is in some way relevant to a decision or programme, then anyone can do that too; and those with particular expertises, like philosophers, will have particular things to say. To put this another way: any public value or rational weight in issuing directives in sense (a) – that is, in simply commanding – will depend on the commands being backed by some kind of good *reason* for the person doing what was commanded. Otherwise one would have to imagine the commander simply issuing orders just for the hell of it, so to speak, or just to exercise his will over others. But then this value or weight can be equally operative in sense (b).

All this is perhaps obvious; but it is interesting to note how, in practical education, this self-denying ordinance on the part of philosophers is paralleled by other disciplines, and has produced an almost complete vacuum in rational decision-making. The empirical workers naturally follow suit: 'It's not for *us* to decide what ought to be done, we're just humble scientists who find out the facts and leave "value-judgments" to others.' The ball is then passed to parents, teachers, politicians, 'the contemporary educational climate', 'society', 'a general consensus', or whatever: the result being that there are very few cases that can seriously be described as rational decisions – what happens, happens as a result of miasmic social and psychic pressures, largely unconscious. I have tried to say something elsewhere[40] about how this situation could be improved, and what part philosophers could in practice play in improving it; but that it exists must be obvious to anyone familiar with the field.

The impression is often created that what is and must be important to human beings (the world of 'values') is wholly disconnected, in point of logic, from human nature or what it is to be a human being (the world of 'facts'). A useful contemporary illustration is Peters'[41] well-known 'transcendental' argument (I shall consider this more fully on pp. 136 ff.). In the present climate of opinion, it is unsurprising that the bulk of criticism directed against this argument has been to the effect that it involves 'concealed value-judgments' or 'tries to derive values from purely formal considerations'. Consider Downie:

> His thesis is rather a logical one: that engaging in the activities is presupposed in the very attempt to assess the value of them. But . . . if this is true, in what sense is it a *justification* of the activities? To see what is meant here, consider a trivial analogy. The activity of asking questions is presupposed in asking the question 'Why ask questions?' and this seems to show that the question is self-answering in some way. But this fact does not show that it is *valuable* to ask questions. Similarly if, as Peters suggests, asking and answering the question 'Why do this rather than that?' presupposes the undertaking of some form of rational inquiry, it is a self-answering question. But this fact does not show that rational inquiry is *valuable* . . . the basic 'Why do . . . ?' itself can mean either 'Shall I do this or that?' or 'Why is this more valuable than that?' (Similarly he speaks of those who ask the question as being 'committed' to theoretical activities, which can mean either 'committed to undertaking them' or 'committed to valuing them highly'.)[42]

This implies a picture of 'value' sharply divorced from the surely connected ideas of intentional action and commitment. The two questions 'Shall I do this or that?' and 'Why is this more valuable than that?' could, at the least, both be thought of as versions of 'Which is the better thing to do?'; the speaker is presumably asking for reasons why one thing is more desirable, more worth aiming at, more worth doing, etc., than the other. Similarly if I am 'committed to undertaking' something, I am clearly in *some* sense 'committed to valuing' it – if not 'highly', at least as something to be aimed at, as a thing seen *sub specie boni alicuius*.

The example given may itself bring us slightly nearer the truth. If a person seriously – that is, here, with some degree of sincerity – asks a question, this at least shows that he 'values' *some* amount of question-asking. There is at least *one* question which he wants (needs, thinks it good) to ask. In fact it would be difficult to see how his sincerity could exempt him from 'valuing' some further questions: for instance, if he wants his question to be understood and taken seriously – and if he did not, we would doubt his seriousness in asking it – then he would presumably welcome questions from a hearer who had not understood him ('What do you mean, exactly?'). What we should *not* conclude, of course, is that he would be logically committed to valuing a *great deal* of question-asking, or the 'theoretic life', or anything of that kind. The point lies in how 'seriously', or how much, he is committed to it.

It seems that there are two ideas here which we have to resist. The first, which is clearly absurd when spelled out, is that we cannot describe a person as serious about or genuinely committed to X unless he is prepared to follow it up with complete single-mindedness, or to make an all-embracing ideal out of it. I can be serious about learning, but also about other things; my other commitments do not *per se* tell against my commitment to learning. They might do so, or at least seem to do so, if they take up so much of my time that I engage in little or no learning at all: overt action is *one* test of the sincerity of seriousness of a commitment. But it is not the only, nor (I think) the clearest: the link between what I value and what I do is more indirect. The second idea is that there is a complete disconnection between what is to be 'valued' and what, as human beings, we are inevitably committed to. Much of the force of philosophy lies in showing that we do inevitably have certain commitments, which are evidenced by our language and other behaviour, even though we very easily forget, repress, deny, or by some other means turn away from them.

Can anything more positive be said about how, in this situation, the philosopher can proceed without joining the ranks of the ideologues? Even if one accepts without question the doctrine that philosophers should be uniquely concerned with 'conceptual arguments', and the connected (though by no means identical) doctrine that this amounts to a concern with 'the meaning of words', it is still possible to distinguish a number of *different* ways in which such concern may have directive or 'substantive' force. There is (a) the fact that, for human beings or rational creatures living in any conceivable (intelligible) world, certain things are logically *given*.

A good deal is given (i) by the notion of an individual creature of this kind, so that concepts marked by 'space', 'time', 'language', 'choice', 'good', 'bad', and many others turn out, on inspection, to be closely interlocked; and a good deal more (ii) by the interaction of such an individual with others like himself, interaction which might turn out to be a conceptual necessity for the continued existence of such individuals. From these could be shown to follow a very considerable number of notions which we often misguidedly regard as contingent: for instance, the (various but numerically finite) basic emotions which such individuals will feel, derivable from the concept of a conscious and choosing creature in a space–time continuum,[43] the necessary features of any human interaction or social group (for instance, promise-keeping and truth-telling in general), and so forth. Some such necessary features, as I hope to show later, are both importantly relevant to education and insufficiently explicated by philosophers.

Arguments which begin with such inexpellable concepts may establish two rather different things, which nevertheless have close connections: (i) what is *minimally* required by the concept, say, of a rational creature, and (ii) what can be seen as at least a *prima facie* good, or reason for action, for such a creature. To use the example quoted earlier, it is clearly (i) a necessary feature of anything we would describe as a rational creature that such a creature should engage in a minimum of question-asking or the pursuit of truth; and (ii) a necessary, if only *prima facie*, good that it should, other things being equal, get as much truth as is possible (since such truth might, as. it were, always come in handy, whatever the creature's desires may be). Similarly, (i) a minimal amount of prudence or 'deferred gratification' is conceptually required (otherwise we should find ourselves describing something even more extreme than a psychopath); and equally (ii) prudence[44] will be a necessary virtue in the sense that it is a permanently useful piece of equipment for gaining one's ends, even though other virtues may on many occasions deserve precedence.

There is also (b), perhaps a little less obviously, the possibility of advancing conceptual arguments which will not establish certain goods of this kind to be such beyond reasonable doubt, but will refer rather to the equipment which a 'reasonable man' (or whatever phrase may be taken as free from dispute) requires in order to make up his own mind about what to count as good. This line may appeal particularly to liberally minded philosophers of education, and perhaps in general to those philosophers who hold some strong version of the doctrine that 'values' cannot be derived from 'facts'; it is in any case clearly a different line from (a) above. To take an extreme case, only a very bold philosopher (at least nowadays) would want to specify just what form of government or political constitution is best either for certain situations or for all men everywhere; but only a very timid, or a very doctrinaire, philosopher would claim that there was not such a thing as being more or less reasonable (sane, sensible, well-informed, etc.) in deciding such issues. In other words, we can speak of criteria of competence or reasonableness in decision-making even when we are not clear about what decisions a reasonable man would actually make – just as, very obviously, we can speak of what makes a good scientist in advance of knowing the answers to particular scientific problems.

These are considerations which apply so long as we intend to go on being human and reasonable; but obviously enough, there are (c) others which apply as soon as we commit ourselves, if only for a part of our time and with some of our resources, to a particular enterprise. Thus insofar as we are serious about people learning things, we commit ourselves (as I shall try to show) to a whole set of conceptual implications which are involved in the notion of serious learning. There will be individual and social requirements and virtues, some minimally to be satisfied for us to be able to describe what is going on as serious learning, or the serious learning of X, at all: and others to be reinforced and pursued, other things being equal, for the proper conduct and flourishing of such learning. One of the reasons why it is important to make a correct or wise delimitation of the enterprise we are to call 'education' is that we can be clear about whether we are considering arguments that apply generally (not just educationally) to human beings (which may help us to assess the *comparative* value of educational goods in relation to others), or working within a roughly delimited area of specifically *educational* goods.

This last is perhaps the most obvious point of entry for the philosophy of education, since it leads most directly to a closer consideration of the form of the enterprise. It is tempting to argue: 'There can be no such thing as a *sui generis* educational good or educational reason: for if something ought to be learned, this will be for some reason outside the business of learning itself – the reason will be a medical one, or a political one, or whatever. Thus if children ought to learn first-aid, this is because it serves the medical good of health: if to defend the state, because it serves the political good of security: and so on. In much the same way there could not be purely legal goods or reasons: if something is a good law, this must be because it enforces or prohibits behaviour which is, for external reasons, good or bad. So the only possible procedure is first to decide what we think to be good or bad for individuals and societies, and then to frame our educational and legal systems accordingly.' But this is, once again, to be obsessed with the idea that the only important thing about education is its *content*. Certain things are logically required for *any* kind of serious or coherent learning; and a good many more things can be added once we have decided (as we must, even if only *pro tempore*) what is to be learned. Similarly there are features of all good laws *qua* laws, whatever their content (for instance, clarity and enforceability): and other features to be added, once we know what their content is to be.

But this is not the only kind of ground that may be gained. Still without specifying any particular content in advance, we may also come to see that some of the goods emerging from the more general considerations in (a) and (b) above are uniquely connected with education: either (i) in that only education can *produce* them, or (ii) in that they are *inherent* in education and learning themselves, and in them alone; and both of these would commit us to the enterprise of education to a certain extent and in certain ways. Not all items of learning or educational content need be valued as *ad hoc* instruments for the attainment of other goods governed by other enterprises. Learning itself, or the results of having learned (some kind of knowledge or control), may perhaps be either (i) a logically necessary, not just an *ad hoc*, instrument, or (ii) valuable 'for its own sake' or 'in its own right', and not to be conceived primarily as an instrument at all. We grant, of course, that all this has to be clarified and demonstrated in detail; my point here is simply that these procedures are possible ones.

These briefly sketched points may at least enable us to preserve an open mind. For it is, in fact, an open – and very important – question how far we may reach agreement about matters of education without abandoning rational discussion in favour of the advancement of particular 'ideologies' or 'commitments'. I believe that we can advance a good deal further than it is nowadays fashionable to suppose. But we can only do this if we are prepared to shelve those specific ('substantive') questions of content on which we are not agreed, and which we do not as yet know how to handle properly, in order to concentrate more closely on the form of the enterprise, and its conceptual connections with what is given in human life generally. Indeed, it is difficult to see what could be meant by 'rational discussion' unless we had at least *some* grasp of inalienable or non-disputable criteria in terms of which such discussion could move towards, if not reach, a conclusion. If in fact we have none at all, we cannot distinguish such discussion from the polite or impolite exchange of, and the more or less dogged adherence to, partisan commitments or fantasies; and how could *that* be thought to be valuable – unless, again, we have some agreed criteria of value?

# Learning

part II

# The implications of learning

3

If we are to work our way towards a better understanding of education and the goods it dispenses, the most obvious connection to pursue is the connection with learning. Even if we refrain (as many psychologists do not) from employing the term in a manner clean contrary to normal usage, we may still find that the concept marked by 'learn' is a curiously elusive one. There are temptations to delimit it too narrowly in some respects, and too broadly in others; and we shall see later that both these errors have important practical consequences for education.

A too narrow delimitation appears in two (connected) doctrines about learning which seem popular among philosophers. The first of these is that learning involves 'mastery' or 'success': for instance

> the process is therefore always related to some kind of mastery of X, to a particular success or achievement. To have learnt, is always to have come up to some standard: for example to know what previously one did not know, or to have mastered a given skill.[1]

This doctrine is sound if we interpret it merely as noting a point of grammar: namely, that 'learn' is a transitive verb and implies some object. But the same is true of most, perhaps all, verbs of the class which Kenny entitles 'performance verbs':[2] 'find', 'build', 'kill', 'wash', 'cut', etc. If talk of 'success', 'mastery', 'achievement', 'coming up to some standard' and so forth is just a way of reminding us that one must, logically or grammatically, learn *something*, we have nothing to quarrel with. In the same sense one must kill, wash, cut, etc., something: without such 'success' the verbs are unintelligible. But such talk at least flirts with the much stronger (and ultimately quite different) idea that the criteria of success are restricted by connections with truth or 'a given skill'. Yet, at least *prima facie*, one can learn to regard Jews as enemies or women as inferior: and one can also learn *not* to bother about being tidy, or about writing grammatical English. One can learn to relax, or to

69

forget (in the Foreign Legion); and though one cannot learn *that* the earth is flat, one can learn to think that it is. The hero of Orwell's *1984* did not learn that Big Brother was lovable or believable: but he learned to love and believe Big Brother. The lack of general restriction on the objects of learning is masked partly by the empirical fact (if it is a fact) that people characteristically set out to learn useful or desirable things, and partly by the particular restriction that we cannot *say* 'He learned that p' unless we believe p to be true.[3]

This particular restriction applies, of course, also to propositional clauses that follow 'learn': as, 'learning who Caesar was', 'learning when William I came to the throne', 'learning where London is', and so on. But it is far from clear what it amounts to. Suppose that today I learn the dates of the kings of England; time passes, and we discover that our chronology was mistaken. It seems odd to say that I did not do some learning, and equally odd to say that I learned *that* William I reigned from 1066, if (as we now think) he actually reigned from 1070. Similarly we want to say that a man can learn astrology or the doctrines of Christian Science, but not that he has learned *that* the planets influence human affairs, or that pain is unreal. Our difficulty, I think, is that learning must have some object: and that these false or unintelligible propositions are non-objects, so that we cannot give an answer to 'What did he learn?' *in that form*. We have to say 'He learned the accepted chronology for English kings', or 'to think that the planets influence human affairs', or 'the doctrines of Christian Science'.

Not only is there some doubt about what is to count as 'success' or 'achievement': there is also a question about whether learning implies actual mastery, or only an attempt at mastery. The same question can be put in the case of other verbs, much discussed by philosophers of education, such as 'teach' or 'indoctrinate'. Was the master teaching the boys Latin even if they learned no Latin, or was he just trying to teach them? Does A indoctrinate B only if A has certain aims or intentions in mind, or is the actual result of what A does sufficient? I do not think anything is gained here by trying to distinguish some verbs as 'task-words' and others as 'achievement-words': that distinction will work only with the obvious – one might say, the classic – cases to which it was originally applied. The problem with 'learn', 'teach', etc., arises precisely because the distinction breaks down; they are not, or not obviously, like 'search' or 'strive' on the one hand, nor like 'find' or 'win' on the other.

It is tempting to say that 'learn' always implies success. Thus Kenny writes: 'Washing the dishes is bringing it about that the dishes are clean: learning French is bringing it about that I know

French: walking to Rome is bringing it about that I am in Rome.'[4]
From this one might conclude that if the dishes are not cleaned, if I
do not come to know French, and if I do not arrive in Rome, then
I was not washing the dishes, or learning French, or walking to Rome.
But this is clearly false, as the last example shows: I have, certainly,
to be making for Rome, otherwise we should not use the description
'walking *to Rome*', but I may be genuinely walking to Rome even
though, like many a pilgrim, I drop out *en route*. To put this another
way: 'bringing it about that' is ambiguous between the task or
process of bringing it about and the achievement of bringing it
about or having brought it about.

Suppose a man spends time in trying to master something: say,
swimming or the principal parts of an irregular verb. If we ask what
he is doing during that time, it is usually unnatural to reply that he
is trying to learn to swim or trying to learn the principal parts.
'Trying to learn' makes most sense in cases where he encounters
obstacles *to* the process of learning, not where he encounters
obstacles *in* the process: for instance, if there is so much noise that he
cannot concentrate, or if the swimming-bath is so fully booked that
he has not enough time for practice. We should more naturally say
that he *was learning*. A great deal seems to turn, in fact, on what
grammatical part of the verb is used. Certain tenses – aorist,
perfect, pluperfect, future perfect – commit us to the idea of
achievement or success. 'He learned (has learned, had learned,
will have learned) X' must imply an actual gain of some knowledge
or control. On the other hand, where (in English) the present
participle is used as part of a tense, there is no such implication. 'He
is learning (was learning, will be learning, has been learning) X'
means simply that he is (was, etc.) trying to achieve something, not
necessarily that he achieved it.

But is the mere trying enough? Must he not have achieved
*something*? Suppose (1) I try to achieve something which is logically
impossible (say, square the circle): we should not say that I am (was)
learning to do it, just as – and perhaps just because – we should
never say that I have learned (did learn, etc.) to do it. What about
(2) things that, though in principle possible, are in practice not
possible for me – for instance, jumping 8 feet high? The same seems
to apply: if X is impossible for me, I cannot have been learning to
X. But now suppose (3) that X is possible for me (say, jumping 5
feet high): that it would take me some time, nevertheless, to achieve
it: and that for some reason or other I never reach the required
standard. *Was* I learning to X in those early stages?

It seems that we would often say 'yes' to this; but the reason we
would be able to give is that I was making some *progress towards* X

(I succeed in jumping 4 feet, raise the bar to 4 feet 6 inches, and so forth). But now suppose (4) that the X is such that the idea of 'progress' seems to have little or no application: for instance, wiggling one's ears. It is tempting to say here that 'learning to wiggle one's ears' makes no sense, since there are no procedures one can follow to achieve this X: nothing counts as 'progress', so nothing counts as learning. But this is too severe: if a man sets himself this task, and tries out various moves which he thinks might help – puckering up his face, massaging his facial muscles, and so on – and eventually is able to wiggle his ears, we should certainly say that he had learned to wiggle them; and we should also have to say that he had *been* learning to, even if he never finally succeeded.

The point is, I suppose, that except in cases of impossibility ((1) and (2) above) there is always *something* that a man can do to achieve any X; so that cases (3) and (4) can be collapsed – some idea of progress is always applicable. However, in case (4), not *any* (haphazard) move the man makes will count as learning. They have to be moves which are necessary to ear-wiggling, or contribute positively towards it, or (at the very least) have some relevance to it – if only as blind alleys which might reasonably be explored. This case shows the minimal sense in which learning is related, however indirectly, to the X being learned. We shall say that such sentences as 'He was learning X' do not imply that he ever actually achieved (learned) X; but that they imply more than that he was just trying to achieve X. The man has, as it were, to have been trying *on the right lines*: that is, again, making some *progress* towards X.

This may already make us hesitate before accepting the second and connected doctrine, that learning entails knowledge:

> it would, I suggest, be impossible to suppose that someone
> could have learned something if he had not in some sense
> acquired new knowledge, whatever form that knowledge may
> take (and it may of course include skills as well as factual
> knowledge). . . . There is a whole range of somewhat disparate
> cases which may fall under the general heading of 'having
> learned to . . .' These may not involve the acquisition of
> knowledge *simpliciter*. Yet I am still inclined to think that
> knowledge enters into the picture in other, more indirect, ways.
> If I have learned to love someone, rather than merely come to
> love them, my love follows upon and exists in virtue of what I
> have come to know.[5]

But what sort of thing have I 'come to know' in those (very many) cases where I have clearly learned to do something, yet have not acquired any new *propositional* knowledge? It is natural here to rely on the much canvassed notion of 'knowing how'; but there seem to be clear counter-examples even to this. I may learn, just by practice, not to look down when climbing mountains, to keep my temper, not to show surprise, and so forth. In these and many other cases there is little or no 'how' *to* learn or know; one just has to set oneself the task and practise doing it. In fact it seems that we only speak seriously of knowing how to X when some kind of propositional knowledge *is* involved, in however shadowy a way: knowing how to fly an aeroplane or solve a quadratic equation, not (or not so easily) knowing how to walk or talk or turn a somersault. If there is no question of attending to some proposition, or at least of following some kind of rule, the 'how' is otiose; philosophers may ask us to 'suppose I am asked *how* I clench my fist, or suck' (my italic),[6] but in fact I just do these things, in much the same way as I just raise my arm. When a child has learned to talk, we do not naturally say 'He knows how to talk': we say 'He can talk.'

There may still be a temptation to say that the *direct* object of learning must be some propositional knowledge, or skill, or understanding, and that the X in 'learning to X' is a kind of indirect object. Thus one learns that Flossie is kind, intelligent, etc., and thus (or thereby) learns to love her; or (according to Socrates at least) learns what is to be feared, and thus learns to be brave. The same manoeuvre can be employed with complex skills: what one directly learns, it might be said, is *how* to X; and thereby, but only indirectly, to X (how to drive a car, and thence to drive it). This fits snugly with the view that learning always involves some kind of knowledge: knowing how or knowing that.

But though many cases of learning to X can be construed thus, there are (as we have seen) too many resisting cases: learning to keep one's temper, learning not to look down when climbing mountains, learning to wait till the light turns green when crossing the road, and so on. What makes the view seem plausible is that, unsurprisingly, a great many objects of human or rational learning do involve propositional knowledge or skill. There is, moreover, usually a background of such knowledge even in these examples of 'brute' learning. No doubt a man learns to keep his temper for certain reasons, just as he learns not to look down in order to avoid falling, and learns to wait for the green light to avoid being run over. But that is a far cry from saying that the learning itself involves knowledge or skill.

Depending on what one learns to do, there are different gaps between learning how to do X and learning to do X: gaps not to be filled by anything we could properly call knowledge. The most obvious gap is a lack of motivation: I may learn *how* to behave politely – that is, I have the required factual knowledge and skill – but not learn *to* behave politely, because I do not want to. It is also, I think, possible to drive a wedge between know-how and ability: there seems to be a clear sense in which someone sufficiently familiar with the proper method knows *how* to solve an equation or fly an aeroplane, even if he cannot in fact solve it or fly it (perhaps the equation is too hard for him, or he always gets giddy in the cockpit). Here again we might well say that he has learned how to do these things, but has not learned *to* do them. It might now be claimed that we are taking the phrase 'knowing how' too seriously: that 'he knows how to X' is more or less equivalent to 'he can X'. But, even if these were the linguistic facts (as, in my judgment, they are not), that move would simply be a short cut to the same conclusion; for now the connection between learning and knowledge, supposedly enshrined in the phrase 'knowing how', has been thrown out along with the phrase itself.

The doctrine might be partially saved by the claim that 'learn' has two senses in English, one of which quite simply *means* something like 'acquire knowledge' or 'come to understand', and is always in force when we talk of learning that p. It is true that there are words in other languages, as for instance *cognosco* in Latin or *gignosko* in Greek, which can often be translated by 'learn' but which – since they have the force of 'find out' or 'get to know' – are not normally used of learning to X. But this in itself shows nothing; for such languages also have words which can be used in either way. Aeneas tells his son to learn courage and conscientiousness, and Hector says that he has learned to behave as a champion ought.[7] The linguistic fact (for what it is worth) is that many languages, like our own, employ one word to cover both contexts; and we ought not to claim equivocation without due cause.

It seems more sensible to say that 'learn' means, unequivocally, something like 'acquire knowledge or control by paying relevant attention' (I shall explain this latter phrase later); and perhaps 'knowledge or control' can be collapsed into some such term as 'mastery'. Certainly there is nothing surprising in the fact, reflected in this unequivocal meaning, that human beings use a single term to mark those (admittedly multifarious) activities by which they acquire both theoretical and practical mastery, and improve both their grasp of truth and their control of action or behaviour. What emerges from these considerations is the fact, obvious in itself and only to be repressed by some philosophical strait-jacket, that the notion of 'control' or 'mastery' cannot be wholly explicated by the notions of 'knowledge' or 'skill'.

We may note here in parenthesis that the disconnection, at this point, between learning and knowledge or truth makes a significant difference to *one* kind of argument characteristically favoured by those who take learning to be in some sense inherently good. It is commonly said that there is always *something* good about acquiring knowledge or truth, although on particular occasions it may be outweighed by other considerations: perhaps the knowledge leads to harm, or – a different point – there is something more important for the person to do than to acquire knowledge; or perhaps both. But even if this were true, it does not always apply to learning, since there are sophistications of experience which are not only not truth-orientated, but may even be enemies to truth and to virtue. The example of learning to see Jews as inferior is one sort of case; others might include learning to close one's ears to criticism, learning to deceive, learning to enjoy torture, and so on.

Someone might still want to say, of course, that there is something good merely in the sophistication of experience which learning involves. An entity who does this, however misguided or wicked, is (he might say) at least acting more like a man and less like an animal: he may be a clever devil, but anyway he is not a beast. To say this is harmless enough, if it means only that learning is a conceptual requirement for being human. But it must not be allowed to mask the important point that there can be *bad learning*: not just in the sense of structuring one's experience along the right lines but rather incompetently, as when a pupil has not learned his Latin grammar very well, but in the sense of structuring it along quite incorrect lines, as when children in certain cultures learn to see aliens as dangerous or women as natural slaves. This point has considerable practical importance for education.

If, then, we reject these over-stringent connections between learning and knowledge, what is it that distinguishes learning as a human performance? How are we to avoid making too loose a delimitation, in the way that most psychologists have done?[8] The natural starting-point is the *manner in which* the person changes; and we might begin by saying that if a man learns to X (rather than just comes to X) he must, at the least, have come to X by paying some sort of *attention* to the world. This is not to say that a man must be paying attention *to X* if we are to count him as learning X: there are all sorts of things we learn on the side, so to speak, and are not even aware that we have learned. But it is to say that he must be paying *some* kind of attention, or making *some* kind of conscious attempt on the world. A boy comes to be able to jump higher and lift heavier weights just by growing older and bigger; he learns to do these things only by some exercise of consciousness. What a man gains by learning, he gains by himself and for himself: it is in this sense that we may talk, though with caution, of 'achievement' or the 'sophistication' of his experience. Thus he may learn not to show surprise only if showing surprise is, in some sense, his natural or unsophisticated reaction. He may *come* not to show surprise by all sorts of methods: by just failing to notice surprising things, or by being under heavy sedation, or by being so strictly conditioned that he simply cannot raise his eyebrows and display other symptoms of surprise. But in these cases he is exercising no option.

Learning, in other words, is a *praxis* and not just a *pathos*. This holds good even in the extreme case, where it may seem that what I have to do in order to learn is precisely *not* to pay attention. Suppose I want to forget my worries, and cannot rely on their natural disappearance in the ordinary course of life; I might learn to forget them by learning not to attend to them when they crop up in my mind (as soon as they appear, I resolutely dismiss them, engage in some task that requires concentration, and so on). I have done more here than come to forget them: I have learned to, because I have paid relevant attention to the worries – if only in the minimal sense that I have a policy for dealing with them when they appear.

All this is connected with the delimitation of education as concerned specifically with the learning of rational creatures. The obvious point is that such creatures, and only such, can learn things which involve conceptual grasp and propositional knowledge. These things include all cases of learning *that* p, but extend beyond this class; for most cases of learning how to X, learning to X, or just learning X involve such knowledge. Thus puppies may learn to walk, or to sit up and beg, or parlour tricks; but not how to read, or to write, or English grammar. But we have to go a good deal further than this. Non-rational entities do indeed learn; but this cannot be learning in the same sense as that in which rational creatures learn, since non-rational creatures cannot pay attention or exercise consciousness – or if they can, not in the full-blown senses of these terms which apply to rational creatures.[9] Kangaroos cannot learn to jump further as a man may learn to jump farther: they just find themselves jumping, or come to be able to jump. With non-rational entities, we locate the distinction elsewhere – very roughly, between things acquired by 'experience' and things given them by 'nature'; and if pressed on the former, we might say something about 'interaction with the environment', 'trial and error', 'reaction to stimuli', and so on. But whatever these terms mean – and perhaps their meaning varies depending on what sort of non-rational creature, and what sort of 'interaction', we are talking about – they do not appear to have the full sense applicable to adult human

beings and (if there are any) other rational creatures. For all such
terms ('conscious', 'experience', 'making use of experience',
'attending', 'modifying', etc.) have a thinner, more strictly 'behavioural', application for non-rational creatures. It is not, then, just
that rational creatures can learn some things which other creatures
cannot: it is also that learning itself is a different sort of enterprise –
a difference apparent indeed, not only in the verb 'learn' but in a
great many other terms which normally contain an element of
intentionality and application of consciousness.

If we accept some such distinction, we have grounds for resisting
the pressure which comes from the 'achievement' element in learning. There are some border-line cases where such pressure is very
strong. Might not a man learn to swim simply by being thrown in
off the deep end, paying virtually no conscious attention at all to
anything but just finding himself (after some struggling) able to
swim? Might not a cripple learn to walk again by hobbling about
in his sleep? If someone puts the right sort of hypnopaedic machine
under my pillow and I wake up being able to construct sentences in
French, have I not learned something? The pressure comes from
the thought 'Clearly he has come to be able to do these things, by
some kind of "experience" or "interaction": why should we not say
"learned"?' Well, of course we *can* say so; but then we have to
remember the difference between these cases and the more usual
cases of attention-paying adults learning to swim, or walk, or speak
French.

I do not think that we should, in fact, even seriously consider
these as cases of learning if they were not also affected by another
kind of pressure, arising from some idea of unconscious or semi-
conscious attention. There is a certain space or scope – mark it by
what words we will – for cases in which people seem to be agents
rather than patients, though not fully or consciously attending.
Some men solve crossword clues without consciously reasoning them
out; some even construct Latin verses in their sleep. It is not, or
certainly not only, the successful achievement which makes us want
to say that *they did* these things: rather we feel that the 'process' or
'mechanism' which produced the achievement is fairly to be counted
as part of 'them', even though below the level of consciousness. Nor
is there much surprising here, since a good deal of intelligent or
rational behaviour seems to be of this kind; part of the expertise of
a good chess-player is precisely that he does *not* have to ratiocinate
consciously about many features of the game – he unconsciously
'screens' or 'scans' the situation on the board and selects only those
features which call for conscious attention. On the other hand, there
are cases like the *idiot savant* who immediately gives the right answer

to a long and difficult mathematical sum; and this we may be tempted to classify along with cases of primitive savages who know what time of day it is and in which direction their homes lie, or even with the powers of homing pigeons – that is, we regard the *idiot savant's* right answer as non-intelligent or non-rational (for one thing, he cannot tell us how he did it).[10]

The most useful criterion here is perhaps whether the achievement, if not directly produced by conscious attention-paying, is at least produced by following rules which had themselves been attended to earlier and which could, at least in principle, be brought to consciousness; this would obviously be true of the chess-player, but not (I take it) of the *idiot savant* nor, more significantly for our purposes, of someone who had just been conditioned to, or fallen into the habit of, making certain moves in chess. The most natural way to deploy this criterion is to ask whether the person had *learned* to behave as he does; and this now clearly seems to mean whether he *had* paid attention to the situation (originally seen the reasons for moves which are now habitual). Learning, we might now say, requires the deployment of conscious intelligence; and even if, as seems necessary, we allow the notion of unconscious intelligence, we allow this notion to operate only where conscious intelligence operated at an earlier time.

There is a further and very important restriction on 'learn', which concerns what a person pays attention *to*. For, though he need not have the description 'X' in mind, he needs to have something in mind which (whether he knows it or not) relates or is *relevant* to that description. Suppose a man, heavily influenced by astrology, who comes to think that Flossie will make him a good wife because their horoscopes are mutually favourable: suppose also that, for quite other reasons, it is true that Flossie will make him a good wife. We should hesitate to say that the man has *learned* that Flossie will make him a good wife. He has certainly done some learning, and he certainly holds a true belief; moreover, he seems to have reached the belief by what he has learned. But this is insufficient: we demand that the means by which he reaches the belief are *appropriate*.

The kind of awareness in question here is, I think, masked rather than clarified by common uses of the word 'know' in our language. In the example above, it seems hard to deny that the man knows that Flossie will make him a good wife; just as it is hard to deny that a pupil who regularly and confidently uses '*livre*' in French, when it means 'book', as a masculine noun knows that it is masculine, even though his reasons might be wholly mistaken (he might think that all nouns ending in -*e* are masculine). We may, of course, follow various philosophers in demanding the insertion of some such criterion as 'having the right to be sure' as a necessary condition of knowledge; but, as cases like those above suggest, this often goes against what we actually say. Moreover, the criterion is ambiguous; in one clear sense the man does have the right to be sure, simply because there is in fact good reason to believe what he believes. If it is now said that *there being* the right does not involve *his having* the right, we shall point out that this too flies in the face of what we normally say: there are all sorts of rights which one has (as a citizen, for instance) without knowing why one has them or even that one has them. All this compels us, I think, to grant that pupils may very often know that certain things are the case, and may even have a sufficient understanding of the concepts involved in the relevant propositions, yet not have *learned* these things; and because of the connection between education and learning, it would not be correct to say that such pupils had been *educated* in respect of them. We shall discuss this further in chapter 5.

One criterion of the appropriateness of attention, then, is that a man should reach his belief by attending to the relevant evidence; and what counts as 'relevant' will naturally be determined by the proper grounds for the belief in question. But where performances rather than beliefs are concerned – that is, where some or all of the learning is non-propositional – it is not so easy to apply a criterion of appropriateness. On the one hand, not every mastery that I acquire just *while* I am attending to something will count; thus the fact that schoolboys may be learning various curricular subjects over a period of years does not at all tempt us to say that they have learned in that time to lift heavier weights, if their ability to lift those weights comes about merely by their growing taller and stronger. We may be inclined to insist that *learning* to lift heavier weights must involve paying attention *to that task*; and that might be taken to imply that a man must (1) set himself (or be set, or anyway *confront*) the task, and (2) actually *engage* in it: then, if we add the condition (3) noticed earlier (in the ear-wiggling case), that he does in fact make some progress in the task, these will suffice to say that he is learning. In a certain sense of 'pay attention', 'confront', 'engage', etc., all this is true; but it must not be taken to imply that the man must *know what* he is attending to, or confronting, or engaging in. He must be directing his attention relevantly: but there is no need for him, or indeed anybody else, to be *aware* of the relevance.

Nor, again, need the task to which he consciously applies himself even be a task of learning (though often it will be). A child may learn to walk partly, at least, just because he wants to get somewhere or enjoy something, not necessarily because he wants to *learn* anything. I pick this example as the clearest, because the point may be masked by the obvious fact that most intelligent adults will be aware of what they need to learn in order to achieve their goals, and hence will consciously address the tasks of learning. But this need not be so: for instance, I may consciously address the task of wooing a girl, and may soon learn to talk softly and sweetly, cast certain glances, smile in a certain way and so on; but unless I am a professional seducer, I may well not have addressed myself consciously to these sub-tasks. Yet we should still say that I had learned (rather than just come) to talk softly, etc., because my mastery arose from some deliberate attempt upon the world, to the success of which these items are relevant.

There are two sorts of cases in which learning may occur in this (as we might call it) non-specific way. The first is the case just mentioned: when I deliberately engage in a task or general X which, whether or not I know it, involves acquiring certain particular skills or sub-Xs. For instance, when I try to speak French, I thereby learn how to move my lips, larynx, etc., in certain ways; and provided this comes about as a result of my general attempt at French-speaking, I must be said to *learn* it whether or not I consciously pay attention to it. Second, I may consciously try to master a number of particular skills or sub-Xs, and thereby (or therein) be learning some general X: for instance, I consciously apply myself to drill on the parade-ground, cleaning my rifle, and so on, and thereby learn to be a good soldier without consciously applying myself to this general task, or even being aware that such a task exists.

These two types of case raise a different question, which applies to all kinds of learning: a question not about what we count as *learning* such-and-such, but about what we count as learning *such-and-such*. We have again to rely here on a distinction between continuous and perfect tenses of 'learn'. In the first type of case, we must say if I have learned the general X, then I have learned all the sub-Xs. The sub-Xs will be necessary for having learned, in three possible ways: (1) they may be part of what is *meant* by the X, (2) they may be logically prerequisite for having learned the X, or (3) they may be empirically prerequisite. Similarly if I *have* (only) learned some sub-X, then I have *not* learned the general X: for, obviously, the mastery of the general X requires more than the mastery of one of its constituents or prerequisites. All that is clear enough; but when we consider whether we are to say that a person *is* learning (was learning, etc.) X when he learns some sub-X, or is learning some sub-X when he is learning X, things are not so easy.

The difficulty is that we allow ourselves some latitude in determining what is to count as *part* of an X as opposed to a *prerequisite* for it. For instance, in order to have learned what check-mate is in chess, a man must be able to identify the king, know its powers of movement, grasp the idea of check, and so on. But, so far as I can see, we have the option of saying either that learning what check-mate is *consists* of learning these sub-Xs, or that the man must *first* learn the sub-Xs (and perhaps only learns what check-mate is at the final stage when he puts them together). Similarly 'learning to solve quadratic equations' might be held to include 'learning to add and multiply' – since these operations are, after all, required in the process of solution – or addition and multiplication might be considered rather as prerequisites, something which pupils had to learn before they even started to learn quadratics.

Much depends here on how teachers and others conceive of, and hence describe, particular goals of learning in relation to what is being learned at any one time. There are no hard-and-fast rules about this, but there is fairly strong pressure to *separate* Xs from sub-Xs when the two have no obviously close connection. Thus it would be unusual to say of a child learning to read that he is learning to appreciate Shakespeare, even though he has to read in order to appreciate: or of a child learning to add that he is learning to do trigonometry: or learning to play the flute, that he is learning to play Mozart's Jupiter Symphony in an orchestra: or even learning to walk, that he is learning to run. We can of course employ some more general description which will bring both the X and the sub-X under a wider X: in these cases, perhaps 'English', 'mathematics', 'music' or 'locomotion'. But any actual piece of learning will usually merit more exact and particular descriptions. For many cases of learning are, as it were, *structured*; and if we have our eyes fixed on the structure, we are more likely to say 'You must *first* learn such-and-such.'

It is hardly surprising that we can reach no determinate overall conclusions here; for we are talking, not about the concept of learning, but about the various concepts marked by descriptions or titles of the various Xs that are to be learned. That is a separate enquiry, and one of great importance: but it does have one significant connection with our main discussion. If we do not much mind just *what* pupils are learning, so long as they are learning something, then we shall not much mind whether they can be properly said to be learning X as opposed to Y; but conversely, if we are anxious that they should learn the *right* Xs (as surely we ought to be), then the very progress of the enquiry into these Xs will tend to structure or stratify what is learned. In other words, as soon as we really get down to the task of delimiting and analysing various Xs we shall close the door on various bits of learning which (we shall then say) are not, strictly speaking, a constituent part of this or that X.

It seems clearly desirable, at least as a first step, that this should happen: that we should, in getting clearer about what is strictly included and what excluded by various learning-titles ('English', 'mathematics', etc.), come to make finer and sharper distinctions. If, for lack of such clarity, we are doing importantly different things under the same uncritically accepted heading, we must first be clear about the differences. Thereafter it is, at least in part, an empirical question whether these differences should be institutionally marked: I mean, for instance, whether different Xs require different periods in the classroom and different teachers. Thus in some cases two Xs – say, 'mathematics' and 'logic' – seem so closely interwoven that it will be hard even to make a clear conceptual distinction between them, let alone to make plausible the suggestion that there should be logic teachers as well as mathematics teachers working in different classrooms; in others, conceptual distinctions may bear practical fruit – there is not much reason, for instance, to think that 'creativity' or 'the education of the emotions' ought to be uniquely the concern of English teachers.

Are there some things that can *only* be learned? A good deal turns on this question, both for the philosophy of education and for the practice of it. If there are some goods of which it would make no sense to say that they can be acquired by other methods than learning, then learning is something we are landed with so long as we wish for these goods; and if the goods are logically entailed by any form of life which is recognizably human, or a mark of conscious and rational creatures, then learning is something we are landed with so long as we wish to be human or rational. On the other hand, if these goods are or could be achieved by other methods, then learning is in principle dispensable; and not much would be gained by a lengthy philosophical exploration of it. For these other methods might be quicker, or cheaper, or in some other way more efficient than learning.

We should be inclined to say, intuitively and with some vagueness, that those things which involve 'understanding', 'the use of reason', etc., *can only* be learned, whereas those things which do not necessarily involve this *need* not be. For instance, one has to learn to solve quadratic equations, but one need not learn to run the mile in under a minute: one may just come to be able to do it by growing bigger and swifter, or by being given a drug or an enlarged heart. Here we seem to have in mind something like the distinction noticed earlier, between descriptions which imply some sort of consciousness, intelligence, or understanding on the one hand, and descriptions of overt behaviour or 'brute' performances on the other.

I think this intuition is right, but there are difficulties. Why should one not just be *given* 'understanding', perhaps in the form of an enlarged brain, as one can be given the power to run faster by an enlarged heart? If there is confusion here, it comes from failing to distinguish (1) the power or capacity to understand, (2) the results or behavioural end-products of understanding, and (3) the act or activity of understanding. It is clear that one can be given both (1) and (2): what one cannot be given, because it makes no sense, is the activity. Thus we may enlarge or repair a man's brain, which may increase his capacity to understand, the *facultas intellegendi*; and we may present him with true propositions to gabble, the results of what has been understood (*intellecta*) by other people. But the process of understanding itself, the *intellegere*, cannot be given.

Some verbs imply others: one cannot arrive without having travelled, nor win without having competed. Similarly one cannot get to know, or understand, or appreciate, without having paid attention to the world: without having reflected, perceived relevant data, seen the point, and so on. Just as one can, logically, only come to arrive by travel, or come to win by competition, so one can only come to know (understand, appreciate) by learning. 'Learning' is the word we use for that particular kind of 'coming to' which is governed (in the case of propositional learning) by the ideas of knowledge and truth. For these ideas, when fully worked out, can be seen to involve the idea of being causally influenced by one's perception of relevant reasons or data. To understand something *is* to have perceived and put together such reasons. The *intellegere* implies a previous *cognoscere*.

Thus in science-fiction stories the idea of hypnopaedia is often extended to suggest that someone could be 'given an education' by some purely technological means (attaching wires to his head, or whatever). The plausibility of this depends on various things that we could, indeed, do by such means: for instance, present the man with what we may call the data (techniques, etc.) for understanding in a quicker or more readily available form. Perhaps we can now implant certain images or symbols in his head, so to speak, instead of putting pictures of them on the walls of the classroom, or making him look them up in a reference book. But this only facilitates his coming to understand, like any good teaching-method or 'visual aid': it cannot do the job of coming to understand for him (the phrase is nonsense). The man still has – with however much added speed or facility – to *make sense* of the data. Similarly by hypnosis or some similar means we can make him recite propositions which (as it were) incorporate understanding; but he still has to understand those propositions if *he* is to have that understanding.

This bears on the question of whether we can *make* people learn things. Many philosophers of education say that we cannot: surprisingly, in view of common remarks like 'I was made to learn Latin at school', 'They made me learn how to salute', and so on. Some stress the point that learning is an 'intentional' or 'voluntary' activity, and say that a person can be 'induced' but not 'caused' to learn:[11] again surprisingly, since it is not (to say the least) clear that voluntary actions do not have causes of *some* kind. A good deal has also been written, sometimes in a rather confused way, about the 'logical impossibility' of attaining certain educational objectives by certain methods – 'conditioning', 'indoctrination', or whatever. Perhaps all that such philosophers really want to say is that learning is something which men do, in a sufficiently strong or specific sense of 'do' to obviate the possibility that someone else can do it for them. That is true: learning implies paying relevant attention, and no one can pay attention for me. I have myself to be a part-cause, a necessary feature in the story of how I came to learn. This holds for all kinds of learning, not only where propositional knowledge is involved. But that, of course, goes no way at all to show that words like 'make' and 'cause', or even 'compel', are not in place. For these words do not imply that my paying attention (or in some other way being an agent) can be neglected or by-passed: that would be implied only by the view, criticized above, that I can simply be *given* understanding or knowledge. The words imply only, what is clearly the case, that various kinds of pressures can be put upon me by others (or I can put them upon myself) which will ensure that I do actually learn. The fact that learning is – if we want to put it thus – an intentional or voluntary activity does not at all suggest that we have always to choose, in some supposed state of causeless freedom, whether or not to learn. There is, indeed, some contrast between 'compelled' and 'free' (not, I think, between 'caused' and 'free', and not always or necessarily between 'made' and 'free'); and questions may be raised about the conditions under which we say that a man is free to learn, as against compelled or forced to learn. But that is a different matter, not to be discussed here.

Is there any logical delimitation on what can be learned? This depends on what we are going to count as a logical delimitation. Certainly there are nonsensical or non-grammatical forms: 'learn to have money', 'learn to be red-headed', as against 'learn to make money', 'learn how to dye one's hair red'. We may say, if we like, that our grammar is such because what we *directly* gain by learning must be some kind of mastery or *power* (more knowledge, or more control over our behaviour), not some other state of affairs: 'having money' and 'being red-headed' represent not direct but indirect objects of learning. 'Learn' is thus more naturally at home with intentional verbs. However, the distinction does not always appear at the level of surface grammar: though 'learn to have' and 'learn to be' are, in general, less common than 'learn to do (win, save, speak, etc.)', there are plenty of exceptions: one can learn to have doubts or to have more sense, and learn to be tolerant, loving, courageous, etc. This is connected, though in fairly complex ways, with the fact that the description 'having money' and 'being red-headed' imply no exercise of consciousness at all, whereas 'having doubts' and 'being tolerant' do imply such an exercise.

It remains an open, and an empirical, question what actual things may be brought under this heading. Nowadays, by the use of sophisticated self-monitoring and feed-back techniques, a man can learn to control the rate of his heart-beat, respiration and so forth. We might still find it more natural to say 'learn to make your heart beat slower' rather than 'learn to have a slower heart-beat'; but this may be simply because we still see a person's heart-beat as something which he does not directly control, any more than he directly controls the colour of his hair: insofar as his heart-beat is no longer regarded as entirely part of his autonomic system, it thereby becomes a possible subject for learning (just as some actresses may learn to cry, or blush prettily). As an intermediary step, we might say 'Learn to *keep* your heart-beat slow', thereby granting some autonomy to the heart-beat but also granting the possibility of the man's will overriding it; and this would be not unlike saying 'Learn to keep cool under fire' (cf. 'aequam *memento* rebus in arduis servare* mentem'). When we recognize the possibility of acquiring what one might call a settled *disposition* – having one's heart, glands, etc., in a calm state, or having courage – we can then more naturally talk of learning to *be* (courageous, calm) or *have* (courage, calmness).

In what directions does this analysis of the notion of learning point us? There are many specific directions, some of which I shall mention in a minute; but there are also, I think, two main points that are none the less important for being general.

The first is that the connection of learning with *particular behavioural performances* – the enunciation of true propositions, the demonstration of useful skills, or the acting out of desirable attitudes – is an extremely loose one. Even the connection with the idea of knowledge is shaky; and in those cases where truth and knowledge are not involved the clear difference between learning X and just coming to X shows that the mere appearance of X as a phenomenon, so to speak, is far from a sufficient condition. On the other hand, there is a very tight connection – indeed, if we have the description right, an identity – between learning and what might be called a certain mental stance, or posture, or mode of operation on the world, which we called 'paying relevant attention'. One might put this by saying that learning, in a manner analogous to education itself, is not restricted in terms of content or value, but is heavily restricted in form. This is most obvious in the case of propositional knowledge, where much turns on whether the person has and uses *good grounds* for his beliefs, and comparatively little on whether what he believes happens to be true. To learn, in this area, is to acquire some degree of rational grasp on the world; and such grasp is better measured by the reasons a man has than by the truths he enunciates – just as a good mathematician, or scientist, or anything else proves himself more by his working out of a problem than by his results.

The second general point, which in practice is essential as a counter-weight to the first, is that learning is nevertheless a goal-directed activity: and we cannot even describe (let alone evaluate) the activity without describing the goal. All cases of learning must involve some particular X: something *to be learned*. Even though (as I have argued) the range of Xs may be wider than some suppose, yet every X sets some standard. What a man does will only count as learning X if it is something necessary or helpful, or at least relevant, to achieving X. We cannot, therefore, assess to what extent a man is engaged in learning X, or how successful he is, unless we are clear not only about what X is but also about what steps are relevant to achieving it. This is most obviously true of propositional learning, or the learning of subjects, but holds throughout.

These two points may be represented, very roughly, by two questions which all educators ought in practice constantly to ask about their students: (1) are they really *learning* such-and-such (rather than just changing in some way related to it)? and (2) are they really learning *such-and-such* (rather than something else)? These questions apply whatever the content of any educational policy. They are extremely difficult questions to answer in practice; and of course, they are interconnected. But they do represent what ought to be our two basic worries. To put them in a slightly different form, we may worry about (1) whether the changes in our students, the propositions enunciated and performances achieved by them, have really come about by a result of our work as educators – that is, by *learning*: and (2) whether or not whatever *has* come about by learning does, in fact, fit or constitute the particular Xs which form part of our educational policy.

There is a certain practical or at least methodological force behind these considerations. People argue, often very fiercely, about what are vaguely described as 'aims' and 'methods' in education: about its content, about what ought to be learned and how. But it would not be absurd to suggest that most of such arguments are premature, since we are not yet clear about *what it is* to learn this or that particular X. We may (to repeat) be unclear about what it is to *learn* such-and-such, or about what it is to learn *such-and-such*: or about both. This is pretty obviously the position when we discuss the rather more vague, or more high-minded, areas marked by (say) 'creativity', 'language', 'moral education', 'religion', 'critical thinking', and so on; but it is, I would guess, almost equally true of even more traditional subjects on the time-table. Do any of us really know just what we are talking about when we speak of 'learning X', where X is (say) 'English', or 'science', or 'a modern language', or 'classics', or practically anything? I do not deny, of course, that we have something, perhaps even something clear, in mind. But we are likely to deceive ourselves precisely because there are traditionally accepted or fashionable pictures of what it is to learn some X, and these pictures are, as it were, institutionalized in classrooms; so that we come to suppose that what happens from 10 to 11 a.m. under the heading of (say) 'science' *is*, in fact, something that can properly be described as 'pupils learning science'. But *can* it, or should it, be so described? To raise this question is, clearly, to raise a number of very difficult sub-questions about just what is going on in the pupils' heads, what is to count as 'science', and so on. It should strike us (1) that these questions are hardly ever raised, at least in an appropriately general or philosophical form, at all: (2) that we do not know the answers to them: and (3) that we do not even have any general agreement about what *ought* to be going on (let alone what is). We cannot assess properly because we are not clear about what we are trying to assess; and to suppose that we know what is going on just because there are time-tabled periods *called* 'science' is an obvious error.[12]

It is premature to argue about the content of education – about what Xs ought to be learned – until we are clear both about what Xs there are to be learned, and about what it is to learn each particular X. We require, in other words, (1) an adequate taxonomy or taxonomies of Xs, and (2) a lot of very detailed work in explicating each X that we have categorized. We shall also need (3) a good deal of factual information about the pupils for whom we are forming our policies, the state of society, the needs of the moment, and so on.

Then, and only then, will we even begin to be able to compare the *value* of various Xs for particular pupils. In our present position we jump far too many guns by taking up partisan positions about educational content.

We may often think it is easier to be clear about some of those Xs which are required by *ad hoc* or, as one might say, grossly utilitarian pressures; that is, perhaps, one reason why those such Xs tend to be prominent and possibly over-valued. We can specify, without too much conceptual investigation, what counts as being able to drive a car, or fly a Spitfire, or count one's change; broader and less *ad hoc* notions like 'mathematics' or 'science' are not so clear. But we must not imagine that *all* the *ad hoc* Xs are easy meat. For, at least in a sophisticated and rapidly changing society, quite a lot of such Xs may be of a rather general kind, and appear under titles like 'literacy' or 'socialization' which may be just as difficult to explicate. There is no *necessary* connection between the kind of reasons for which an X is valued and the ease or difficulty of explicating it.

Here again some people are likely to claim that the taxonomic or explicatory procedures of categorizing Xs and analysing their constituents cannot be wholly divorced from our 'commitments' or 'values'. I do not deny some connection, but this may be at worst harmless and at best beneficial – provided always that we make the right connection. Certainly it seems *prima facie* possible (and highly desirable) to explicate particular Xs without making the wrong kind. For instance, we may explicate the subject-title 'classics' in a traditional way (Latin and Greek grammar and prose composition, etc.) or in a more modern way (the culture of the ancient world); 'religious education' may be explicated in a confessional or sectarian way, to mean roughly 'learning to be a Christian (Buddhist, etc.)', or in more 'open' ways which might involve the study of comparative religion and perhaps the education of the emotions. Granted that these explications are, in practice, often conducted tendentiously, because the conductor has already taken up some option and sets a greater value on one interpretation than another: nevertheless they do not *have* to be tendentious. We may simply *lay out* the options, and defer taking any of them up until we are clearer.

It is also possible, indeed probable, that we may come to settle some of our 'value' problems just by laying out the options and distinguishing them. For not infrequently what lies behind clashes of 'value' is some kind of monism or essentialism: I mean, the concealed idea that what is marked by (say) 'classics', or 'religious education', or 'philosophy' itself, has to be some *one* thing. Thus there may be a place for the immersing of pupils in, and the advancement of, some particular sectarian world-view – Christianity or Marxism, for example; but there is also clearly a place for the consideration and analysis of various world-views in a context of enquiry which is, relative to any such views, neutral. It may be, at least, that there are a number of goods which we are more or less bound to acknowledge *if* we are willing to elucidate each and reflect sufficiently on it, and each of which we can attain by judicious allocation: and that it is chiefly the obsession with certain particular goods which causes us to forget about the others. This may still leave us with problems about priorities; but perhaps it will be best not to anticipate them until we have made more progress.

Apart from these general considerations, there are a great many specific points which follow conceptually from the idea of learning: more points still if we bring in the other criteria which govern the concept marked by education: and yet more if we assume certain practical parameters (such as that at least some of the learning will have to be done collectively in groups, rather than in a one-to-one relationship between pupil and teacher). I want to stress that these points are not dependent on any *particular* views about what should be learned or how (any particular 'ideals of education'), but rather upon the ideas of learning and education themselves. They may be as important for both the theory and the practice of education as are more disputable arrangements whose merits and demerits would turn on such particular views. A rough parallel can be drawn with medicine: whatever particular disputes there might be about the merits of this or that form of treatment (or even about what constituted 'health' in a particular case), there are plainly certain requirements which are necessary for the effective and serious practice of the enterprise as a whole. For instance, there would have to be people perceived or accepted as *authorities* or experts, both in the sense that they would be thought to know more than the rest of us, and in the sense that they would be empowered to tell us what to do in this field – that the nurses and patients should, at least characteristically, do what the doctor ordered; in other words, there would have to be some kind of *discipline*. Again, part of their expertise would necessarily consist in their having fairly *close contact* with their patients and intimate knowledge of their patients' bodies; and there would have to be procedures of assessment, checking up, or *examination* of their patients' progress, the notion of progress itself being entailed by the mere enterprise (even though what counted as progress might be disputed).

It is impossible to work out all these points at length here, and I have discussed some of them in detail elsewhere.[13] But they deserve some comment of a general kind for a number of reasons: most obviously because without a clear grasp of what any activity conceptually (and hence, in some appropriate form, empirically) requires we cannot pursue it coherently at all. In practice this grasp is not achieved merely by our being clear, in this case, about what is meant by the *word* 'learning', unless we put a great deal into the notion of 'being clear about'; we have also to achieve a full and vividly imaginative understanding of all the conceptual trappings (as one might call them) of serious learning, and hence the ability to recognize whether and how far practical and institutionalized situations actually instantiate them. Without this understanding, we too easily tend to take for granted that what is said to be, or institutionally supposed to be, learning actually *is* learning. This has considerable practical importance at the present time, when (some might argue) a lot goes on under the heading of 'education' or 'learning' which is, in fact, nothing of the kind.

It is not too difficult to outline some of these conceptual requirements in a general way; most of the detailed work consists in determining the point at which conceptual truths need to be supplemented by empirical ones. I will give one or two (very sketchy) examples, to show something of this important interface:

1 If the enterprise of education is to be successful, we must delegate enough *authority* and *power* to ensure that whatever educational policy we adopt is put into effect – that whatever Xs we want our pupils to learn are in fact learned. Hence it is clear that those responsible for educational practice (and this means, in effect, the teachers) must have sufficient *disciplinary* powers to do the job effectively; this is indeed an obvious conceptual point, since to be effectively in charge of any enterprise is to wield power along with authority, and the notions marked by 'discipline', 'obedience', 'rules', 'sanctions', etc., are tied together in the same web.[14] On the other hand, it is clearly an empirical question whether corporal punishment (whatever that may be taken to mean precisely) is necessary. But that *some* effective sanctions are available to the authority of educators is, once more, a conceptual requirement; for effective authority involves the notion of effective rules, which in turn involves the notion of effective sanctions. If it appeared, as in some supposedly educational institutions today it does appear, that the educators did not in fact possess effective sanctions, we should have doubts about whether such institutions could be regarded as seriously concerned with education at all, at least in respect of those pupils for whom such sanctions would be necessary.

2 More generally, we have to ensure that educational institutions are adequately defended against corruption from external sources – 'corruption' here being defined as whatever may impede

or vitiate serious learning; and this would include, for instance, not only political and economic pressure but also any gross impediments in the pupils' homes or social environment. Serious educators will require a 'potent' school, the values of which will stand in contrast to (often in defiance of) what goes on in the outside world. Thus, whoever is supposed to be initiated (whether voluntarily or compulsorily) into some kind of educational régime must in fact turn up (rather than playing truant), and turn up in a suitable state (rather than drunk, under the influence of drugs, or whatever); and this might perhaps require some powers over parents to ensure that the pupils were looked after sufficiently well to be reasonably educable – not, for instance, prevented from doing homework because of constant family quarrels or other such causes. Again, *how* this is to be ensured is, clearly, an empirical matter; perhaps parent–teacher associations, efficient public-relations exercises, the natural respect which members of a society may have for education, and the eagerness of politicians to delegate power and influence to educators may be sufficient to do the job (though it seems to me, speaking merely as an experienced amateur, that only a person tender-minded to the point of idiocy could believe this of our own society today). But only to the extent *that* it is ensured can educational institutions effectively educate.

3 The scope of the educator's authority will naturally be co-extensive with his function; he is empowered only to enforce or discourage what is necessary for *education*, and must employ only educational reasons for his decisions. He is not simply to 'pass on' cultural values or practices just because they are approved by his society, or his pupils' parents, or his own tastes: he is to encourage *learning*. How certain rules (for example, rules about school uniform or sexual behaviour) would fare under this criterion is an empirical matter, about which we know very little; but it is clear that there is a difference between arguing for such things on educational grounds and arguing for them on grounds of tradition, respectability, personal taste or public relations. (This criterion is not, so far as I can judge, properly understood and adhered to in most educational systems.)

4 There is clearly a necessity for some assessment or examination of what is learned. Part of what is meant by a person's seriously wanting to learn anything is that he will need to know what progress he is making, which involves the notion of examination in some form or other; and also, though the connection here is looser, it is difficult to see how he could avoid wanting to compare his progress with other people. Certainly the notion of competition in a broad sense, or at least comparison, is hard to get rid of altogether.

How this is to be realized in practice – whether we need this or that particular *form* of examination, prize-giving, etc. – is again an empirical matter.

5 Some kind of segregation or selection seems to be a necessity for group-learning. Pupils can only learn together, or as a group, if they are able to learn the same thing. It is a conceptual point that learning X is only possible for pupils (a) who do not already know X and (b) are already in possession of the knowledge prerequisite for learning X. This sets quite severe logical limits on the class of pupils who can learn any X, because entry into that class will be a function of having certain attainments. Empirically, we can only avoid the force of this point (a) by giving such wide descriptions to our Xs ('language', 'the environment', etc.) that more or less *anybody* can learn *something* in that area: (b) by abandoning group-learning in favour of letting individuals learn by themselves: or (c) by ceasing to worry very much about whether learning is actually going on.

It will, I think, be obvious – particularly to anyone who has been involved in educational theory or practice over the last few decades – that points of this kind have considerable practical force. What may be rather less obvious is why they are neglected. Why, for instance, is the need for them so clear in the parallel case of medicine, but so disregarded in education? One might hazard two general reasons here, in themselves perhaps fairly obvious but worth a brief discussion. First, and because there is in fact agreement on what is to count as health, we find it easier to feel confident about structuring the enterprise of medicine along those lines which are demonstrably required for it to prosper: we do not feel demoralized by having to confront 'value-judgments' and 'ideologies'. This is a bad reason, since *any* serious attempt to improve or alter a patient's physical constitution by coherent and sustained treatment would involve the same conceptual trappings. We might dispute *who* should hold authority and exercise discipline, what *sort of* close contact and examination was necessary, etc.; but in the end we should either have to agree on this and put it into practice, or give up the idea of serious medical treatment altogether. But the reason, though bad, is understandable; various parties to the dispute might prefer to give up the idea, rather than allow the necessary concepts to be empirically realized in (as they would see it) the wrong sort of way.

It is, of course, quite possible to believe that existing institutional-izations of an enterprise are so dreadful that we ought not to entrust ourselves to any of them. Any schools, hospitals and political systems that are actually available to us may seem worse than useless. But unless we make the mistake of identifying the enterprises with their institutionalizations, we do not therefore abandon the enterprises altogether. We teach our children at home, or treat our own illnesses, or restrict our communal life to a social group whose politics are more tolerable. Total abandonment of the enterprises involves either denying that the goods which they aim at are real, or claiming that we have absolutely no idea about how to realize them (so that things had better be left to nature or chance). In some cases, one or the other of these beliefs might not be absurd; for instance, we might believe that neither the doctors nor ourselves had any idea at all about how to treat a particular disease, so that it would be better to do nothing at all and let nature take its course – though it would be more difficult to hold the more general belief that there was *no* expertise as regards *any* aspect of health. But with education and learning, as we have seen (pp. 35 ff.), these views are not credible. Education is a necessary enterprise; there will always be *some* things which each man thinks he and his children ought to learn, and *some* scope in the practical world for such learning to go on. This gives sufficient foothold for the realization of the necessary concepts.

The second reason, though closely connected with the first, is not a dispute about the value of different Xs to be learned, but a practical (and often conceptual) confusion between educational and non-educational goods: that is, between goods directly connected with learning and other goods. Any actual educational *system* – that is, any set of institutions theoretically supposed to promote learning – is likely to affect its participants in other ways also. One might roughly distinguish three such ways, all notorious in current politico-educational discussion. (1) Attending a certain type of institution, or occupying a particular place within it, might exercise what we call a *psychological* effect on a person; he might, for instance, come to 'feel a failure' if he is put into an under-privileged school or fails all his examinations. (2) Attending an institution might affect the *social* rewards which the person gets in after-life; thus simply having been to Oxford (Harvard, Eton, etc.) might be thought productive of social rewards (or, of course, counter-productive, depending on what circles one moves in): still more if the person has satisfied whatever standards these institutions demand for success. (3) The fact that a person *has actually learned more* at a particular institution, and that this can be verified by examination results or degrees or whatever, may bring him increased social or psychological rewards (more money or more self-esteem).

This is a very rough classification, which needs to be expanded and sophisticated by those interested in non-educational goods connected with educational systems, if we are to have any very clear idea of just what sorts of goods they are talking about and just what conditions produce them. But it should suffice here to show that none of these, not even (3), is *necessarily* connected with the general enterprise of education in any *specific* way or direction. By this I mean that, though it is (I think) necessarily the case that in any society there will be *some* effects of the kind suggested in (1), (2) and (3), it is not necessarily the case that these effects can be specified in terms of particular psychological or social goods, such as more self-confidence or more money or a better job. We could quite well imagine societies (there may indeed be actual instances) which did *not* bestow these goods on those who had been highly educated, or individuals who did not acquire them for themselves. In other words, it is not an *educational* question whether or not particular effects need to be attached to particular cases of learning: it is a question for politicians, or economists, or psychologists, or child welfare officers, or whatever experts deal with the kinds of goods these effects may produce. But if we are passionately concerned with non-educational goods – money, status, social class, or whatever – we may simply forget or deny the distinction altogether. 'Education' will mean to us 'the educational system', and our main concern with the system will precisely *not* be the extent to which it actually educates, but rather the extent to which *other* features of it bestow various social and psychological goods on various individuals or deny them.

This is, of course, only to scratch the surface of what the enterprises of learning and education require; but it does, I think, illuminate yet again the disastrous effects of premature adherence to a particular ideology. For when some of these requirements are absent – as they clearly are absent in nearly all societies – it seems to be this which ultimately causes us to overlook the fact. Some general term like 'ideology' is required here, because it is not just that we tend to be fixated on a particular *educational content*. If we genuinely accepted a number of Xs that we wanted our pupils to learn, were quite clear what constituted each X, and made all necessary arrangements for the learning of them, things might not be so bad – provided, of course, that our Xs were not excessively narrow and partisan, such as 'learning to be a good Nazi'. But only too often we forget about learning and its requirements altogether, and judge what goes on in schools and other educational institutions simply by their *style* or *tone*, as one might call it. Battles are fought with terms like 'progressive', 'traditionalist', 'integrated', 'socially divisive', 'élitist', 'revolutionary', 'Christian', and so forth, none of which bear any necessary relation to learning at all; indeed they smack more of politics or sociology. This is not to deny that socio-logical and other features of educational institutions are important; but it is to assert that their *educational* importance must be derived from what the pupils are supposed to learn. Until we have some rational agreement on this, sociological and other such enquiries are certainly premature and may well be irrelevant; and such rational agreement cannot be reached without seeing something of the range of possible options, the Xs which are available for learning. To this we shall now turn.

# What there is to learn

If we are to 'lay out the options' (as we expressed it earlier) of what there is to learn, the question at once arises of what categories to use. One point must be ceded in advance: that categorizations or taxonomies derive part (not all) of their merits or demerits from the purposes they are intended to fulfil. It is clearly possible – i.e. not logically contradictory or even lunatic – to set up more or less *any* set of categories, provided they are clear and their items discrete. We could consider various Xs to be learned in terms of their cost, the availability of people to teach them, the difficulty or interest experienced by various types of pupils in learning them, their 'relevance to the modern world' (whatever that may mean), the likelihood of getting grants to do research on them, or even the letters of the alphabet with which their titles began. Clearly much depends on what one is setting up the categories *for*; and few if any criteria could not be imagined to have *some* purpose (to take the last and apparently most absurd example, the compilation of an encyclopaedia).

However, it would be odd – or at least somewhat despairing – to suppose that we do not need, or cannot get, some set of categories which will give us a rather broad or *general* view of what sorts of things human beings can learn. One possibility here is to eschew any reference in our taxonomy to *subject-matter* (I include here not only Xs like 'Latin' but also Xs like 'being kind'), and stick to such terms as 'skill', 'facts', 'concepts', 'competence', 'disposition', 'attitude' and so on. (We may even try to arrange these, as one very influential psychologist has done,[1] under general headings, like 'cognitive', 'affective', and 'psycho-motor'.) For instance, it might be said that in many actual pieces of learning, a person will learn *that* certain things are so, acquiring certain concepts and grasping the truth of certain propositions: also *how to manage* certain things (his limbs, a sailing boat, the calculus, a Latin sentence, a philosophical argument): also *to see it in* some way or other (as boring or interesting, difficult or easy, manageable or intractable, and so on). These three categories might apply, then, to the learning of most things (not all);

but they can still be assessed separately, in however rough a form. Thus a person may (1) know all the facts and have all the concepts relevant to, say, doing a scientific experiment or giving a dinner-party, but (2) be impossibly clumsy in the laboratory or tactless in the dining-room, and (3) find the whole thing too boring, or too alarming, to carry out successfully. We can thus score him, as a good scientist or a good host, under these three categories: propositional/conceptual competence, non-propositional skill or 'know-how', and attitude.

However, there are (at least) two major difficulties with this. First, it is clear that these categories interact with each other in a much more complicated way than has been suggested. We may in principle start by subdividing something to be learned under these three headings; but most practical ('phenomenological') descriptions will lack this purity. For instance, (2) a man's 'know-how' or skill, except in very simple cases, will have an important admixture of propositional knowledge and attitude (he knows that the test-tubes are easily upset, and cares about keeping things tidy, as well as possessing a certain 'pure' dexterity). Similarly (3) his attitude will partly consist of, or be based on, some kind of propositional belief or knowledge; indeed if this were not so, we should probably not talk of attitudes at all, but rather of allergies or *penchants* unmediated by conscious or unconscious beliefs of any kind. Nor is it even clear that (1) propositional knowledge can, in practice, be made totally independent of some kinds of skill or competence in handling or managing the concepts involved, or of a man's attitude towards them. A vast amount of extremely important work in education, and in psychology generally, consists in sorting all this out: that is, in determining exactly what is happening – what is going wrong or right – in particular practical cases: a task as yet hardly understood, let alone attempted, by most scholars and researchers.[2]

Second, how would this task be possible at all without some prior delimitation of the subject-matter? The nature, admixture and interrelations of skills, concepts, attitudes and so forth will clearly vary from one case to another. Hence the importance of this sort of categorization seems to come into play chiefly when we have *already* determined on the necessity for some one kind of thing to be learned; and that involves using *other* criteria for what counts as a 'kind of thing'. We may decide that we want children to learn to be good scientists, good hosts, good husbands, or good citizens: to know some French: to be able to express themselves clearly: to be enthusiastic, courageous, artistic, and so on. Having decided this, we then have to get down to the business of sub-categorizing these areas, or working out in detail what these descriptions imply. In some, straightforward propositional knowledge seems to satisfy most of the description: in others, some kind of competence or know-how figures as obviously important: in others again, the person's basic attitude or disposition appears crucial. But until we have decided this, the categorization will be empty. We cannot identify the proper items in lists of propositions, competences and attitudes independently of the subject-matter, for the *kind* of skill, attitude, etc., that we want to list is only describable by reference to the subject-matter. Often this is quite complicated; for instance, we require concepts marked by (say) 'party', 'entertain', 'property' and so on before we can understand the notion of tact or competence *in a host*. At best such a categorization could function only as a sort of check-list, to be used after we have thought our way through some subject-matter, or in conjunction with it. That is, in explicating our ideas on (say) 'a good scientist', 'a morally educated person', or whatever, we shall find ourselves listing a number of features (or characteristics, or components, or attributes); and it may be helpful to ask in each case 'Does this represent, or is it an instance of, "skill", "attitude", "factual knowledge", or what?' But the actual explication has to come first.

If we plump for categorization in terms of subject-matter, we have to be careful to cast our net wide enough. Most recent philosophical writers have plunged straight into a taxonomy in terms of different kinds of propositional or conceptual knowledge. We may guess at various reasons for this move: the false idea that learning is uniquely connected with propositional knowledge, the philosopher's peculiar concern with truth, the tendency to regard institutionalized learning (in schools and elsewhere) as a set of subjects, and the idea that 'education' or 'the educated man' ought somehow to be peculiarly sophisticated along these (as one might say, 'intellectual' or 'cognitive') lines. But, as we have seen, this already loads the dice in favour of *one* partisan, and highly specialized, picture of education. Any good taxonomy must deal, not only with the ignorant man, but also with the soulless man, the wicked man, the neurotic, the servile man, the despairing man, and many others.

There is thus a danger in construing the question 'What is there to learn?' as 'What is there to learn *about*?': for then we shall already have committed ourselves to a particular option. We shall think of a person primarily as one who needs to develop his mind by acquiring information, concepts, and theoretical understanding of the world; and from this it is a short step to discussing how we are to chop the world up under various 'subjects', 'disciplines' or 'forms of knowledge' in a curriculum. But knowing about things is not the only possible end-state of having learned. When Aeneas told his son to learn virtue and true industriousness from him,[3] he did not mean only that he should learn what virtue and industriousness *were*: he meant that he should learn to *be* virtuous and industrious.

One natural way of trying to form some general picture of what there is to learn is by picking up some cues from our delimitation of education in chapter 1: in particular, the twin ideas that education is concerned with learning which has at least some kind of semi-permanent, rather than just *ad hoc*, significance; and that what one educates is always a person, not just a role-filler or task-performer. From this we may come to consider the possibility of some educational content, or set of Xs, which may be distinguished by being (1) of *permanent* importance to people, (2) of *universal* importance – that is, of importance to *all* people, and (3) of importance to people *as such*.

I shall not attempt here the considerable task of distinguishing clearly between these three criteria, nor of showing any conceptual connections that may exist between them; although some points relevant to this task may become clear as we proceed. The important thing, at this stage, is not to confuse whatever distinctions we may make by these criteria with two other distinctions. First, we are not distinguishing between what is of *greater* ('real', 'true') importance and what is of *lesser* (transient, sublunary) importance. Clearly, learning necessary in reference to *ad hoc* pressures arising from (say) plague, famine, or barbarian invasions is not less important just because the pressures are *ad hoc*: whether arms should yield to the toga depends on circumstances. The importance of the things roughly separated under our own distinctions – their 'value', if you like – has to be argued for; and this we shall try to do below (pp. 194 ff.). Second, we are not distinguishing between things that are important 'for their own sakes' or 'intrinsically' and things that are only 'instrumentally' important or important 'as a means to an end'. The chief difficulty here, admittedly, is to make sense of these phrases; but at least it seems plausible to say that some things may be of permanent but primarily 'instrumental' importance to men (obtaining food, for instance); and equally some things may at least seem desirable 'for their own sakes', but perhaps have only an impermanent and non-universal value – they might, for instance, suit only certain individuals or age-groups or societies.

These confusions have to be noted because, again, philosophers have characteristically lumped the distinctions together. They have, as it were, seized *ab initio* on a certain content or subject-matter which is supposed to be not only significant in terms of its permanence and universality, but also (1) 'important' in the crucial action-guiding sense: that is, the chosen content that pupils (or those who can manage it) really ought to learn in preference to other things; and (2) 'worth while' (or 'valuable') 'for its own sake'. They may, as we have noted, even make the move of regarding this content as the only thing deserving the term 'education'. We ourselves have followed normal usage in not insisting on (1) or (2) for applying the term. So far as our own three criteria go, and for this purpose lumping them roughly together, we have seen earlier (pp. 22 ff.) that there is *some* linguistic pressure from the word – and similar pressure, though variable in quality and quantity, from parallel words in other languages – which makes us hesitate over learning which is purely *ad hoc*. But the issue is not ultimately a linguistic one. For reasons also noted earlier (pp. 35 ff.), the position is rather that, insofar as individuals and societies reflect seriously on what is to be learned (as they are bound to do), they can hardly avoid some such distinction. They are bound, that is, to consider the question of what (if any) things that can be learned *are* of permanent and universal importance to men as such. Whether or not they tighten the screws on words like 'education' to fit this general criterion, or – though this is certainly to tighten them against normal usage – the criteria (1) and (2), does not matter here.

Somebody might, I suppose, try to deny either that there were any things of permanent and universal importance to men as such, and/or that these things could be learned; denials which, if made good, would of course invalidate the practical value of the distinction. But both these seem difficult to argue for convincingly. It is hard to maintain either that there are *no* universal features which men, so long as they remain and wish to remain men, need attach some importance to or that these are features which cannot, at least to some extent, be acquired or improved by some kind of learning. Such features as health, food, language, a degree of rationality, the following of some sort of social rules, and many others spring (heterogeneously) to mind. I doubt whether such denials need be taken seriously; provided they are not mixed up with the quite different questions of (1) the *comparative* importance of such features as against others, and (2) the *kind* of importance they have (the kinds of arguments we might use in advocating them), their adherents would be few in number.

The force of the distinction can perhaps best be shown by an example. Many people have the feeling that education should relate to 'the needs of society'; they may react against the idea, admittedly much canvassed by a certain philosophical tradition, that 'the educated man' is one who engages in some kind of higher culture which has little or no connection with the needs of his fellows or the state of the nation. Such a reaction may be justified, but need not (though it often does) lead those who have this feeling to concentrate on those kinds of learning best put under headings like 'socialization', or 'what is relevant to modern society', or 'social adjustment'. Our distinction calls on us to separate (1) things that (we might reasonably believe) must necessarily be learned by *any* man in *any* society – the concepts, know-how and desirable attitudes that go along with such general notions as law, morality, promise-keeping, justice, authority, discipline and so on: and (2) the particular learning relevant to his own society (which might change, or be misguided, or could be circumvented). We fairly describe (1) as permanent and universal, for obvious conceptual reasons (one cannot generate men without some kind of society, and any kind of society has to have some concepts and rules of this sort). Again, it does not follow (a) that it is always or ever *more* important for a particular man to know about law and authority in general than for him to know that (say) the police in his own society have certain powers, and to obey them: nor (b) that we have to argue for (1) on the 'intrinsic' merits of its content, as against the 'instrumental' merits of (2) – we might think, not that it was particularly interesting or 'fulfilling' to learn about rules and contracts and authority, but simply that it was pragmatically disastrous not to know about them.

The notions of permanence and universality are in themselves perhaps fairly non-problematic; but something must be said about our third criterion, that the serious learning should be of permanent and universal significance to human beings *as such*. To talk of 'human beings as such' or '*qua* human beings' is to attempt some kind of distinction between what is conceptually or necessarily, as against empirically or contingently, part of a human being. If we were to cast this in linguistic form – say, 'what is meant by "human being" ' – it would make a great difference what terms we actually chose: 'human being', 'man', 'person', '*homo sapiens*', 'rational creature', and so on. For clearly these terms carry different conceptual implications: '*homo sapiens*' is specified in ways different from 'rational creature', inasmuch (at least) as Martians may be rational creatures or *sapientes* but not *homines*; moreover, some candidates ('man', 'person') are less specific than others – it might be thought, for instance, partly a matter for decision whether Martians were to count as people. It is better to explore the claim that there are certain features which we, as human beings, are bound to see as central to ourselves: that is, features contributing to a concept which is virtually forced on us – whether or not it is exactly marked by 'man', 'human being', etc.

The term which most nearly covers these features is perhaps 'rational creature'; roughly, a creature with a conscious *mind* –

which, of course, includes what we normally classify under headings like 'emotion', 'will', 'feelings' and so on, as well as 'reason'. Whatever the complex philosophical problems concerned with personal identity, it seems that I can hardly avoid thinking of myself primarily as an entity which thinks and feels certain things, and which has certain memories, desires, values, and points of view; rather than, for instance, primarily as an entity who performs certain social roles, or has five fingers on each hand. By 'primarily' I do not, of course, mean – a point again to be remembered – that I take my central features to be, always or even often, more *important* from the viewpoint of practical action than the peripheral features. The practical importance of a feature will clearly depend very much on the context of action. Nor do I necessarily *more often* think of myself in this way; I may spend more time thinking of myself as, say, a butler or a midget than (what we might naturally say here) as a person in his own right. It is rather, to put it in a somewhat high-sounding way, that I should not feel that I had lost my essence or identity if I changed my physical characteristics or my job: I should still be me. Certainly in any kind of reflective or decision-making activity I cannot avoid seeing myself in this way; for such activity is an activity of the mind. There is always a 'me' which can stand back from and consider my role, physical attributes, and other peripheral features.

Once again, just as (a) central features may be of less practical importance than peripheral features at a particular time, so too (b) we need not always argue 'intrinsically' for education in respect of the central features, nor always 'instrumentally' in respect of the peripheral ones. For instance, there may be certain central features involved in developing consciousness and having a mind which require a good deal of education if a man (any man) is to be happy, productive, a good citizen, or whatever we want to use as a criterion; and we argue for this education in terms of this 'extrinsic' criterion, not necessarily in terms of it being a good thing in itself (whatever that means) to 'develop our minds'. Conversely, it is not a central feature of being a person that, say, he appreciates Shakespeare and Bach; yet we might want to argue for educating him to do so in a quite non-instrumental way.

Like the former addition ('permanent and universal'), the notion of what is relevant to 'people as such' may seem to do little more than adumbrate some conceptual truths which apply to human beings. What (it may be asked) is the point of doing this, if it is simultaneously admitted that there is no correlation either (a) with the practical importance of, or (b) with certain types of argument for, particular bits of education? The reasons here are strategic;

what we are doing is to consider a general criterion which may have importance at the level of categorization.

The first strategic argument for its importance is that we reasonably wish to achieve some degree of immunity from change. Precisely because descriptions of certain features are logically connected with descriptions such as 'a person' or 'a rational creature', the *actual* features they describe are inevitable for *actual* people.[4] This means that, working (as we are) with people, we can feel safe in claiming that these features are permanent in a deeper and hence stronger way than is given us by empirical facts. Hence it seems useful to push some arguments in a conceptual direction. For instance, an adequate supply of food and air might be taken as an example of what is of 'permanent and universal importance' to human beings; but it is at least conceivable that, with the advance of science, men might come to be able to do without either. By adding 'human beings as such' we acknowledge this fact, and turn rather to features of the mind and heart which (in a stricter logical sense) could not be otherwise so long as human beings remain rational creatures.

A tactical move to the same effect would be to generalize the concepts of impermanent needs, so that they become conceptually necessary. Food and air, for instance, could be taken in a broad sense as something like 'whatever input keeps the physical properties of the creature in working order'; just as 'the use of one's limbs', sometimes quoted as something it would be hard to imagine a person not desiring, could be suitably generalized as 'the use of whatever organs the creature possesses to manipulate its environment'. For that any creature would want to, or at least want to be able to, alter its environment follows conceptually from various other features, e.g. that any such creature has desires, that it is rational to be secure in the satisfaction of those desires, and so on.

There are, in fact (as even these few examples may have shown), quite a large number of features generated by the concepts of a rational creature and the connected concepts of space, time, choice, desire and others. They are of the utmost importance for educators because they provide the highest possible degree of immunity from change. The practical value of this is fairly obvious: we do not, and perhaps cannot, know what the world will be like even in our children's lifetimes, let alone our grandchildren's. To bet on the impermanent is to bet on what is uncertain and may become rapidly obsolescent. A too-specific concept of thrift or chastity, for instance, may be useless in the face of inflation or easy contraception: the time-free and culture-free virtues for which 'thrift' and 'chastity' may be made to stand remain secure (see p. 130).

A second and obviously connected argument has to do with the feeling of unjustified *imposition* on pupils which underlies the use of such words (whatever they can most profitably be taken to mean) as 'indoctrination', 'partisan', 'hidden values' and so on. This is not, or need not be, a worry about whether we are entitled to educate people at all, or force children to attend school, or anything of that kind. Nor, again, is it a worry necessarily confined to certain areas of education – morality, politics, religion and so on. We worry rather about those bits or aspects of practical education which may either become obsolescent or irrelevant, or appear to be based on irrational or parochial ideas. We look back on, say, making boys learn not to cry, or pupils to adopt a Victorian copper-plate style of handwriting, and wonder whether our own specific objectives are any less liable to the charge of prejudice or doctrinaire ideas. Much has been written about the practical difficulties of enforcing on young people, at least in most contemporary societies, pieces of learning which we cannot justify either *sub specie aeternitatis* or as of immediate practical benefit to them; but usually from the point of view of maintaining the pupils' interest and good behaviour on an *ad hoc* basis. Equally important, however, is the loss of nerve which will overtake teachers who have no solid belief in, because no solid justification for, what they are teaching: a loss of nerve particularly apparent in many societies nowadays, when the severe weakening of accepted values and traditional authorities leaves a vacuum which can only be properly and permanently filled by an adequate understanding of what men as such need to learn. Without this, teachers and other educators will – in a way, quite rightly – be under constant pressure from their pupils, from society, and from their own uncertainty.

Third, this criterion gives us some guidance on a very important issue, to be considered later: namely, what things *everybody* ought to learn, and what things can be regarded as in some sense optional. There are of course may criteria which would affect our practical decisions here. A may find it strictly impossible to learn something, or B may find it extremely hard, because he lacks ability, or because he hates the subject. But the criterion would enable us to distinguish, for instance, between knowledge (or some other result of learning) which was important to have available in a community or society – that is, which *some* people at least should have – and knowledge which *every* man ought to have. Here, yet again, the use of the criterion is not (or not directly) a function of *how* important we take the knowledge to be. It may be extremely important that there should be some people in a society who are able to prevent bubonic plague or keep our guided missiles in good order: more important than that pupils should learn, say, good manners or the major features of adolescent psychology. But the former might fairly be regarded as something which could, without much loss, be entirely delegated to specialists; whereas the latter involves learning whose main point would be lost if it were delegated in this way – indeed, it might be nonsensical to suppose that it could be. For there are some things which a person can only do for himself: somebody can keep a plague away from me, but nobody can be good-mannered for me. The criterion allows us to place the former in one category and the latter in another: how much *weight* (time, resources, etc.) we put into either is another matter.

What practical force, to put it in a rather general way, do these (it may seem, rather heavy-handed) conceptual manoeuvres have? At this stage I want primarily to stress their taxonomic value. Suppose that we actually apply this criterion, and end up by agreeing (schematically) to take A, B and C to be areas of permanent and universal relevance to human beings as such, and D, E and F to be otherwise. At the least, we then have a framework in which to conduct arguments about their practical importance: arguments which, it must be remembered, we cannot avoid bringing to provisional conclusions, inasmuch as we have in fact to teach pupils one thing rather than another. We may assume, then, that we shall single out some things in the former group – say, A and C – as of great importance in this sense; and we shall do this, even though our judgments may not be correct, or the 'consensus' which we reach may not be wholly rational.

We now have something which I take to be of immense method-ological and organizational value: namely, the notion of a perma-nently important and permanently defensible area, in reference to which we can add or subtract arrangements whose importance is *ad hoc*. A and C, at least, we feel secure about, and will want to promote so far as is consistent with *ad hoc* pressures. We would then naturally try to 'fix', or circumvent, many of the requirements of D, E, and F, so as to leave more scope for the acknowledged importance of A and C. For instance, automation or an improved economy may take care of the pressure to train pupils for particular jobs: improved diplomacy may prevent the barbarians invading: improved medicine or agriculture, the onset of plague or famine. Many of these pressures, obviously but importantly, would be reduced or abolished by enterprises which had nothing directly to do with education at all: leaving us, thereby, more time and resources to educate in other ways. We have at least a clear picture of what we would *like* (and have good reason) to do with our pupils if these pressures were removed: a clear picture of what to count as a (tiresome if important) pressure and what to count as permanently valuable learning. And only by having such a picture can we know what we want to work towards.

Indeed it might not be unduly puritanical to say that the use of education to gain *ad hoc* goods was, other things being equal, a *misuse* of the enterprise. Of course other things are often not equal, and to talk of an 'ideal use' is not to provide practical arguments for practical situations. Nevertheless, there is a clear sense in which to use education for the provision of such goods is regrettable. It is the goods *peculiar* to each enterprise that each enterprise should – again, 'ideally' – be devoted to promoting. From this point of view we are bound, I think, to regard educational objectives in a defeasible sort of way: that is, to begin with those objectives which are most securely justified, and allow *ad hoc* objectives to encroach on their space only under pressure from the practical world. I am not arguing here either that this is, in fact, how most societies normally proceed in their reflections about educational policies, nor that most societies are more likely to value the *ad hoc* than the permanent: both these are empirical points. The suggestion is rather that a rational policy-maker would proceed on that basis.

To these we may add a semi-practical argument. The more sophisticated, complex, and rapidly changing a world we live in, the less we are able to specify with any confidence the particular *ad hoc* demands which we wish to make on education. Machines become out of date, defending one's country takes on totally new forms, and pulling one's weight economically does not commit one unequivocally to the learning of specific skills. Even for the meeting of *ad hoc* demands (whatever, indeed, these may turn out to be), it appears that we shall chiefly need individuals with certain *general* characteristics: mental flexibility, reliability, a critical intelligence combined with an understanding of the need for authority and discipline, together with some basic competences which would probably form part of anyone's education and hence would not be in dispute – for instance, literacy and elementary mathematics.

I describe this argument as 'semi-practical' because it is, obviously enough, quite possible that societies may regress to a position in which easily-identifiable skills may be crucial: trapping deer or fending off sabre-toothed tigers. But there is some conceptual pressure here: an *a priori* likelihood that societies (if we do not blow ourselves completely off the face of the planet) will become more sophisticated and rapidly changing, more able to deal with *ad hoc* pressures by non-educational methods (e.g. automation, injections against disease, and so on). Again, it may also be thought probable that authoritarian or totalitarian methods of ensuring that the *ad hoc* demands are met cannot (perhaps in principle, as they plainly cannot in practice) be seen as permanently effective, if only because they must necessarily rely on a sufficient degree of consent among those governed; and the notion of consent or obedience implies some *general* quality which (arguably, as Plato argued) the citizenry ought to learn. Whatever the force of particular conceptual or practical arguments, we may at least claim that, without a firm basis of education in such general qualities, any attempt to meet the demands by highly specified training will be extremely *fragile*. Indeed, their rapid obsolescence is such that we should probably not want to bring them under that idea of a 'general policy' which is a necessary condition of counting them as education.

Finally, there is perhaps *something* to be said about the substantive (as against the methodological) importance of this category. The importance of the permanent and the universal, as against the contingent and particular, derives from a number of general considerations which are themselves in the former category, and many of which are given by Plato. Briefly, the point is that the notion of reasoning itself involves paying attention to the general rather than to the particular: we have to see the particular – 'I', 'my', 'this', 'that' – as *a case of* the general. This enterprise is conducted in the teeth of opposition; for all sorts of reasons, some of which we shall look at below (p. 163), we find it more natural to cling to those particulars which are closest to us. We very easily 'value' or 'commit ourselves' to those particulars, and fail to perceive that – in point of reason – there is no special justification for valuing them rather than others. Indeed, because of our failure to grasp the general – the Form, one might say, of whatever it is – we do not even *see* the particulars correctly, let alone value them justly.

Much of the business of education is a struggle against this enemy. Thus behind notions represented by 'justice', 'consistency', 'fairness', and so on lies the idea of some pressure on the individual to put his individual particularities and *penchants* in the background. This idea applies to all forms of reasoning and justification; though it is perhaps most obvious in the moral sphere itself, where the crucial move is from 'Why should *I*?' to 'Why should *one*?' Insofar as it makes sense (as I think it does) to talk of justifying or giving reasons for accepting such demands, and insofar as there actually *are* good reasons for accepting them, then to that – so far, undetermined – extent they have to be accepted, and education is concerned with getting pupils to do so.

In particular cases, at least, it is difficult to see how the idea of serious learning or of advanced understanding and rationality can be sustained without bringing in reasons and concepts of a fairly general kind. For example, we may start with the idea of colour prejudice or racial prejudice, just because these particular kinds of prejudice may be very evident in a particular society at a certain time; but any serious educational attempt on these areas immediately leads the student to consider in more general terms what counts as prejudice, what features of men are relevant and what irrelevant to certain kinds of judgments, and so on. The particular features (being black or Jewish) come to be seen as just two, among many, irrelevant features. Even if we were interested, from a psychological or sociological point of view, in why it should be *these* features to which prejudice attached itself in particular circumstances, we should have to be able to see the features and the circumstances in the light of some wider generalization; there are perhaps general reasons why colour, or endogamy,' or whatever, should function in this way. We should inevitably see these things as *cases of* whatever generalization we thought appropriate; just as, rather more obviously, a natural scientist sees particular objects as cases of things having mass (and hence subject to the law of gravity), or having a certain kind of atomic structure and hence subject to certain laws about radioactive decay.

It is even possible to think that there may be some correlation between those areas of understanding which are well established and the recognition of this point. Because mathematics and science, for instance, are in this fortunate position few serious men feel the temptation to talk of British (German, Russian, etc.) mathematics or science; indeed, when the temptation is yielded to, people stop doing mathematics or science and start engaging in some kind of politics, as was the case with Nazi ethnologists and Soviet biologists. The temptation is clearly stronger to think of morality in such terms, as if our purpose was to produce British gentlemen (or 'true Germans' or '100 per cent American boys' or 'the traditionally Japanese virtues'); and with religious and other ideals the temptation is stronger still. In these latter cases it is clear that we have, *pro tanto*, ceased to be interested in the general advancement of under-standing and rationality (perhaps even in serious *learning*) at all, and turned our attention to preserving or inculcating what we take to be worth while in some other way; just as it is one thing to run a seminar on the general problem of minority groups in societies, and another thing to run a political party with the specific purpose of making (say) Wales or Quebec independent.

I am not, of course, saying here that 'freeing Wales', for instance, could not be something one might seriously learn how to do; nor that it could not be something one overridingly ought to do without bothering to learn very much at all. The point is rather that anyone who could fairly be said to be primarily concerned with *education* would, at the least, wish to gain as much understanding as he could about Welsh freedom. He would want to ensure that there were good reasons for freeing Wales, which would involve seeing Wales as one case among many (though no doubt with its own particularities, also to be reflected upon); and especially he would not tolerate any embargo on general discussion about the problem – that is, any suggestion that certain values, or ideals, or political aims should be taken for granted – while reasonable men did in fact disagree. For this would show that his prime allegiance was not to serious learning, but rather to some particular ideology. If as a result of these discussions freeing Wales appeared as a clear desideratum, that would be a kind of spin-off, so to speak, from the education or serious learning which had been going on. For such learning to be sufficiently serious, the participants would have to be sufficiently removed from their immediate contingent interests.

What then *are* these things which are of inalienable significance to all men – which we are landed with, so to speak, whether we like it or not? Traditionally philosophers have laid out (if in a rather haphazard or partisan way) two sets of options, corresponding roughly to knowledge and character. On the one hand, we may try to categorize a set of Xs which we might call subjects, or disciplines, or forms of thought; and on the other, a set comprising certain virtues, or qualities of mind, or excellences. This has some initial plausibility. Any responsible parent or other educator, we might suppose, will have an interest (1) in what his children (pupils) *know* – whether they are literate, or have some grasp of basic mathematics, or whatever: and (2) in what sort of people they are turning out to *be* – whether they are kind or cruel, clever or stupid, courageous or cowardly.

It is not to be denied that such an attempt will leave a lot of questions unanswered. Are these categories exhaustive? (There might be important cases of learning how to do, or at least simply *to* do, certain things which could not easily be subsumed under either.) Are we to fill them with items representing kinds of knowledge and qualities we think desirable, or inevitable, or traditionally accepted, or what? Would not some items in the two categories overlap (since some virtues at least involve knowledge, and any serious pursuit or acquisition of knowledge seems to involve certain virtues)? But I do not think these questions should deter us from some examination of such categorizations, if only as a starting-point. Some of the answers may become clearer *en route*: others may require additional discussion. We shall at least be able to see how far we may advance by this particular path.

I shall begin by considering one contemporary taxonomy, not just because it is well known and philosophically sophisticated, but because it illustrates the nature of our difficulties very well. The following quotations from its author, Hirst, will be enough to start us off:

(a) In the developed forms of knowledge the following related distinguishing features can be seen:

(1) They each involve certain central concepts that are peculiar in character to the form. For example, those of gravity, acceleration, hydrogen, and photo-synthesis characteristic of the sciences; number, integral and matrix in mathematics; God, sin and predestination in religion; ought, good and wrong in moral knowledge.
(2) In a given form of knowledge these and other concepts that denote, if perhaps in a very complex way, certain aspects of experience, form a network of possible relationships in which experiences can be understood. As a result the form has a distinctive logical structure. . . .
(3) The form, by virtue of its particular terms and logic, has expressions or statements (possibly answering a distinctive type of question) that in some way or other, however indirect it may be, are testable against experience. This is the case in scientific knowledge, moral knowledge, and in the arts, though in the arts no questions are explicit and the criteria for the tests are only partially expressible in words. . . .
(4) The forms have developed particular techniques and skills for exploring experience and testing their distinctive expressions.[5]

In a passage written later, the same author distinguishes seven forms: logic/mathematics, physical science, interpersonal knowledge, moral knowledge, aesthetics, religion and philosophy. He adds:

(b) The differentiation of these seven areas is based on the claim that in the last analysis, all our concepts seem to belong to one of a number of distinct, if related, categories which philosophical analysis is concerned to clarify. These categories are marked out in each case by certain fundamental, ultimate or categorical concepts of a most general kind which other concepts in the category pre-suppose. . . . It is these categoreal concepts that provide the form of experience in the different modes. Our understanding of the physical world, for instance, involves such categoreal concepts as those of 'space', 'time' and 'cause'.

Concepts such as those of 'acid', 'electron' and 'velocity' all presuppose these categoreal notions. In the religious domain, the concept of 'God' or 'the transcendent' is presumably categoreal whereas the concept of 'prayer' operates at a lower level. In the moral area the term 'ought' labels a concept of categoreal status, as the term 'intention' would seem to do in our understanding of persons. The distinctive type of objective test that is necessary to each domain is clearly linked with the meaning of these categoreal terms. . . .

The division of modes of experience and knowledge suggested here is thus a fundamental categoreal division, based on the range of such irreducible categories which we at present seem to have. That other domains might, in due course, come to be distinguished, is in no sense being prejudged: for the history of human consciousness would seem to be one of progressive differentiation.[6]

This general line, and the list of the forms of thought, is followed more or less *au pied de la lettre* by many other philosophers of education (e.g. Dearden, whose exposition of them in a well-known book is extremely clear, if thin).[7]

There are some obvious holes to be picked here, of which perhaps the most obvious is visible in the 'religious domain'. This is supposed to be a 'fundamental category'; and the examples we are given of 'central' and/or 'ultimate' concepts in this domain are, in quotation (a), 'God, sin and predestination'; in (b) 'God' again and 'the transcendent'. Unless one gives a monopoly of the term 'religion' to certain types of sophisticated monotheism, these examples plainly will not do; it is not clear that any religion must operate with all these concepts, and in fact many religions do not. Unfortunately Hirst reinforces this impression elsewhere: 'In religious discourse you cannot use the term God in any old way. He is not an object or being in space and time, he has no extension or colour. He does not act as a human being acts.'[8] This will do for certain versions of, for example, the Christian God, but not for other 'religious discourse': for instance, the Zeus and Poseidon of Homer. We should say here that the account of the 'religious domain' is too particularized.

Conversely, the account of the moral domain seems not particularized enough, at least in the quotations above. 'Ought', 'good' and 'wrong' are plainly not peculiar to moral judgments, on almost any account of moral judgments; we can have right and wrong answers to sums, good and bad shots in tennis, and kettles that ought to be boiling by now. Elsewhere, however, Hirst particularizes very strongly: 'Actions are judged morally when they are assessed in relation to such fundamental principles as the consideration of interests, respect for persons, freedom and equality'[9] (a list of principles borrowed from Peters[10]). These principles represent *one* general kind of *genre* or morality (a Kantian–utilitarian tradition): and this is a monopolistic move which I and other philosophers have criticized elsewhere.[11] Briefly: imagine how hard it would be to bring the morality of a Homeric hero or Japanese samurai within this circumscription.

These and similar points raise the general question of what a 'form of thought', as Hirst conceives it, is supposed to *be*. We are offered various criteria: 'central concepts', 'a distinctive logical structure', 'distinctive expressions that are testable against experience', 'particular techniques and skills', and 'categories . . . marked out by certain fundamental, ultimate or categoreal concepts.' Hirst sees that these are 'related', rather than logically independent, and adds 'The central feature to which they point is that the major forms of knowledge . . . can each be distinguished by their dependence on some particular kind of test against experience.'[12]

*Prima facie* this is a revisitation of familiar philosophical territory. We are to say something like this: there are different kinds of propositions, and one way of classifying them (a particularly important way not only for philosophers but for those who teach children to understand the reasons for them) is by their 'method of verification'. Thus we notice that some sort of distinction can be made between 'analytic' propositions and 'deductive' knowledge on the one hand, and 'synthetic', 'inductive' or 'empirical' on the other. Hirst's logico-mathematical form seems to fit the former, and the rest of his forms (except perhaps 'philosophy'?) the latter. Then we may go on, and say that the way we verify propositions about the physical world is different from the way we verify propositions about the intentions and purposes and rule-following of rational creatures. We might have worries about this, since it is not clear just how we *do* verify the latter (by asking them? by observation of their voluntary behaviour, and/or involuntary symptoms? by some kind of non-observational knowledge, at least in the case of our own intentions?); but at least we notice that the 'why?' in 'Why do planets move in ellipses?' seems to bear a different, or at least a simpler, sense from the 'why?' in 'Why do gentlemen raise their hats to ladies?' – though even here we shall have trouble with, for example, 'Why do gentlemen prefer blondes?' (are the gentlemen following rules in any sense?). But we might feel tolerably happy with some sort of distinction between 'scientific' and 'personal' knowledge, even though some might regard the latter as a rather sophisticated sub-section of the former.[13]

Even at this point, however – and certainly when we look at some of the remaining forms (morality, aesthetics, religion) – we feel a certain malaise. Rather than just glaring at 'propositions' and their 'method of verification', we want to enquire into the general background of what is said and what is claimed as known. We need to know more about what is *going on* when people do and say things we might feel tempted to categorize under 'morality', 'art' and 'religion'. What *sort* of enterprises are these, what are the people *doing*? When we know this, it will be time enough to delineate 'forms of thought'. This too is now familiar philosophical territory.

Since Hirst does not enter this territory, and since his demarcation of these latter forms seems inadequate, we are bound to raise again the question of what this list of forms is a list *of*. Now from what we have said so far, the answer we might expect is something like this: 'Look, all over the world people have to make decisions about what to teach children. Obviously it will be useful for them to have a sort of logical guide-book to what *kinds* of knowledge there can be. Some of these areas that we've demarcated – morals, religion, aesthetics – may be a bit obscure; but there's surely a case for saying that there just *are*, from a logical point of view, these different kinds of knowledge. What we're offering is a timeless, culture-free sketch of the logically different kinds of things that rational creatures can know, or the logically different modes of knowledge that are possible.'[14] In other words, we would expect this to be a strictly philosophical enterprise along traditional lines.

In fact this is not a correct interpretation, as appears from the final remarks of Hirst quoted in (b) above on p. 111: 'categories which we *at present* seem to have . . . other domains might, in due course, come to be distinguished.' The general intention is echoed by Dearden: 'What actual forms of understanding men have evolved . . . can be determined only by an examination of the knowledge that we do now have, and not in any high-handed *a priori* way.'[15] But now we have a worry which can be represented as follows:

1 If the concern is with what 'men have evolved' or 'we at present seem to have', then who are 'men' or 'we'? Pygmies? Witch-doctors? Astrologers? Are 'we' the *avant-garde* of 'human consciousness', or just typical representatives of it, or what? Insofar as this is an empirical thesis about what 'men' have done, it ought to be made much clearer *what* 'men' we are talking of. *Some* 'men' (social groups) do not distinguish or differentiate as 'we' do – for instance, they do not count morality and religion as separate domains; and the 'we' who have 'evolved' the highly monopolistic concept of religion ('God', 'the transcendent', 'predestination', etc.), or the particular utilitarian-style version of morality ('respect for

persons', etc.), may not be either typical or, necessarily, more sophisticated or 'progressive' in our 'differentiation'.

2 If now we want to say that 'we' are the *avant-garde*, that people *ought* to differentiate because in some sense there just *are* these distinctions (whether or not people actually make them), then this (sociological) interpretation becomes incoherent. For on what basis could it be said that the distinctions are there, other than on some strictly logical basis which is not intended as culture-bound or time-bound? We can of course investigate, *qua* philosophers and not just *qua* sociologists, distinctions which are drawn and recognized, albeit vaguely, by 'us'. But either we face the question of whether these are 'real' (i.e. logically sound or necessary) distinctions, or we do not face it. If we do not face it, then this is just a rather sophisticated sociological thesis – and certainly we should have no valid reason for recommending these distinctions for curricular purposes. If we do face it, then we must have some culture-free criterion for determining whether the distinctions are 'real' or not; and this criterion must presumably be found somewhere in the realm of logic or conceptual necessity.

It might be thought that this is to wield too sharp an axe. Consider a parallel with animal taxonomy. Some societies may not distinguish mammals, vertebrates, reptiles, etc., as zoologists do, preferring perhaps other distinctions (edible and inedible, easy or hard to trap). Nevertheless we can say (1) that there really *are* these zoological distinctions, and (2) that we are still not operating 'in any high-handed *a priori* way'. We are not precluded from saying that there may be other kinds of animals which we have not yet discovered, or new kinds that may arise, which would add to our taxonomic list; yet we might also feel able to claim that our taxonomy was in some ways more profound than one based on such distinctions as edible–inedible – that ours did more justice, so to speak, to the real nature of the animals.

That is the best I can do for this interpretation of the forms of thought; but it is still not quite good enough. One consideration is that taxonomies have to be judged on their purposes. There would be no point in the distinctions of zoology if they did not help us to make sense of certain problems and phenomena – the evolutionary history of animal species, for instance. If we can understand evolution, or the distribution of species in the world, or something of that kind, only by the use of these distinctions, then (only) are we justified in claiming that the distinctions are important *irrespective* of whether particular social groups made them – we would now say, *recognized* them – or not. For then they are underpinned by culture-free considerations. In the same way, the forms-of-thought taxonomy must ultimately be justified by whether the logic of different forms really *is* different, not by whether 'we' or any other social group actually make these distinctions. This is perhaps the sort of thing Austin had in mind when he said of philosophy 'this clarification is as much a creative act as a discovery or description. It is as much a matter of making clear distinctions as of making already existent distinctions clear.'[16] To repeat: if 'we' *qua* philosophers are trying to produce a list each item on which is *sui generis*, then 'we' cannot ultimately rest content with the 'differentiations' which 'we' currently make *qua* members of certain twentieth-century cultures. 'We' (*qua* philosophers) have ultimately either to endorse these differentiations or reject them.

This does not mean that there is anything wrong with using the 'categories which we at present seem to have' or 'the knowledge that we do now have' as a basis: that is, as data – even perhaps as a *prima facie* taxonomy – to be philosophizing *about*. Nor, equally, is it necessarily false that 'other domains might, in due course, come to be distinguished': but this will have to mean, not just that some social group may come to *make* new differentiations (rightly or wrongly), but that the distinctions are logically sound – and this means, in effect, that more progress will have been made in logic (in a broad sense) or philosophy. To use our parallel: it is not so much that new species of animals may be discovered on Mars, for instance, and that we cannot do anything about categorizing these until time passes; it is rather that, by very hard thinking about the animals we already have available, we may be able to notice new distinctions.

Whether or not these considerations would be acceptable to Hirst and others, it seems clear that they are relevant to the obvious deficiencies in the more suspect forms (morality, aesthetics, religion). In this light, we should surely not adopt a programme of *waiting to see* whether, for instance, various societies severed religion from morals, or regarded literacy, musical and artistic criticism as different *genres* (as we now to some degree regard biology, chemistry and physics as different). For we should still have to say whether these moves were proper or improper. And this involves wrestling with the enterprises or 'forms of life' which have thrown up such subject-titles as 'religion': what we have to take seriously is not the titles but the *genres*. There is no short cut to this.

Of course the process is extremely difficult. But it is not made easier, more down-to-earth, or less 'high-handed' by representing the programme as just a matter of *observing* the 'progressive differentiation' of 'human thought'. For we immediately run into well-known difficulties which recent philosophical debates have brought out. For instance: one author says of a particular magical or superstitious belief of the Azande that

The Azande do not intend their belief either as a piece of
science or as a piece of non-science. They do not possess these
categories. It is only *post eventum*, in the light of later and more
sophisticated understanding, that their belief and concepts can
be classified and evaluated at all.[17]

Now one might well doubt whether there could be any society in
which, as the author says,[18] there was a *total* 'absence of any practice
of science and technology in which criteria of effectiveness, in-
effectiveness and kindred notions had been built up': rather as one
might doubt whether there could be any society without a norm of
truth-telling, or any language without subjects and predicates. But
one's doubts here are logical and (if you like) *a priori*, not sociological
doubts. We might end up, with the Azande and other cases, by
saying something like 'Well, in a way they differentiate and in a way
they don't', or 'They don't differentiate as clearly (consciously) as
we do.' In other words, it is not just a matter of seeing whether the
Azande have 'science' on their school time-tables: it is a matter of
classifying 'in the light of later and more sophisticated understanding' – and to do this, we have to be sure that our understanding
*is* more sophisticated (that is, more philosophically and timelessly
*correct*) rather than just 'later' or different.

From this point of view we may not only find the categorization of
the suspect forms (morality, religion, aesthetics) in Hirst to be over-
hasty: we may well think the categorization of the first two or three
to be over-modestly presented. Whatever distinctions may be valid
here – for instance, some sort of distinction between analytic and
synthetic knowledge, or between our understanding of persons and
our understanding of physical objects – they are surely not just
valid for *our* language or our society or our planet. If somebody said
that there were or could be Martians who did not make some use of
these distinctions, and who operated without such concepts as
'space' and 'time', 'person', 'intention', and the like, I think we
should be unable to understand him. His picture would be as
incoherent as that of monsters from outer space whom science-fiction
writers try to represent as 'rational' but totally without 'feeling' or
'emotion'. Arguably also there are conceptual reasons why *some*
mode of moral thinking, some kind of aesthetic experience, and
perhaps even some religious activity are inevitable for rational
creatures: or at least (we might for some purposes want to add) for
creatures that develop from children into adults, rather than
springing fully-armed and equipped into immediate maturity. This
possibility is what makes the task of delineating these forms or modes
worth a philosopher's while to attempt; whereas (to put the point

extremely) a more sociological programme might conclude that 'aesthetic experience' was merely a curious cultural phenomenon originating in Bloomsbury in the 1920s.

Hirst's more recent remarks do not, in my judgment, make his position any clearer. On the one hand he says

> As distinct from a Kantian approach, it is not my view that in elucidating the fundamental categories of our understanding we reach an unchanging structure that is implicit, indeed *a priori*, in all rational thought in all times and places. That there exist any elements in thought that can be known to be immune to change, making transcendental demands on us, I do not accept.[19]

Even in its context, this is very hard to understand. If someone said that notions like subject and predicate, truth and error, non-contradiction and many others were not 'immune to change', I think we should be at a loss to know what he meant by such a phrase. The notion of a logical or 'transcendental' demand has sense just because we recognize paradigm cases of it, which we contrast with what is changeable. To put this another way: for something to *count as* 'an element in *thought*', it would have to satisfy certain criteria: there are analytic truths and logical entailments which set the rules for what we can intelligibly think and say. If someone were to claim, for instance, that there could be coherent or rational thought that paid no attention whatsoever to the law of non-contradiction, we should not understand him. If this were not so, philosophy and logic would be indistinguishable from sociology and empirical linguistics.

A further passage reads:

> Nothing can any more be supposed fixed eternally. Yet none of this means that we cannot discern certain necessary features of intelligibility and reason *as we have them* . . . we can pick out those concepts and principles which are necessary and fundamental to anything we could *at present* call understanding. . . . Intelligibility is itself a development in this context, and one that is of its nature hedged in and limited by it. To assume that this framework is in any sense necessarily fixed now seems absurd. But to imagine it is not setting limits to what is *right now* intelligible is equally absurd [my italics].[20]

But the trouble here is the same as before; the ideas fall halfway between sociology and logic, between the empirical and the conceptual. 'Intelligibility' and 'reason' are normally taken to mark transcendental notions: that is, either something is intelligible (reasonable) or it is not. Certainly we may *come to see that* something is or is not intelligible, by the usual processes of philosophical clarification; and certainly we may start to speak a different language, whereby (the rules being changed) collections of signs that were intelligible become incoherent, and vice versa. But that is all that could be *meant* by the italicized phrases ('at present', 'right now', etc.).

There are, surely, some considerations which would make it worth our while construing our procedure along lines opposite to those taken (perversely, as I see it) by Hirst. We need not specify these lines in advance by terms such as '*a priori*' or 'transcendental': but we have to show, by conceptual rather than empirical argument, that certain basic types of experience giving rise to certain structures of thought and language are inevitable for any rational creatures living in a space–time continuum. In fact, our difficulties here are due mostly to the fact that philosophers have paid remarkably little attention to those experiences and structures which (to put it briefly) have more to do with emotion than with perception; hence it is quite unsurprising that our specific doubts about Hirst's forms of knowledge increase, as we saw earlier, the further we remove ourselves from logic and science.

We can, without too much difficulty, see what sort of conceptual arguments make it inconceivable for such a creature to have absolutely *no* kind of logical, scientific, or personal knowledge. To advance much beyond this would involve constructing a conceptual network based on the (given) fact that the creature has desires and emotions as well as intelligence, and the logical inevitability that these desires and emotions will be characterized by what might be called a common case-history (see p. 175). It seems reasonable to doubt whether we could proceed very far without paying rather more serious attention to the unconscious mind than philosophers have hitherto been accustomed to do; and it is certainly on the cards that existing titles – 'morals', 'personal relationships', 'art', 'games', 'humour', 'religion', 'politics', 'ideals', 'ideologies', etc. – will need a good deal of revision.

Nevertheless, it seems clear that these are the lines on which some significant part of philosophy ought to proceed, for the benefit of the educator. The underlying difficulty is, as so often, taxonomic. We are attempting *one* sort of answer to the general question 'What is there to learn?' by listing those forms of life which are, as it were, available for rational creatures and into which they can be initiated; and the items on our list will turn on what criteria of similarity and difference we are prepared to use. Strict or formal considerations of logic, of the kind that Hirst seems to have in mind when he speaks of 'categoreal concepts' and 'tests for truth', may not take us very far; some distinction between analytic and synthetic propositions seems inalienable, but to distinguish usefully between different kinds of synthetic propositions only seems possible against a background of a fuller understanding of the enterprises in which they figure.

An important part of such understanding, without which it seems dangerously premature actually to list or *number* various 'forms of thought', will involve trying to grasp what might (not without risk) be termed the point or *purpose* of the activities.[21] The evident problem here, which in effect constitutes the taxonomic difficulty, is that many of the activities are not consciously undertaken and deliberately conducted for overt purposes at all; they are, if not hopelessly then at least very profoundly, tied up with various unconscious purposes and perceptions. This of course gives us an additional reason to be dissatisfied with any programme of classification which takes the knowledge which 'we at present seem to have' as a starting-point.

We are saying, in effect, that the 'progressive differentiation' of which Hirst speaks has simply not yet progressed far enough. Nevertheless, it is of the highest importance for the educator that it should progress further. At present we are able, for instance, to distinguish science from astrology and crystal-gazing, and to hold up science as at least *one* tolerably clear 'form' in which the mind may develop. But we can do this only because we have, at great pains and after much psychological and social striving, achieved a certain seriousness and clarity about asking and answering a particular type of question: we might say, about facing reality in a particular mode. We may now, indeed, be able to talk of 'categoreal concepts', 'conceptual structures', 'specific tests for truth', and so on: but this only becomes possible after, or at most during, the process of getting clear and becoming serious about what we are or should be trying to do.

How far 'philosophy' is a satisfactory title for this process is an open question: but, insofar as it may be one, it is certainly *not* the case that 'philosophy leaves everything as it is' – or at least, it should not be the case. Naturally if 'philosophy' confines itself to reminding us of what, in some fairly superficial sense, we know already – that is, bringing to consciousness various structures of thought which are, though buried, nevertheless coherent in themselves and discrete from one another – then our language and our actual practice will remain unchanged. But insofar as, whether under the heading of 'philosophy' or not, we are concerned with deeper and more miasmic areas in which at present we can hardly distinguish belief from fantasy, then our concern should produce clearer differentiations which will themselves result in linguistic and practical change.

If we fail to consider human enterprises in their own right, and in some transcendental or culture-free way, we thereby set at least two limitations on the value of this procedure. These limitations emerge, in a general way, when Hirst grants that his theory

> explicitly excludes all objectives other than intellectual ones, thereby ignoring many of the central concerns of, say, physical education and the education of character. Even the intellectual ends it seeks are limited. Linguistic skills, for instance, are included only as tools for the acquisition of knowledge in the different forms. . . . The lack of concern for moral commitment, as distinct from moral understanding, that it seems to imply, is a particularly significant limitation.[22]

This betokens an undue obsession with concepts and propositions in themselves, and generates the (clearly false) implications that 'commitment' is relevant only or chiefly to certain specific areas, like morality: that we have a workable distinction between 'intellectual' and 'other' objectives: and that we can distinguish these in particular areas, as with 'moral commitment, as distinct from moral understanding', without doing violence to the areas themselves.

The first limitation involves the exclusion of what might be described as specific *virtues* (or dispositions, or attitudes) which are part and parcel of the learning in question. This emerges clearly if we consider some of the later forms labelled 'aesthetics', 'morality' and 'religion'. We have already seen that there are various questions to be raised about just what ground each is supposed to cover. But, more importantly, we might regard it as *prima facie* odd to describe education in respect of human activities, instances of which might be quite ordinarily called 'enjoying a concert', 'worshipping God' and 'loving one's neighbour' as centrally concerned with forms of *thought* or *knowledge*. This oddity does not entirely disappear when we grant the importance of beliefs and appraisals in these activities or in human emotion generally.[23] Nor is much gained by restricting 'education' to the 'cognitive' aspects of the activities. For, first, we are not wholly clear about what the activities *are*, and hence not clear about *how* or what *kind* of 'cognition' enters into them: second, on Peters' 'initiation' model of education[24] (which is here a particularly good one), it seems in these cases impossible, or at least empty, only to initiate pupils 'cognitively'.

In these respects the activities are radically unlike Hirst's first two forms (the logico-mathematical and the scientific), and sufficiently unlike the 'personal knowledge' form (which includes history). We may indeed (with Peters) make some degree of 'caring' a criterion for applying the term 'education' in all these areas; thus we shall say that a person is not really educated in science or history if (so to speak) he just goes correctly through the intellectual motions – he must also care about the subject as a whole. But this is not enough to make the relevant distinction. Somebody who solves an equation or conducts laboratory experiments is in a clear sense engaged in doing mathematics or science, whatever his motives and degree of involvement. But more is required for somebody to be seriously engaged in morality (as against moral philosophy), art (as against art criticism), or religion (as against the philosophy, history, psychology, sociology, etc., *of* religion). His feelings must be involved in a quite different way: otherwise he is not, so to speak, really in the game at all. We can distinguish (1) between the man who just 'goes through the motions' in the 'intellectual' aspects of morality, art and religion, and the man who cares about these aspects: but we need also to distinguish (2) between the man who is (or is not) concerned about *these* aspects and the man who is (or is not) emotionally involved in the whole enterprise.

The phrase 'emotionally involved' may be misleading. For the kind of thing missing in the person to whom religion or morality or art does not, as we say, 'mean anything' is not necessarily any kind of *passion*: it is more like what is missing in the person to whom certain activities (some kinds of painting, interior decoration, dress) do not 'mean anything' because he is colour-blind. The man with a sense of colour *can* at least enter into these activities: it is then another question whether he cares a great deal about them as a whole (how much time and energy he likes to put into them), and another question again whether he cares about doing each of them well – i.e. how concerned he is to follow the appropriate criteria internal to each activity. What we are talking about is the initial ability (so to speak) to play the game at all.

One difference connected with this is that, in these activities, education seems *prima facie* less concerned with making pupils *do* things. In many areas of education, we are concerned with reasoning and knowledge and *action*: we want to make the pupil think in the right way, use appropriate reasons, and produce right answers as a result of that reasoning. It is true that we also want him to *care for* the subjects: to enjoy, or be in some sense keen about, finding out mathematical or scientific or historical truth. But in 'aesthetics', for instance, it is plainly different. Here we want the pupil not (only) to do or know something, but to feel something. This applies, in some degree, to education in religion and morality (*pace* philosophers who insist on seeing morality as solely concerned with overt action): but 'aesthetics' is a pure case of it. Anything that an 'aesthetically educated' person overtly *does* as a result of his education (e.g., I suppose, go to more concerts or buy the right pictures) is in a way peripheral. What is central is his feelings.

For similar reasons, a clear sense can be attributed to a regulation which stated that the school day should commence with a compulsory half-hour's mental arithmetic; but it is not so clear what can be meant by 'compulsory religious worship', 'moral interaction' or 'aesthetic enjoyment'. If under some Leavis-like dispensation an ordinance was proposed which required that the whole school should begin the morning with 'a compulsory act of literary appreciation', we should be inclined to regard this as some sort of philosophical joke. This is not because of a basic misfit between the notion of compulsion on the one hand, and the notions of *any* kind of learning, coming to understand, etc., on the other. 'He was made (forced, compelled, etc.) to learn Latin' is perfectly good English and quite clearly intelligible. 'He was forced to appreciate Shakespeare' is more baffling, because we recognize a gap between anything we could compel children to *do* overtly – turn pages, recite lines of poetry, utter aesthetic judgments, etc. – and anything we would seriously want to call 'appreciating Shakespeare'. 'Worship' is on the border-line: 'forced to worship Baal' will make sense if 'worship' is restricted to a series of acts (bowing down, uttering words); if it includes feelings and emotional appraisals (seeing and/or feeling Baal as worshipful), the sense becomes more doubtful.

It seems fairly clear that this is not, or certainly not just, because the *concepts* are more complex or intellectually sophisticated in these areas, as against the areas of mathematics and natural science. The point is rather that there are important differences between what lies *behind* the possession of the concepts in either case. We could no doubt teach certain concepts to pupils who had no aesthetic sense (those marked by 'baroque', 'sonata', 'chiaroscuro', and so on), just as we can and do teach colour-blind people the meaning of 'red' and 'yellow'. But this would not be central to aesthetic education, though it is no doubt a part of it. On the other hand, to teach certain concepts and develop certain cognitive abilities in science precisely *is*, centrally, to educate them in science. We should not have the uneasy feeling that we might be operating in a vacuum.

The second and closely connected limitation involves the exclusion not of virtues which are specific to particular enterprises, but of virtues of a general kind which may run through a great many enterprises. Hirst and Peters say:

(i) There are no general 'powers of the mind' that can be
    exercised in a vacuum. They are rather adverbial to activities

and modes of experience in that they are connected with the manner in which they are conducted. Men can cook, paint or construct theories creatively; they can feel compassion imaginatively and with great objectivity and integrity; they can be autonomous and critical in their thinking and in their dealings with other men. These excellences are qualities of the mind that have to be displayed in specific activities which have their own specific standards, if they are to be distinguished from mere self-expression or contra-suggestibility. Nevertheless, it does not follow that there is nothing in common between the exercises of these excellences in different spheres. . . . What does seem to follow, however, is that these general qualities of mind, which have been called excellences, cannot be thought of as general 'powers of the mind' of a person in separation from the modes of experience . . . they can only be exercised in the modes of experience.[25]

The section-heading for this rather obscure passage is 'Human excellences'; and the argument is developed in the next chapter (on the curriculum), in which there is the following crucial 'bridge' passage leading on to the 'forms of thought':

(ii) It has been argued that underlying all the more sophisticated objectives such as autonomy, creativeness and critical thought, there must necessarily be the achievements of objective experience, knowledge and understanding. If this is so it suggests that the logically most fundamental objectives of all are those of a cognitive kind, on the basis of which, out of which, or in relation to which, all others must be developed.[26]

It would be fair to interpret the general drift on the following lines: First we take a number of words – 'creative', 'critical', 'autonomous', etc. – and we enforce two criteria of meaning on to them: (1) they are to be names of 'excellences' or 'sophisticated objectives', and (2) they are only to make sense in reference to their operation in some public cognitive sphere, in particular to *achievement*, 'displayed in specific activities which have their own specific standards'. Then it will seem to follow that 'the logically most fundamental objectives of all' are the 'forms of thought', to which these 'excellences' are 'adverbial'. If challenged on this, we go back (as it were) to chapter 1, in which 'education' is itself defined in terms of (1) desirability characteristics, and (2) a sophisticated kind of cognitive understanding; so that any terms, or any interpretation of terms, not bringing in both (1) and (2) can be thrown out as logically irrelevant to aims of education.

In (i) above, the existence of 'powers of the mind' is recognized, but only in the sense of 'excellences': by which the authors seem to mean, roughly, the 'intellectual' virtues. In (ii) we are told that 'underlying' all these 'must necessarily be the achievements of objective experience, knowledge and understanding.' Consider now ordinary cases of mental characteristics (powers, traits, dispositions or what you will): carefulness, curiosity, persistence, or independence of mind (I suppose 'autonomy' might mean this). Some or all of these might be related to 'intellectual virtue' and hence fit the authors' picture: but what can be *meant* by saying that they 'can only be exercised in the modes of experience'? Either this just says that, e.g., independence of mind, like any trait, is normally and perhaps necessarily *shown* by people living in the empirical world, in relation to *some* kind of experience or other: or else the type of showing is being tied down to '*the* modes of experience' – that is, the forms of thought to which all this leads up. But unless the notion of a 'form of thought' is stretched to the point of vacuity, this second interpretation is grotesque. You can show independence of mind in learning to walk, talk, read, use a knife and fork, and a million and one other things.[27]

But we have to go a good deal further than this. For these examples can, at least, all be brought under the idea of 'achievement' without too much obvious distortion. It is plausible for Peters to say, for instance, that 'Creativity without competence is cant; being critical without a mastery of some content and without training in argument is just being captious', etc., so that 'these excellences' can be conceived of as 'adverbial'.[28] To get behind this idea we might consider things like the ability to love, to enjoy oneself, to concentrate, to relax, to worship, to make friends, and so on. Here of course we *can* talk of 'achievement' – these are all things that people *do*; but to talk of doing them well or badly 'by public standards' will mean no more than that we have to be able to attribute some (public or agreed) *sense* to phrases like 'good at making friends', 'bad at enjoying himself', 'not much good at loving' – and even these phrases sound rather odd, because these activities are not supposed to have public *point* in the same way that, for instance, building bridges and writing symphonies have. We normally take them as modes or aspects or areas in which we want our pupils to be happy, or 'to be themselves', or be free from certain kinds of crippling handicaps: not in which we want them to *perform*.

Similarly in a passage immediately following quotation (ii) above we read:

For only insofar as one has the relevant knowledge and forms of reasoning can a person be creative or critical in, say, atomic physics. Only insofar as one understands other people can one come to care about them and actively seek their good. Enjoying and valuing the arts is impossible without the concepts that make aesthetic experience possible.[29]

Of these propositions, the first is obviously true. The second is, I think equally obviously, false as it stands: 'understanding' and 'caring' are to *some* extent (as the jargon has it) 'independent variables' – plainly one can care a lot for someone whom one understands only a little, and vice versa. The third seems hard to understand: what sort of *concepts* must I have to 'enjoy and value' a pretty tune or a pretty dress, or even the late Beethoven quartets? Of course it may be said, *à la* Plato, that unless we have some deep and accurate knowledge of people and art-objects we cannot care about them as they really are: we just think we do, but in fact care only for shadows. But, at the very least, this needs arguing for; and in the meantime we are made to believe that quite ordinary activities, together with the powers of the mind which operate in them, must somehow be squeezed into some 'form of thought' if they are to survive at all.

The authors might admit this, but claim that it has nothing necessarily to do with education; or not quite that (since these powers obviously *have to do* with education), but that they cannot be taken as *aims* of education. For (the story goes) one can be creative, critical, curious, etc., without being educated; and (perhaps) one can be educated without being any of these things. These traits might be taken care of by parents or psychologists: why should the educator be professionally concerned with them? Perhaps some of them might be essential preconditions for becoming educated; but so is a minimal degree of physical health – yet teachers are not doctors. All this rests on a concept of education fully discussed in the literature. It emerges in remarks like: 'Would they (*sc.* 'human excellences such as autonomy, creativeness') satisfy the knowledge conditions (of 'education') as well? Surely not necessarily; for a man could display such excellences and lack breadth of understanding.'[30]

That this concept of education is unduly restrictive has been shown earlier: that it is internally inconsistent may be a little less obvious. Peters in particular places a good deal of stress on the importance of 'caring about' or 'being on the inside of' various curricular activities or forms of understanding: denying, indeed, the term 'educated' to anyone who lacked these attributes. But then we necessarily import features of another kind – powers of the mind, 'motivational factors', character traits, and so on – into our picture of education; and now, these will be as 'logically fundamental' as the forms of thought. In plainer English, we shall have to say that an educated person must not only be able to study science, history, etc., but must *want* to do them – out of curiosity, a desire to make sense of the world, or whatever motives we are willing to allow. Having and using these powers will now be, not a sort of precondition or essential piece of 'motivation' for *getting* educated, but part of the concept of *being* educated; and developing them in pupils will be, for teachers, not merely a background to the educational process, but part of their educational aims.

In their use of the term 'logically fundamental' the authors seem to have in mind a particular epistemological doctrine, which I shall not try to expound or criticize more fully; partly because I am not at all clear just what it amounts to, and partly because it is too closely bound up with the authors' specific notion of education. But the effect is rather as if we asked what was 'logically fundamental' to a person's learning chess, and took this to be the question 'What is it to learn *chess*?' (as against draughts, halma, etc.) so that we ended up with appropriate answers in terms of the concepts and rules specific to chess; whereas we might equally take it as 'What is logically required for *a person to learn* chess?'; and here, although we shall not forget about the word 'chess', we shall want to add other and quite different answers (e.g. it seems to be a logical requirement that the person should be able to attend or concentrate to some degree, be at a certain level of 'conceptual development', and so on).

Nobody, I think (including these authors, when they are not bewitched by their own specific concept of education), seriously doubts that there are a number of mental or spiritual powers or attributes marked by such words as 'courageous', 'sensitive', 'determined', 'intelligent' and so forth, which are not all confined in their meaning or application to any specific form of knowledge, or indeed any specific form of life; some of them may run through most or all such forms. Our difficulty, as usual, is with classification: words like 'intellectual' and 'cognitive', with their even vaguer counterparts such as 'emotional', 'affective', 'moral', 'spiritual', etc., do not help. However, there are a number of points worth considering, which may at least enable us to see the limitations as well as the possibility of this particular approach.

If the approach is to be of any use at all, we have to avoid the error already criticized in discussing the forms of thought: that is, we have to produce some list of 'virtues' or 'powers of the mind' which can be demonstrated as necessary or desirable for men in some time-free and culture-free way. There would be little point, and much danger, in listing (to parody a quotation) 'the virtues which we at present seem to have', if that means simply listing those qualities or behaviour-patterns which are counted as 'virtuous' by a particular society, or even by all contemporary (or past) societies. It is worth saying a little more about this, if only to show how much hard work is involved in such a procedure.

To begin with, we shall want to be sure that the actual *words* we use will be understood in the right sort of way: that is, roughly, as referring to attributes which are necessarily to be seen as desirable, and not to attributes which are either only to be seen as virtues within the framework of some partisan ideal or commitment ('being a good Nazi') or have no permanently valid desirability characteristics at all ('having red hair'). The difficulty here emerges very clearly when Hirst and Peters ask themselves or their readers: on what grounds is autonomy singled out as a desirable state?. . . . What arguments can the lover of liberty advance against the kindly despot who puts more emphasis on the virtues of conformity and obedience?[31] We want to know whether 'autonomy', 'conformity' and 'obedience' are being used exclusively as the names of virtues (so that, for instance, we use 'bloody-minded' instead of 'autonomous', or 'servile' instead of 'obedient', when we have good reason to disapprove of what the person is or does); or whether these terms are to be used in a purely descriptive way (in which case we should happily say that it is sometimes *wrong* to be 'autonomous' or 'obedient').

Connected with this is the need to free such title-words from cultural or contingent bias. Concepts marked by, say, 'thrift', 'honour', and 'chastity' may obviously be descriptively filled out in a biased way: that is to say, 'thrift' may be used to *mean* 'saving one's pennies', which in a period of inflation may be unwise; or 'honour' to mean 'committing suicide rather than surrendering', which may be wrong for a man whose wife and children will then starve; or 'chastity', that a woman should never be seen on the streets alone, which might be misguided for all sorts of reasons. The procedure to adopt here is not that of trying to sever 'fact' from 'value' (which may have the result of leaving us with no substantive virtues at all), but rather to generalize the concepts. If 'thrift' were to mean something more like 'the ability to defer gratification' and 'to save up when necessary', 'honour' something like 'living up to a correct image that one has of oneself as a virtuous person', and 'chastity', perhaps, 'preserving oneself from what is truly corrupting', it could more easily be seen that these were virtues necessary for any person: just as it is not hard to see why any person requires prudence, courage, justice, determination and so on.

A further and perhaps more intractable problem is the tendency of various cultures or intellectual climates to *classify* these things in some pre-empted way. The word 'virtue' itself, which has come a long way from its roots in the Latin *virtus* (courage or manly qualities in general), is still apt in our own culture to be interpreted in a specifically 'moral' way, more easy to sense intuitively than to describe. Indeed many philosophers, attempting to justify some distinction between 'moral virtues' and other human desiderata, find it hard to say much more than that the former are supposed to be 'under the control of the will'; an extremely mystifying notion, if only because there is no clear-cut distinction between those things which one cannot and those which one can – if only in the long term – try to do something about. It is better to begin, at least, with some much broader notion (like the Greek *aretē*), and try to determine what qualities or attributes (even 'excellences' is misleading) human beings as such need to have. We can, without too much difficulty, appreciate that clarity of mind, whole-heartedness, determination, cheerfulness and other qualities are desirable for men without becoming involved in questions about whether these are 'under the control of the will' or not – questions which, even when we are clear about what this phrase should mean, must surely to a large extent be empirical. It will be time to classify these qualities, and investigate their causal origins, when we have a proper list of them to work with.

Despite these difficulties, there is no reason to suppose that we could not produce some such list; and contrary to a good deal of current opinion, it seems actually *easier* to list items that we should want to call 'moral' than items in other categories. This is perhaps not very surprising, since any plausible delimitation of morality will include the idea that it is in some way an enterprise in which men are inevitably, not just optionally, involved (see pp. 220 ff.): just as men are inevitably involved in some of the forms of thought and can be clearly seen to be so involved, provided that we describe the forms in an appropriate manner (for instance, 'logic' and 'science' must not be restricted to what professional logicians and scientists do).

An example may help here. Suppose I say that courage is a good thing for anybody to have, so that children ought to learn to be brave. There are two ways in which this might be misinterpreted. First and most obviously, somebody might think that by 'courage' or 'being brave' I had put my money on some particular instances or cases of courage, perhaps those socially approved at the time: as if, for instance, I *meant* by 'courage' something like 'not crying if you're hurt', 'being prepared to die for one's country', and so on. But this is not my meaning: indeed I might prefer to call these cases by another name. Second, somebody might think that I was advancing some particular moral thesis: that I was 'valuing' or 'making a value-judgment' about courage, putting some kind of preferential weight on it which other people might not want to put, or commending it in a way in which they might not wish to commend it. But though I may be doing this, that is not all I am doing. I want to draw attention to courage as something which everybody *needs*, whether they know it or not, and whether or not I or they like it, or commend it, or choose it, or 'value' it.

Asked to explain, I say something like this: 'Every human being, indeed any conscious ('rational') creature living in space and time, will have certain ends or goods which he thinks to be worth achieving. If danger or some unpleasantness, fear or boredom, makes it hard or impossible for him to achieve them, he will wish to be equipped with a disposition or a virtue which enables him to overcome these obstacles without undue pain: if he did not, he would not be serious in regarding the goods as goods. "Courage" is the word we use for the disposition or set of dispositions which enables him to do this, or by virtue of which he does it. By courage he overcomes, or can disregard, or is not influenced contrary to reason by, these obstacles.' Then there will be complications about whether we can talk of courage when a man does not really *feel* the fear or boredom: about whether there are two kinds of courage – the 'charging ahead' kind and the 'endurance' kind: about how we are to distinguish courage from determination and persistence: and no doubt other complications also. But the kind of thesis I want to present is now a bit clearer.

What kind is it? Clearly it is not meant to be an empirical thesis, if by 'empirical' is meant the kind of thesis I would be presenting if I said 'Everyone needs air.' Maybe all human beings need air, but there is nothing peculiar in supposing that Martians do not. There is no conceptual connection between being human and needing air (unless we deliberately make one, e.g. by defining 'human' or '*homo sapiens*' as 'an air-breathing creature'). Somebody will now say 'Very well, I see it is a conceptual thesis: ultimately, a thesis about the meanings of words. You are saying that if we take a number of concepts marked by words like "space", "time", "conscious creature", and so on, and explicate these properly, we shall see that it makes no *sense* to deny the virtue of courage. That's fine, but then all you're doing is to elicit something which was, somewhere, already in the conceptual premises. I suppose the, or a, crucial point is that your creature will have certain ends or goods which he thinks to be worth achieving even in the face of some danger or unpleasantness. Such a creature has, clearly, thereby in effect committed himself to valuing courage. This is where the evaluative or prescriptive element lies. But it is *his* element and not yours. He does not *have* to make this value-judgment:'

Much of this need not be denied. But the point is that any rational creature does have to make (*have* to make, since this is part of what we mean by a rational creature) *some* judgments of value, just because he has desires, and he lives in a world. He can, of course, resign from it: he may think there are no goods worth having, or nothing which makes life worth living. But so long as he remains in it, there will be virtues which are desirable for him *whatever* his particular goods. *He* may not desire these virtues: perhaps he does not properly understand what they are. But that does not mean they are not desirable. I am suggesting, what is perhaps obvious enough, that we could not even describe human existence without reference to virtues *qua* virtues, and certain desirable practices *qua* desirable, which form the essence of what we mean, or should mean, by such terms as 'courage', 'justice', 'honesty', etc.: just as we could not describe it without such terms as 'love', 'hate', 'fear', and 'satisfaction'.

Nevertheless, the limitations of this procedure are, in their own way, just as stringent as the limitations of the forms-of-thought procedure: indeed, there are close parallels between the two. Certainly we may say that there are *some general* qualities (both 'moral' and 'non-moral', however we distinguish these) which all men need: and we may even show that the concept of a human being logically requires a minimal possession or enjoyment of some of these. This is rather like saying (in the forms-of-thought mode) that men could hardly be men without certain basic kinds of knowledge or cognitive competence – a minimal grasp of logic, of cause and effect in the physical world, and of their neighbours' intentions and purposes. But if we want to go further than that, by way of listing more particular virtues, we have to show what the *point* of such virtues is: nothing is gained, because nothing much could be understood, by just producing a list of 'excellences'; and this is like the way in which the forms-of-thought advocate, as we saw above (p. 122), needs to show what some of the forms (aesthetics, religion, etc.) are *about*, if the concepts and 'tests for truth' inherent in them are to make much sense. In other words, we cannot advance very far along either line without a clearer understanding of the particular *enterprises* in which men can or must engage, and of the goods which such enterprises pursue: only then can we perceive and justify both the knowledge and other 'cognitive' elements, and also the virtues, which the enterprises require.

It may be thought, with some justice, that in this chapter we have done nothing but laboriously expound certain obvious truths, which might be summarized thus: (1) There are some things to be learned which are, in a more or less strong sense, of permanent and universal significance to men as such, and which can be distinguished from those things which are of impermanent or *ad hoc* significance. (2) Some of these can be described as 'forms of knowledge', representing epistemologically different kinds of truth, all of which are (as it were) inescapable for rational creatures. (3) Others can be described as 'virtues' or 'powers of the mind', which are inescapably desirable. But even this, however laborious, has some force – particularly at a time when many educators talk as if they denied it: as if there were *no* fixed background of this kind at all, no categories which could be used as reference points. The importance of accepting such a background is, as I have tried to stress throughout, methodological rather than normative. I mean that, though it may not give us direct answers to the question 'What Xs ought to be learned?', it may help us to answer the question 'Just what *sort of thing* is this or that X, and how does it relate to what is given to human beings in the world?'

It may still be said, and rightly, (1) that there remains a big gap between categories created at such a high level of abstraction and the particular Xs which may come up for discussion ('classics', 'literacy', 'kindness', 'creativity', and so on). That is entirely true; and the only way of filling the gap is to engage in a great deal of much more particularized philosophical investigation of various Xs. It is also true (2) that we have said nothing, or very little, about priorities: about just what, in fact, ought to be learned. For to have shown the inevitability, or (as it were) the minimal necessity or desirability, of certain forms of knowledge on the one hand and certain virtues on the other, is not to have advanced any particular policy. Granted that all these must have some minimal scope, nevertheless are not some more *important* or *valuable* than others? And, if so, how are we to show this without yielding to some ideological pressure, or taking some 'doctrine of man' as a given starting-point?

However, we ought not to repent our procedure hitherto. As I have suggested, most of us (whether philosophers or not) have been far too quick to take up particular options: a quickness whose results, both in the academic and the practical world, have reduced many people to a kind of despairing relativism. Nevertheless, I think it is possible to produce something like a 'substantive' policy, or at least a set of priorities, based primarily on conceptual arguments of a non-ideological kind. Such a policy will, of course, have something to do with 'the nature of man' or 'the human condition'; but the central features of it can, I believe, be best observed by trying to get clearer about (1) the general point or *object* of learning, and (2) an *attitude* which is basic to learning. To these we shall now turn.

# Education and human nature

part **III**

# Happiness and learning

5

We have seen enough of the ideas marked by 'education' and 'learning' to be able to face three questions which naturally arise from them. First, is there some *general point* or *object* to these activities? Granted that we could not conceive of a human being who had learned nothing at all, nevertheless what *sort* of gain, or good, or advantage do men derive from them? And how do we weigh or compare this sort of good with other sorts? Second, there is a general question about how men are placed, or how they stand, in reference to this sort of good. Is it easy or hard to attain? What obstacles do we face, what dispositions do we need, and what help can we get in trying to attain it? Third, can anything general be said about the most important aims in education, or about what the central content of education ought to be – about *what* men most need to learn?

These questions are connected, and need to be considered in that order. There is a *prima facie* case for this: unless we first had some idea of the point, or purpose, or object of the whole exercise, and of how men stand in relation to it, how could we tell what specific aims or content it ought to have? In much the same way, I think, we should need to be clear about what such enterprises as religion, or morality, or politics were *for*, and about the sort of difficulties or obstacles that we encountered in trying to enter upon them wholeheartedly, before addressing questions about what particular gods should be worshipped, or what specific moral or political principles adopted. I shall, in fact, try to show that most of what can usefully be said about the third question follows from what can be said about the first two questions: in other words, paradoxical though it may sound, that a better understanding of the general form of the enterprise, and of its relation to human nature, is the best guide for determining on any specific aims or content. The effect of trying to answer the last question first – that is, of setting up some kind of specific content and then arguing for it – is inevitably to distort the enterprise in the interests of that content, and to prejudge possible answers to the first two questions. For premature adherence to a specific content must rely on the support (usually tacit) of some particular idea about the point of the enterprise, and some particular view about how human beings stand in relation to it.

It is instructive to consider a sophisticated example. Peters' arguments for 'theoretic' activities – that is, roughly, the kinds of enquiries and enjoyments found in the various 'forms of thought' – include a number of different *genres*.[1] (1) These activities provide 'unending opportunities for skill and discrimination'[2] and hence 'constant sources of pleasure and satisfaction'.[3] (2) They have certain practical advantages: 'questions of scarcity of the object' or 'of the object perishing or passing away' cannot arise.[4] (3) 'They are "serious" and cannot be considered merely as if they were particularly delectable pastimes, because they consist largely in the explanation, assessment, and illumination of the different facets of life';[5] so that 'any rational man who seriously asks "Why do this rather than that?"' needs these activities, 'instrumentally', to answer his question and gain his ends.[6] (4) The 'transcendental' argument that 'To ask the question "Why do this rather than that?" seriously is . . . to be committed to those enquiries which are defined by their serious concern with those aspects of reality which give context to the question . . . they are involved in *asking* the question . . . as well as in answering it.'[7] (All these arguments, with the possible exception of (4), are found in some form in other philosophical writing: more particularly in Plato, Aristotle and Spinoza.)

Of these arguments, (3) and (4) – certainly (4) – are conceptual arguments in a sense in which (1) and (2) are not. I mean that if, or to the extent that, a person is 'serious' or 'seriously asks' questions in the way Peters describes, his commitment to 'theoretic' activities is taken to follow as a matter of logic. In (4) this is obvious: in (3) slightly less so, since it might appear a contingent matter that these activities alone supply his needs. But if we ask 'What else, in principle, could supply them?', there appears to be no possible answer; roughly, if you ask the sort of question which necessarily involves you in understanding the world, you are logically or rationally bound to go in for at least some of the various forms of understanding available. It is not just that 'these sorts of inquiries are all . . . relevant to answering the sort of question he is asking';[8] it is that only they could (logically) be relevant – rather as 'food' is conceptually connected with 'hunger' (whereas fishcakes are only contingently connected). Arguments (1) and (2), on the other hand, can be said simply to specify certain contingent facts about the activities: they are alleged (1) to give more 'rich opportunities'[9] than low-brow activities at the level of the 'necessary appetites',[10] and hence to be less intrinsically boring; and (2) to be safer because they are less perishable goods.

Even this is a shaky distinction, however, because it is always possible to turn contingent arguments into conceptual ones by *fiat*. Peters flirts with this move in (1) and (2) also. Thus in (1), the notion of spending hours washing glasses 'must surely appal any *reflective* person' (my italic),[11] and anyone 'who is thinking *seriously* about how to spend his time cannot but go in for' theoretic activities (my italic).[12] Here a conceptual link between 'reflective' (or 'seriously') and certain activities (as defined) is allowed to appear. Similarly in (2) we are told 'It is absurd for a man to be jealous of another philosopher in the same sort of way as he might be jealous of his wife's lover, or of a business rival';[13] and if we were to say that philosophers do become jealous of each other in just this way, we should be told that this only means that they are not committed to *philosophy* (but rather to reputation-seeking, or whatever), or not 'seriously' committed to it – and now it is to be a conceptual rule that this sort of commitment excludes jealousy.

I do not want to investigate these arguments in detail[14] so much as to consider the general difficulties which they raise, in relation to our original question about the point or object of learning and the kind of arguments to be used. As they stand, the conceptual ones do not much help us, because they are too tightly conceived – that is, they move within too small a circle. If, or insofar as, anyone is 'serious' in the required sense, the conclusions may follow; but many people are not often very serious, and we want arguments to show why, or how far, or when, they ought to be. We may of course connect the concept of being serious with other concepts – being human, or rational, or a language-user; and we can no doubt show that sentient or rational creatures are necessarily sometimes, and to some degree, serious enough for the arguments to start – thereby offering a somewhat larger package deal. But even this does not really touch the substantive nature of the questions. For we can still ask how far, and when, people ought to operate in the context of *all* these concepts; and the fact that the questions cannot be raised except *in* this context is irrelevant.[15] (We can even raise questions, surely intelligible if admittedly unclear, about why we should be 'rational' or 'sentient' at all.)

This does not mean that there might not be *other* 'conceptual arguments' relevant to our questions; but the chief difficulty is to determine what *sort* of arguments we need here. For the contingent arguments have the opposite weakness of being too loose. Given most men as they are (not ideally 'serious' or 'reflective'), clearly it is the high-brow or 'theoretic' activities which are (1) boring in comparison with the low-brow ones, and even (2) 'a bad bet *sub specie aeternitatis*',[16] and if we now say that men as they ought to be – i.e. 'serious' – would not find them so, we are back to the need for arguments on behalf of seriousness. Further, (1) it is odd to describe the satisfaction of the 'necessary appetites' as *boring* just because there is less opportunity for discrimination, skill and 'standards'. They are boring only to those who insist on such things: and why should we not represent this as some kind of neurotic compulsion? Similarly, (2) we might say that the avoidance of attachments to perishable objects looks more like some fantasy than like acceptance of the world and of human needs as they actually are. As with most neurotic symptoms, it gains safety only by a corresponding loss of contact with reality: no wonder, it might be said, that philosophers invent ideal forms or other such things to invest in, if they cannot endure losses in the real world.

Another doubt might also arise, in itself different but similarly generated by the movement from conceptual to contingent consider-ations. If our interest now lies in the relations *between* the package deal ('being serious', 'raising questions', 'reflecting', 'engaging in forms of thought', etc.) and whatever description we use for a successful outcome to our practical problems ('the promotion of happiness', 'the good life', etc.), then we might simply want to argue that we need the former as a means to the latter: that we need to be rational, or 'serious', or pursue truth, just in order to gain our ends. But we can now ask awkward questions about the composition of the 'we' who need to be 'serious' for this purpose. Must everybody go in for this? Could we not have very sophisticated philosopher-kings, or perhaps psychologist-kings, to reflect on various issues and just *tell* most of us the answers? *Pace* most recent moral philosophers,[17] there is no obvious conceptual incoherence about this. If a choice or an answer is not arbitrary, then there must be some criteria or methods of judgment; and there must also be some people who are better at deploying these than other people. However we explicate some such phrase as 'being good at making such-and-such a decision', it seems that we must in principle be able to identify certain people as better at it than others – either that, or one decision is as good as another, which nobody believes. Is it so clear that Plato was wrong about this?

This of course drives us back to a conceptual consideration again: roughly, to the idea that there are some things which a man can (logically) only do for himself. (Deciding or framing his own ends, as against the best means to them, might be taken as one of these things: though this seems less straightforward than is usually assumed (see p. 221).) Clearly this applies to most of the contents of the package deal: there is obviously a sense in which one man cannot be rational, 'serious', etc., *for* another. But though these may be things which a man must do for himself if he does them at all, it does not follow that he must do them at all. Even if we bring in the argument that he must do them to some extent if he is to be human, conscious, a language-user, etc., it still does not follow that he must do very much of them. And now we are back again in the realm of contingent arguments: for what else (it may seem) could show the importance of doing a lot of them?

What difficulties do we meet, then, if we eschew any particular content, and consider the point (purpose, justification) of learning in general? The first and perhaps most obvious difficulty is whether 'learning' *in general* is really a very plausible candidate for inspection. We might reasonably think it to be so wide a notion that practically everything depended on *what* was learned (or, perhaps, on what sort of learning was involved); rather as it might seem absurd to take the idea of, say, 'thinking', and ask how much thinking should go on and what reasons we could give for various answers – we might want to say that it depended on what one thought *about* or what *kind* of thinking went on. Clearly there are some things that everyone ought to think about, others which are (so to speak) more or less optional, and perhaps others again which it would be a mistake to think about. Indeed, this last category applies much more definitively to the idea of learning; as we saw earlier, one can learn *bad* or disadvantageous things (habits and attitudes): so that the view that *any* case of learning must represent some gain or advantage is a non-starter. We would add that much also (perhaps even more) depended on other contextual features: perhaps in particular on *who* was learning – what his character or temperament was like, what conditions of life he found himself in, and so on. These and other similar points might well make us give up such an enquiry altogether; or else, as most philosophers have done, to narrow it by taking a pre-emptive view of what in fact ought to be learned, and tying the justification of learning to that content.

Nevertheless such despair would be premature. For clearly 'learning' is just *one* (admittedly very general) kind of activity that men can go in for; and if there is something generally good about it, or most cases of it, we want to know what it is. Granted, that contextual features will play a very large part in all our practical decisions: but such decisions can only be sensibly taken if we have some adequate view of the value of learning in general. Granted also, what is rather a different point, that we *may* be able to establish some things to be learned as of much more importance – in a quite context-free way and for all men everywhere – than others: nevertheless it is clear that the weight of *this* importance *will* lie in what is learned rather than in learning itself – and that is a different enquiry.

The real difficulty, as I see it, lies in identifying exactly what it is we are trying to justify or see something good about; and this is, in effect, the same as the difficulty of trying to make sense of phrases like 'in itself', 'for itself', or 'for its own sake' when applied to learning. At the root of this difficulty is the fact that 'learning', unlike (say) 'walking' or perhaps even 'thinking', is logically tied to some kind of goal or end or successful outcome: roughly, as we have seen, some sort of knowledge, or understanding, or control. A person who spends a lot of time in the Latin class but ends up knowing no Latin at all may have tried to learn Latin, but has not in fact learned any; 'learning', as we might put it, is an 'achievement' word, and perhaps is not properly used to mark any specific *activity* at all. So how, it might (though prematurely) be thought, could it be justified 'in itself', or other than 'instrumentally'? Any good must surely lie in the knowledge or control which is the successful outcome: just as there is nothing particularly good in finding or winning, only in what is found or won. Is not the idea of 'learning for its own sake' just a misconception, better replaced by 'knowledge for its own sake' – unless of course 'learning' is used in the old-fashioned sense to *mean* 'knowledge'?

But to this we might reply that it is surely possible to identify and defend learning at least as a set of activities or processes; and the fact that it is impossible, at least simply by means of the word 'learn', to *specify* the activity independently of its success, does not tell against this. As we saw earlier, 'learning' (along with many other verbs) behaves like 'going to Greece': while it is true that I did not go to Greece last year unless I actually arrived there, it is also true that I am going (was going) to Greece as I pass (passed) through France and Italy, or even as I leave (left) London, whether or not I actually arrive. Perfect tenses of 'learn', we argued, imply success; but the process or activity of gaining that success still exists, and is apparent in the continuous present and imperfect tenses. Similarly my going to Greece, even if used in a tense which implies my actual arrival, cannot be wholly *translated* by 'arriving' – it takes time and involves the activity of travelling. What one enjoys may not be the arrival itself but the travelling: not the knowledge or control, but the learning.

It does, nevertheless, appear rather difficult to see how there could be any desirability or *species boni* merely in the activity, if we divorce this wholly from any possibility of achievement. Suppose (not too fanciful a supposition, in terms of practical education) that we immediately or almost immediately forget everything or almost everything we have learned. It might of course still be possible to defend the learning of it – more precisely, the state of *having* learned it – on the grounds that the learning of it had trained the mind or improved the soul; yet this would be to defend the activity of learning not for itself, but instrumentally. Would it be possible to defend the activity 'for its own sake', shorn of all connection with knowledge or other achievement? One could point to various features that might be contingently connected with the activity: the security of the classroom, the intimacy of the tutorial, and so on. But then one would say that it was not learning as such that one enjoyed; just as, if there were no question of arrival in Greece, a man could only enjoy going *to Greece* because of the contingent pleasures of travel in France or Italy.

Might he not, though, enjoy France and Italy not in themselves but only as being *en route* to Greece? We might want to say that what he enjoys is going *towards* Greece; but is this not perfectly possible? Might a man not enjoy building houses, in a clear sense of that phrase, even though every house he builds collapses before he finishes it? It does not matter much here whether we say 'building' or 'trying to build'; the substantive question is whether a purposive or goal-directed activity can be enjoyed for its own sake: that is, independently of any question of success. On the one hand, it seems that this is, in everyday experience, quite common: I can enjoy the activity of wrestling with brain-teasers or crossword clues whether or not I find the right answers – indeed if I were simply handed the answers on a plate it would take all the fun out of doing it. On the other hand, it seems that if we take away the notion of success the activity loses all *point*.

If we do remove the idea of success, then there must be some other, quite different, *species boni* under which the activity is enjoyed. Strictly speaking it cannot be *learning* that is enjoyed for its own sake, but a particular kind of activity which is co-extensive with the process of learning: or which (accidentally, as it were) results in having learned. But what could this activity be? For just as what is learned differs enormously from case to case, so (and necessarily) does the activity of learning it. We think of rote-learning, the learning of motor skills, facts, concepts, techniques, attitudes, and so forth: is there, in fact, any *one* activity which embraces all these? Are they even *alike* in significant respects? Well, of course we can say what we have just said – that they are all cases of learning; but it is not clear that this adds up to anything very helpful here. The significance of the worry is that, if we are casting about for some *species boni* (some 'basic motivation', if you like) which will make the enjoyment of learning for its own sake intelligible, nothing seems to fit all cases.

A man might want to recite the multiplication tables till he has them by heart; to relax or drop his defences progressively until he can communicate adequately with other people; to appreciate music and art; to fight his way through the complexities of a philosophical problem, and so forth – and these are only a few cases; have these different wants really anything in common? Of course we can say that they are, substantively, all cases of wanting to acquire more knowledge or control; which is to say, linguistically, that they are all instances of the concept marked by 'trying to learn'. But that could only lead to the suggestion – the much more plausible suggestion, as I see it – that the activity in itself is not and cannot be undertaken for its own sake, but only for the sake of its end-product – knowledge and control (see more on this question, pp. 156 ff.).

What then is the point of knowledge and control? I shall argue that this sort of question can only be answered by reference to the idea of human happiness. Many people, perhaps particularly those who are not already committed to some fairly specific and sharply delineated outlook or ideology, may (like myself) see it as entirely natural to make this move. They may also, as I do, find considerable difficulty in understanding how other candidates that are commonly canvassed – not only particular ideologies or 'isms', such as Christianity or Marxism, but also more general outlooks marked perhaps by words like 'honour', 'scholarship', 'authenticity' and so on – can have any reason-giving force, or any right to bestow justifications, except via some connection with happiness. This is by no means a universal opinion; but I shall try to show that the natural move is in this case also the right one.

Apart from a predetermined commitment to some ideology, there seem to be two general reasons why this rather obvious criterion is not more widely accepted. The first, which involves far too many considerations to be dealt with fully here, is that the criterion has been enshrined in particular forms which may, indeed, be questionable. It has, for instance, been specifically connected with 'morality' or with 'utilitarianism' (whatever those terms may mean), the general headings under which most recent philosophical criticism has in fact appeared.[18] Second, and partly for this very reason, insufficient attention has been paid to what the word actually means; and this may have led some philosophers to assume either that we all know what we are talking about, or that the constructions which past writers have (tacitly or overtly) put on the word are in fact correct.

Happiness[19] has one frontier bordering on good fortune, and another bordering on joy or pleasure. Etymologically, 'happy' has more in common with the former than the latter ('hapless', 'by an unhappy chance', 'a happy thought'): but in modern English it is different from both. The three concepts come out most clearly in Latin,[20] and similar distinctions can be observed in Greek. Many words, of course, may be used in more than one of these categories; but whatever the relationship between words and concepts in various languages, the concepts themselves are reasonably distinct. You can be happy without being either fortunate or joyous. 'Happy' is closest in English to 'contented'; 'unhappy' to 'worried', 'anxious', 'sad' or 'wretched' (*miser*, not *infelix*). We might say, as a sighting shot, that to be happy is to be generally 'pleased with life'.[21] This is to deny, not only that happiness is the same as being well placed in life: but also that happiness can be defined by reference to (rather than being caused by) the satisfaction of particular desires. 'Dissatisfied', like 'discontented', can be opposed to 'happy'; but 'unsatisfied' cannot, because 'unsatisfied' is normally used of specific desires. Thus one can have an unsatisfied thirst, yet still be happy. One can even be in pain and be happy. And certainly one can be quite happy at a particular time without positively liking or enjoying any *specific* thing or activity at that time.

A man may be fortunately placed (good health, enough money, a nice job, etc.) but not be happy, and vice versa. A happy man will say things like 'Everything's fine', 'It's good to be alive', etc., but here he expresses his happiness and does not state facts about the world outside. Everything may not be fine, and he may know it: but he may not mind. No doubt there are always causes of a man's happiness, and if 'fortunate' (or a synonym in another language) is used to refer solely to sufficient causes of happiness, then it will be necessarily true that a man cannot be happy without being fortunate: for 'fortunate' will now mean 'having those things which make one happy' – including, for instance, a contented disposition. But to call a man 'fortunate' will still not mean the same as calling him 'happy'.

Happiness can be ascribed only to conscious creatures (although they need not be conscious that they are happy). The dead or the permanently unconscious are not happy or unhappy. But we can say 'He is a happy man' even though he is asleep at the time. This is because ascriptions of happiness can be framed to fit a shorter or longer time-period, or a particular department of life. Thus the time-period may be a man's whole life, or it may be brief – there may be 'fleeting moments of happiness'; or again, we can ask if a man's marriage is happy, or if he is happy in his work. Nevertheless, asking about a man's happiness, in most contexts, implies somewhat longer–term considerations than asking whether he is enjoying himself at that moment.

Happiness is conceptually tied to a man's state of mind only in the sense of a man's enjoying or (better) welcoming his state of mind, and not to any other features of that state of mind. If we try to describe these features by the use of such words and phrases as 'tension', 'harmony', 'stress and strain', 'anxiety', 'contentment', etc., then either our descriptions will be neutral with regard to the man's happiness, or we shall have described the welcome or lack of welcome he gives to these features. Thus 'tension' either simply describes a state of being keyed up, alert, etc., in which case it is neutral (one man may be happy when keyed up and another man may not); or else it implies that the man is anxious and worried, in which case the man does not welcome tension and is hence unhappy.

A man can say 'I'm happy' (or 'I'm unhappy') *and be wrong*.[22] A phrase like 'That suits me fine', although it can function as a true-or-false report, can also be an adequate-or-inadequate expression of feeling, or a felicitous-or-infelicitous performative (meaning something like 'OK, I (hereby) agree'). But 'I'm happy' is not characteristically used, and is never only used, in these last two ways, except in one or two casual or slangy instances. Normally it is a statement of fact. In making the statement (as in all utterances) a man can be sincere or insincere, attempt to deceive or attempt to tell the truth. Further, in the course of inspecting his own feelings with a view to making the statement, he may in some sense deceive himself or be dishonest with himself. But he may not: he may simply be lazy, forgetful, or careless. Then he might be said, loosely, to be deceived (better, 'mistaken') about himself, but not to deceive himself. And in any case he does not thereby deceive us. There is perhaps some sense in which a man is, either generally or in principle, in a better position than anyone else to know what he feels; but this is no excuse for saying vaguely that if he misreports those feelings he must, somehow, be being insincere. He can also be mistaken.[23] This is particularly obvious in those cases, perhaps the most characteristic as well as the most frequent, where what is in question is not momentary happiness but happiness over a time-period or in a whole department of life. For here the possibilities of a man being mistaken about his own state of mind are more evident: he may, for instance, have forgotten how he usually feels. Even in momentary happiness, however, a man may fail to notice or pay proper attention to how he feels. A man can be mistaken, not just because he does not understand the word 'happy' (another kind of mistake), but because he does not attend closely enough to the evidence.

Evidence of whether a man is happy may come from many sources: from his circumstances, which may be more or less likely to make him happy; from what he says in general, or what he says about his state of mind; from what activities he tends to pursue; from other parts of his voluntary behaviour; and from involuntary symptoms (whether his mouth droops, his eyes look tired, etc.). The relationships between all these are complex; and no particular piece of evidence is by itself conclusive. Perhaps the most reliable type consists of a man's involuntary or semi-voluntary symptoms (including his cries of joy, sighs, etc.). For (1) what a man says, and his voluntary actions, may be faked, insincere, false or misleading in a way in which his involuntary symptoms cannot be; (2) human nature is so varied that it is hard to be sure, without further evidence, that any particular set of circumstances makes a man happy; (3) a man may well fail to be happy even in those activities which he voluntarily undertakes and looks forward to, not only because something beyond his control may upset him, but because he may be mistaken about what sorts of things he actually enjoys. There is no difficulty at all in denying that a man is happy, even though the evidence in (1), (2) and (3) may suggest that he is happy. But it would be very hard to assert that a man was happy if his posture, facial expression and involuntary behaviour was of a certain kind (if, for instance, he always sat hunched up, bit his nails, never smiled, wept, groaned, etc.). The tie here is not conceptual (the characteristic symptoms of happiness or unhappiness of Martians might be quite different): but it is nevertheless very close.

Whether we call other people happy or not has nothing to do either with whether we can imagine ourselves having their desires, or with whether we can stomach the idea of having them.[24] Only philosophers hesitate to call young children or certain kinds of madmen happy; and if we hesitate to call a wicked person happy this is not because we do not like the sort of desires he has, but either because we somehow feel that the wicked ought not to be happy, or because we feel that on a very close examination they would turn out not to be. But we could not even ask whether wicked people were happy or not, if we did not recognize that ascriptions of happiness were not logically tied to our own views about what desires one ought to have. Similarly we can at least ask whether Martians are happy, however strange their desires might be to us.

It is important to remember that happiness is not only dependent on the satisfaction of wants. I may wake up one morning feeling happy, and another morning feeling miserable or depressed: and this may have nothing at all to do with my wants, except in the sense that I want to be happy or don't want to be depressed. Here we might talk of being 'unreasonably' happy, or feeling sad 'for no reason'. Such cases may be due to unconscious wants (desires, fears, hopes, etc.): but they may also be due to my liver, or drugs, or excess oxygen. Wants only come into the picture when I know, or think I know, why I am happy or unhappy.

What then is the relation of happiness to the giving of reasons in practical living? It is well known that such phrases as 'because I enjoy it', 'because it gives me pleasure', 'it hurts', etc., are often the final words, the longstop answers, to questions about why I choose to do something. There is a logical connection between reasons for action and the notions of pleasure and pain. So too there is a connection between reasons for action and happiness. The connection is looser, because (to put it briefly) the concept of happiness covers more ground than the concept of pleasure. If we ask a man why he engages in a specific activity at a specific time – why he has eggs for breakfast, for instance – it is sufficient for him to answer 'Because I enjoy it.' But there are many questions to which this reply is inappropriate. If we ask him a question which refers to a whole slice of his life – why he remains a bachelor, or lives in the country, or goes to bed early – he will more naturally say something like 'Because I'm happier that way.' Such a man claims, rightly or wrongly, that certain states of affairs contribute to his happiness or contentment; and this is quite different from claiming that he enjoys a specific activity or finds it immediately pleasurable. Thus if we press him about living in the country, he may say 'Well, I enjoy hunting, shooting and fishing, and I'm free from the noise of traffic; it's nice for the children: it's true that I can't go to concerts, but that doesn't worry me too much', and so on. He is defending the general arrangements of his life, or of one department of it: the strategy he has adopted to deal with his particular wants, the activities he enjoys, the kinds of discontent to which he is liable, and so forth. In adopting this strategy, the sensible person will attend to certain criteria of rationality: he will arrange for his wants and pleasures not to conflict, give priority to those which give him most pleasure, and so on. To do this with an eye on that state of mind which we call 'happy' is to seek happiness. There is neither a logical contradiction, nor any psychological oddity, in failing to seek happiness in this sense. Many people have no overall strategy at all, and most fail to apply any such strategy in certain departments of life. The point is rather that it is (in a number of very different senses) irrational not to plan in this way.

This point comes out in the falseness of the dichotomy which some critics of utilitarianism try to impose on utilitarian writers. Thus either 'The injunction "pursue happiness", when happiness has been given the broad, undifferentiated sense which Bentham and Mill give to it is merely the injunction "Try to achieve what you desire" ',[25] or we should treat the injunction as referring to specific activities (wine, women and song, for instance). But 'You ought to pursue happiness' is a way of saying 'Your life ought, if you're going to be reasonable about it, to be arranged in a certain way, i.e. to avoid conflict, etc.', and neither a way of saying 'Pursue your desires', nor a way of saying 'Choose this object of desire rather than the other.' So Mill's recommendation is not empty, yet it is not a first-order recommendation. (Its logical status is more like saying 'Check your facts', or 'See if the experimental results confirm it', in science, which are not empty phrases meaning 'Discover the truth', nor yet enjoin specific scientific beliefs.) It points to some of the criteria of rationality in practical living.

Critics of naturalistic ethics will say, 'But if it's a descriptive concept it must be logically possible not to commend it, because of the naturalistic fallacy and the centrally prescriptive role of words like "ought" and "good" ' and so forth. Certainly it is logically possible not to commend happiness: what is logically impossible is to commend something else, as against happiness and in defiance of it, *for good reasons*[26] (just as it is logically possible to commend illogicality, refusal to face facts, etc.; but not logically possible to do this as a general policy with any show of reason). This is because 'happiness' marks out a concept specifically designed to include all good – perhaps all ultimately intelligible – reasons for choice.

The connection between happiness and having good reasons for action is simply that 'happiness' labels a state of mind in which we welcome the world: in which we say to ourselves, as it were, 'Everything is *all right*' or at least 'Nothing now troubles me, nothing is badly wrong.' When we wake up in the morning feeling like this, we do not first say 'Wait a minute, let me check that my major desires are fulfilled or likely to be fulfilled today: that my wife and children are safe, that I have interesting work to do, that there is enough to eat', and so on. If we do this, we are not (or not yet) happy. Rather we wake up free from anxiety or depression or tension, with a 'sense of well-being' or 'euphoria'. Things in or aspects of the world – often very simple things, like our own bodies, or the fact that a new day has dawned – seem to us *good*: 'It's good to be alive.' We may of course wish to add to the stock of these good things ('I'm hungry, I'll have two eggs for breakfast, that would be lovely'): that is, to make ourselves more happy. But we have no reason, or no good reason, to act except in order to stock our world with more goods in this way, or to avoid bad things now or in the future; and this is in effect just another way of saying that we have no good reason to act except in order to increase happiness.

Reasons run dry when we ask such questions as 'What's the point of being happy?', 'Why enjoy oneself?' or 'Why seek happiness?' If we ask, of some other 'values', such questions as 'Why use one's reason?', 'What good is freedom?', etc., we may easily show by conceptual argument the necessity of *some* degree of reasoning, truth or freedom for human life. Indeed, we may even be able to show some conceptual incoherence in the question. But if we ask these questions in reference to particular contexts – 'Why should I use my reason *for the next ten minutes*?', 'Why shouldn't I have a bit of compulsion in *this* area of my life?' – the reasons do not run dry. (We would, in practice, very often answer them by some reference to happiness.) But in the case of happiness they do run dry, even with context-dependent questions. It may be that I ought not to be happy for the next ten minutes: but the reason must be, not that happiness is not always a good, but (roughly) that I or other people will be happier in general if I abjure happiness for the next ten minutes.

There is, however, one important way in which the notion of happiness as a criterion ought *not* to be used. The notion may tempt us either to over-determine, or to determine prematurely, the *content* or *causes* of happiness and the *nature* of 'standard interests', 'human goods', 'desirability characteristics', 'benefits', or however we may describe them. This temptation operates in one or other of two general directions. First, there is a kind of down-to-earth, no-nonsense, 'utilitarian' approach which lists as 'standard interests' such obvious things as food, health, money and so forth, and which usually displays an incredulous or unsympathetic attitude to what falls outside the scope of these interests. In philosophy this approach is associated with Mill and the classical utilitarians; in practice it tends to dominate societies like our own in which politics is conceived of chiefly as an enablement for efficient economics. Here the content and causes of happiness are unduly *narrowed*. Second, there is a much wider, 'anything goes' approach, according to which the attachments or 'commitments' of individual people (or the human race in general), however 'non-utilitarian', are given weight in their own right, and the notion of happiness is abandoned as a criterion. Here one's worry is that the content of what is desirable, or satisfying, or worth while seems to have broken free from any rational criteria at all.

The various dangers here emerge clearly in some recent philosophical writing,[27] mostly of an anti-utilitarian nature. Thus some writers make considerable play with the possibility that there may be certain features of life which a man either ought to regard, or cannot but regard, as in some sense absolute, untouchable, or at any rate not to be subjected to any kind of hedonistic calculus. 'Ought to', perhaps because such subjection would (in some fairly literal sense) demoralize any man: 'cannot but', perhaps because human nature is so constituted that these features are inevitably objects of profound and (so to speak) non-negotiable emotional attachment, not to be written off as 'taboos' which we can be educated out of easily (or at all). Such things (whatever they are) have to be accepted as given. Nevertheless, we have to be careful in distinguishing these from what may quite fairly be called irrational taboos, compulsions or fantasies which we would be better off without; and where there is scope for reasoning and change, we have to use it. We cannot just say 'That's how I feel' or 'That's part of my way of life'; or at least we can *say* this, but in saying it we disclaim any attempt to *justify* what we do, or feel, or are.[28]

But in any case, young children do not – or not in anything like the same way – have these 'deeply-rooted attitudes' or 'commitments'; or, if there are basic elements in the 'human condition' which are going to be non-negotiable *whatever* educators do (Hampshire mentions such features as killing, sex, and the 'celebration of the dead'),[29] then we need to know what these are, and the sense in which they are 'basic'. Children are not, indeed, *tabulae rasae*, and the deep attachments of which Freud and others write are not, of course, to be regarded merely as tiresome aberrations. But they are not 'committed' as religious believers, or samurai, or those who ardently pursue the 'theoretic' life are committed. The educator's problem precisely arises from the fact that children are *not* formed in these ways: that we can take less as 'given': that the *content* of their 'integrity' is not established. The notion of the 'unthinkable', for instance, demonstrably *shifts*, in all sorts of curious ways, during a child's development.

Thus whatever may be fixed for our own lives, the lives of our children are more negotiable. There is at least scope for argument on the part of those many parents and other educators who may themselves have non-negotiable 'projects', 'commitments', or 'rooted attitudes', but have doubts about whether these should be passed on to their children. One such 'rooted attitude', for instance, might itself be that children should follow exactly in their father's footsteps; but this is just the sort of attitude we might want to question – and if this threatened the 'integrity'[30] of (say) a Nazi father, we might want to say something like 'So much the worse for that sort of "integrity"'. It is this line of thought, which must inevitably be pursued in the particular enterprise of education, that drives us towards considering the questions of what can fairly count as a reason (justification) for choices in this area, and how we are to identify ourselves as reasoning rather than indulging in fantasy or rationalizing some compulsion.

To steer a course between these two temptations we have to bring in the notion of unconscious reasons. If somebody entertains an ideal, or engages in intentional action, or produces a reason for some piece of behaviour, which seems to us odd or peculiar, we have to avoid saying either (1) that the reason is no reason at all, and that the ideal or the behaviour is 'unintelligible' or 'makes no sense': or (2) that anything can count as a reason, and that the behaviour is quite unproblematic. The miser may seem to accumulate or hoard money without getting any kind of good out of it; and the sadist may seem simply to enjoy hurting people: they can give no other reasons than just 'It adds to my hoard', or 'I like seeing them squirm'. We have to say (1) that these are, indeed, reasons or even good reasons *for them* to behave thus, because for them the behaviour is symbolic; for instance, the miser is insecure and unconsciously believes that he can fend off insecurity by accumulation, and the sadist that he can come to feel potent by dramatizing his power. Security and potency may be called 'standard interests', in that it would be impossible to conceive of any entity in any world for whom these were not goods. There has to be some such unconscious belief, if they are acting for a reason at all. But (2) the behaviour seems problematic, just because the unconscious belief is inappropriate. The behaviour has to be referred to *some* intelligible advantage, some good which will contribute to happiness, if it is to be seen as human behaviour. A reason like 'I need to feel secure' is not on all fours with a reason like 'I need to hoard money'; with the latter we can ask 'What for?', but not with the former, because security is a necessary constituent of happiness.

If we raise the traditional question 'Do all men seek happiness?', we may answer 'No' if 'seek' refers to their conscious intentions and goals; but 'Yes', if we bring in the idea of unconscious intentions and symbols. It is true to say that people can use whatever they like as a reason if it means either that there is nothing logically contradictory in *saying* 'He does it just to add to his hoard' (to see them squirm, etc.), or that there are no logical limits on what a man might in fact *suppose* (consciously or unconsciously) will make him happier or gain him some good. But it is false if it means that one reason is ultimately as good as another: people make mistakes both about what good they are really trying to obtain, and about what means are appropriate, particularly if they are not properly conscious of what they are doing. This is not to say that the unconscious mind may not have a wisdom of its own (so to speak). Perhaps the hoarding and the squirming do, if only temporarily, help the wretched miser and sadist to feel more secure and potent; the form or outline of a good reason may be perceived even in these cases (and even in wilder ones). The men would rightly not be satisfied by being sharply reminded that there was no 'point', or 'advantage', or 'standard interest' in hoarding and torturing. For them as they are there is a point; and we can improve their rationality and satisfaction only by uncovering their goals and ministering to them in more effective ways.

I have argued that 'happiness' marks a descriptive concept, and can thus be verified without the need for any evaluative stance. No one denies that it is often difficult to verify it in practice; but that is different from denying the possibility. Many writers have spoken of the difficulty or impossibility of 'measuring happiness'; yet in fact (unless the word 'measuring' is unfairly pressed) this is something we do every day, and could hardly imagine not doing. Very often we have choices to make in education which illustrate both our acceptance of happiness as an overall or controlling idea, and our ability to deploy this idea in the assessment of particular cases. In general it seems clear that we want our children to grow up happy, and we want them to grow up into more fully conscious, aware and rational people if they can thus be more happy. If disaster strikes or we meet insuperable obstacles – Mary will die in a year anyway, or Johnny needs to earn a living more than to enjoy Sophocles – then (other things being equal) we rightly drop our concern to give them more awareness or understanding, because they will derive no benefit and hence no happiness from it. Crippling one's children's feet, for instance, or forcing them to enter competitions for pain-endurance, would make no sense unless connected with some benefit – whether or not ancient Chinese and Spartan parents made this connection.

We may profitably take a quick look at what goes wrong (1) when the idea marked by 'happiness' is distorted, and (2) when a particular content is ascribed *a priori* to education. The combination of these two errors appears in the following passage:

> increase in education and sensitivity brings with it increase in the number of desires, and a corresponding lesser likelihood of their satisfaction. Instruction and emancipation in one way favour happiness, and in another militate against it. To increase a person's chances of happiness, in the sense of [?] fullness of life, is *eo ipso* to decrease his chances of happiness, in the sense of [?] satisfaction of desire.[31]

But it is not at all good English to suggest either 'fullness of life' or 'satisfaction of desire' as a translation for 'happiness' (both may be causes of happiness, but neither is part of what 'happiness' normally means). Similarly there is the fixed idea that the educated ('sensitive') man is in some way bound or compelled to seek satisfaction for his peculiarly sophisticated tastes, and cannot help but be unhappy at those things which are, as it were, substandard. But to the extent that he was under this sort of compulsion, we might prefer to say that he had not been properly educated: that is, resisting the over-intellectualist picture of education criticized earlier (p. 57), we might say that he had not learned at least one important capacity – namely, how to take pleasure in simple or even substandard things. 'Emancipation' is just what such a person does need. We may demand that the educated man is capable of finding happiness (1) in more things than the uneducated, and perhaps also (2) in things which contribute in a peculiarly potent way to happiness (whatever these are: we do not know that they *must* include such things as art, philosophy, or sophisticated human relationships). But it is hard to see how anyone could reasonably demand that he should suffer from, though of course he will recognize, substandard products or activities.

It may still seem as if there is a certain inevitability about this: surely to be educated in (say) art necessarily implies that, in recognizing some art as 'good' and appreciating it, one is forced to recognize other art as 'bad' and hence deprecate it. The 'force' here is not some kind of brute psychological compulsion, but merely inherent in the subject: as a good mathematician is forced to recognize some answers to sums as wrong. This is true; but whether or not such recognition brings unhappiness depends on the person's other qualities and attitudes. In particular it depends on his ability to view things and people under other *species* than those roughly describable as 'coming up to scratch' or 'meeting certain standards'. This is entirely clear in the case of personal relationships: a father's happiness need not depend on having a son who wins scholarships and is captain of the school team, nor a husband's on having a wife who constantly wins the Miss World competition. It depends more on their ability to love them for what they are: to find some other *species* in which to view them and enjoy them.

'Emancipation' is better seen as the freedom required for a person to see good, or at least opportunities for interest and pleasure, in as many things as possible: an idea entirely consistent with preserving one's critical faculties. If the office discussion is not philosophically sophisticated, it may be psychologically interesting; if the office painting is 'tasteless', it may be welcomed as giving some kind of pleasure to his colleagues. Even if he considers them initially under the standard-dominated *species* of 'philosophy' or 'art', he may see them as opportunities for helping his colleagues to see more clearly and for improving their own happiness: just as sin or ignorance may be seen by the parson and the schoolmaster as opportunities for the deployment of love than as inevitable causes of depression. If this were not so, no person – whether 'educated' or not – could both perceive the ills of the world and retain any chances of happiness at all.

We need now to consider more closely the relationship between happiness on the one hand and the goods of learning – that is, knowledge and control – on the other. There are two mistakes here which have to be avoided. First, we may be tempted to suppose that we are dealing with quite different kinds of goods, having no logical relationship to each other: that the idea of happiness is, after all, of no use as a controlling idea for practical choice, since there just *are* radically different 'values' in life. Second, we may suppose that all other goods stand in relation to happiness as means to an end, in some simple sense (for instance, as fish-cakes may stand to the satisfaction of hunger). But this also turns out to be not true.

A simple-minded example may show us the way between these two errors. Suppose we see a TV programme about some unsophisticated Polynesians. They seem calm, happy, cheerful, spontaneous, 'at one with nature': they are nice to their children, pacific to each other: their superstitions and ancestor-worship appear to us as pleasant rituals. They do not have Chartres cathedral, or atomic physics, or Shakespeare: but neither do they have war or pollution or suicide or (apparently) mental illness. They are contented and carefree. In considering such a case, we might very well find ourselves tempted to balance two opposing 'values', which we could fairly call 'happiness' and 'awareness'. This is not a bad starting-point, because in our individual lives most of us do not even reach as far as recognizing that there is *some* important general choice to be made here. We just follow our noses. We *find ourselves* more or less attracted to sophisticated or unsophisticated pursuits, and instinctively pick the mixture that we think suits us (though we may be wrong). If pressed by philosophers, we should argue – often rightly – that we are what we are, and cannot easily change. But when we consider how to bring up our children, or (as with the Polynesians) what sort of society and individuals we would like to create, the questions begin to seem more real.

One move attempts to strangle the issue at birth. There are people who speak very wisely and accommodatingly and say 'Well, yes, if you like, there is "happiness" and there is "awareness", and there just are two values here; both are (in some measure) conceptually necessary goods for rational creatures, neither is superior or subordinate – it's like politics, where we have liberty and law-and-order and some other high-level principles, and why should you expect to be able to settle every issue between them?' As a negative thesis (e.g. that not all principles stand in a tight hierarchy, that some issues are not to be settled by deductive logic, etc.) this is intelligible: as a positive one it is queer – is it being suggested that the choices are arbitrary? Does it not *matter* what mixture of 'happiness' and 'awareness' one feeds into oneself or one's children? If it matters, is the issue amenable to any kind of reason, procedure, or unprejudiced *modus operandi*? Certainly philosophers have spoken as if they accepted the view that, in politics (and perhaps in personal life and ideals), there just are a number of important 'values' – say, 'freedom', 'law-and-order', 'security' and one or two more – which cannot (so to speak) be mixed at full strength. Life is inevitably a compromise between these; the notion of an 'ideal society' ('ideal life') in which we have all of them at 100 per cent proof is an incoherent or unrealistic notion. But there is an obvious muddle here between maintaining (1), as above, that one cannot have 100 per cent of everything: and (2) that there are no criteria for making the mixture, that some mixtures are not better than others, or even that it may not be sense to speak of an 'ideal mixture'. Car design is a compromise between speed, weight, space and safety; but there are better and worse compromises, more or less well-designed cars. The problem is there. Either there are criteria of judgment, or else the matter is arbitrary. Nobody, I think, seriously believes the latter.

A more significant move consists of questioning the Polynesians' happiness by wondering what – so to speak – they are happy *about*, or just *what* they enjoy. It may be misleading to take very blank and open judgments like 'He is happy'. If we use verbs with objects, like 'He is enjoying fishing', or tie the happiness down to particular contexts, like 'He is happily married', the points emerge a bit more clearly. (1) A drunk or dazed man may (perhaps) be enjoying something, and may certainly be happy, but he cannot be enjoying *fishing* if he is not sober enough to attend to it. Similarly 'fishing' will *mean* something different to simple Polynesian fishers and to sophisticated fly-fishermen; we begin to wonder whether the Polynesians really enjoy *fishing* very much at all – there is not, as it were, very much to enjoy, the way they fish. (2) Lots of people are married, and happy, achieving this by a very remote relationship with their spouses (remote in real or in psychological distance): this does not mean, even in ordinary English, that they are 'happily married'.

To be happily married, we might say, you have to take marriage seriously. This does not mean that you have to keep having intense and painful and arduous psychological confrontations with your spouse, but it does at least mean that you have to *attend* to the other person, mesh in with her (him), 'relate', and so forth. Otherwise it is not really a marriage at all (and now nobody needs a linguistic philosopher to point out that they went to church together and said this and that, so they married, and so on.)[32]

Yet this would show, at most, that we might prefer to speak of the Polynesians 'enjoying themselves' (their own feelings and fantasies, perhaps), rather than as 'enjoying life' (the various activities and realities of life). And why *should* we bestow this sophisticated 'attention' on the world? Why must we devote ourselves to 'reality', or 'knowledge of the good', or however we choose to describe it? After all, human kind cannot bear very much reality; or (from a mental patient told to 'face reality') 'Anybody familiar with reality knows better than to try to face the bloody stuff.' Why shouldn't we be autistic? Why should a minimally conscious three-year-old, happy with his bottle and his rattle, grow up? Of course it will be said 'This question could only arise for grown-up language-users who go in for things like reasons and arguments; and if you're grown-up (or sophisticated, or repressed, or corrupted, or whatever you like to say) then it's not a real issue.' Yes, but it arises for grown-up parents (teachers, etc.); shall we turn three-year-old Johnny into a 'grown-up' or not?

Nevertheless, there is a point here about the relation of 'happiness' to 'awareness'. One reason why philosophers have been dissatisfied with happiness as an overall criterion is that it seems, *prima facie*, to justify a contented pig or Polynesian as against a discontented Socrates; and some have produced bizarre arguments to show that this is not really so, only at the cost of abandoning 'happiness' (in its normal sense) as an overall criterion. But pigs are not contented or happy in the sense in which conscious creatures are. This suggests that in statements like 'X is happy' we need to attend to the subject as well as to the predicate.

We ascribe predicates like 'contented', 'satisfied', 'happily married', etc., to what look like the same subjects – 'he', 'she', 'they', 'human beings'. We acknowledge a point at which these predicates are inapplicable because there is no longer a person in the required sense; thus pigs are not happy (at least in the same sense in which humans are), a man is not happy when he is dead because he is no longer a man, and we might have doubts about whether people are happy when they are drugged. But we also have the feeling that, as we move along the scale from persons to pigs, or philosophers to

Polynesians, the subjects of these predicates get *thinner*. It is not so much that they exist in full up to a certain point, and then vanish (when the subject loses consciousness, goes very mad, or dies); it is rather that (we feel tempted to say) there is less and less of a person, a progressively narrower consciousness. If there is anything in this, it is not a linguistic point at all: indeed language masks the point by continuing to apply the same subject-words and predicates ('he is happy') all along the scale.

Thus we feel that the Polynesians are happy all right, but that there is (so to speak) less of them to be happy. They are less conscious precisely by virtue of being more 'at one with nature'. What would we say of Socrates half-drunk? He is, we suppose, still partly conscious, so that the predicate is still applicable; but can we say without hesitation that 'he is extremely happy'? Well, of course we can and do *say* this, and rightly: such is our language. Do we mean the same thing when we say of, for instance, Socrates enjoying a philosophical discussion that 'he is extremely happy'? Again of course there is an obvious sense in which we 'mean the same thing': but not a very interesting sense. Why should we not say that the 'he' in these two sentences has a very different content?

In our language we have only two forms of pronoun: the personal (he, she, you, etc.) and the impersonal (it). This brutal distinction masks a sliding scale of consciousness, along which we might place drug addicts and drunks, very young children, certain kinds of mentally ill people, rigid conformists, and so on up to Socrates. We do not have to say that 'he' *means* something different in all these cases. But to assess the amount of happiness a person has involves assessing the degree and extent, as well as the quality, of his consciousness. For though 'conscious' (like 'happy' and 'rational') can be used absolutely – either one is conscious or one is not – it can also admit of degrees.[33] In this second sense, the 'amount' of the consciousness necessarily depends on the availability of the objects of attention which are *separated* from the self; one might say, the more objects, the more ('fuller', 'richer', etc.) consciousness.[34] Socrates is happier than the pig-person, because there is more of him to be happy; or, if this form of words is inappropriate, let us say that Socrates experiences more happiness (and perhaps unhappiness). The reason why few people would lose (though full of pain) this intellectual being is not that there is another value, 'awareness', to be set against happiness; it is that though 'intellectual being' involves a lot of pain, it involves a lot of happiness also. (When it does not, people may – often rightly – try to 'forget their troubles', take drugs, or commit suicide, thus filtering or 'screening' the input to consciousness, or cutting it off altogether.)

Awareness, then, is not contributory to happiness in the way that other things (health, money, etc.) are contributory; rather, the area of awareness *defines the extent to which we can talk of a conscious person who experiences both happiness and unhappiness.* But neither is awareness an independent value to be set against happiness; its desirability has to be cashed out, in the short or long run, in terms of happiness. These considerations emerge, I think, in philosophical discussion (which goes back at least as far as Aristotle) about what the happy man will *do*, and in particular whether he will engage in the theoretic life. As we saw above (p. 136), those who defend the theoretic life sometimes seem rather uncertain about whether this is to consist of, or be justified as, an activity; and there is a certain ambiguity inherent in the markers 'activity', 'action', 'doing', and so forth which needs some exploration. Happiness certainly requires consciousness – other things being equal, as wide a consciousness as possible. Nor can 'experience' be taken as simply 'input'; to be conscious means, at least, that *we* are – in a broad sense – doing something, being active or in touch with the world. This broad sense of 'doing' or 'activity' is unobjectionable. There can, however, be narrower senses in which certain things count as 'active' and others as 'passive' experience, as *praxis* or *pathos*; an extreme case of this might be the Victorian parent who says to the child 'Put down that novel and find something to *do*' (not, 'something *else* to do').

Aristotle seems sometimes to imply a narrower sense of 'doing':

> For in 'doing well' the happy man will of necessity *do* (*praxei*). Just as at the Olympic Games it is not the best-looking or the strongest men present who are crowned with victory but competitors – the successful competitors – so in the arena of human life the honours and rewards fall to those who show their good qualities in action.[35]

But in fact his preferred activity is speculation or contemplation (*theoria*); and it is not altogether clear how far, for Aristotle, this is confined within a fairly narrow sense of 'doing'. That it might be so confined is suggested by his insistence on the 'intellect' (*nous*), and the dubious remark that 'we can think about intellectual problems more continuously than we can keep up any sort of physical action.'[36] On the other hand, he also says that 'it stands to reason that those who have knowledge pass their time more pleasantly than those who are engaged in its pursuit';[37] which suggests that the pleasure at least (if not the happiness) of the theoretic life lies not in the process of learning itself, but in the enjoyment of what has been learned – its 'appreciation', as we might say; and this seems somewhat to require a rather more tolerant sense of 'doing'. Whatever account we give of the pleasure in, say, enjoying good music or appreciating a good poem, there is as much *pathos* about it as *praxis*.

Indeed there appear to be difficulties in seeing activities which would fall within a narrower sense of 'doing' as *per se* constituent of happiness. For either such activities are simply means to an end, as when a man travels simply in order to arrive; or the *species* under which they are enjoyed turns out to demand a wider sense of 'doing' – when a man enjoys travelling 'for its own sake', it is not mere physical movement or action that he seeks, but (perhaps) the opportunity to appreciate different cultures and climates in fairly rapid succession. There must be, as it were, certain *objects of attention* which are good or desirable in his eyes; conscious enjoyment is the enjoyment of *something* to which he is attending. This may, indeed, be his own body, or his own sensations, or his own efforts and actions; but these must still appear to him as in some way good if his enjoyment is to make sense. Thus on the running track he may see himself as strong and swift; he may enjoy simply that, not any kind of more sophisticated phenomenon (pacing himself, competitive running, or whatever). But the *species boni* now lies, not in the mere fact that he is (in the narrow sense) doing something; rather, it lies in the notions of strength and swiftness. It is not wholly a contingent fact that he has to run, or perform some similar activity, in order to see himself as strong or swift; but there is a clear sense in which he cannot enjoy running *per se* – that is, divorced from the feeling of power or speed that it gives him, or from the 'appreciation' (as we might put it) of his own power or speed.

Aristotle advances something like these considerations, in a briefer and more pungent form, when he asks what kind of actions we can rightly attribute to the gods. Dismissing all forms of 'virtuous activity', he says:

> Nevertheless men have always thought of them as at least
> living beings and, if living, then doing something (*energein*): for
> we cannot suppose that they are always asleep, like Endymion.
> But if from a living being there is taken away action (*prattein*),
> not to mention creation or production (*poiein*), what is left him
> but contemplation (*theoria*)?[38]

Activities, we might say, have point or justification only in relation to certain states by virtue of which a man is in touch with and enjoying something good. Of course this would justify – in the sublunary world – 'virtuous actions' and different kinds of 'creation or production', because these *produce* goods which can then be enjoyed ('contemplated'). But if, no doubt *per impossibile*, we had a

world in which all possible goods already existed, only the enjoyment of them would remain.

A good deal of the 'doctrine of function', as found in Plato,
Aristotle, Spinoza and others, and characteristically written off by
many modern philosophers because it 'shares the defects of all
naturalistic arguments',[39] is best seen in this light. Some of the time,
admittedly, Aristotle may appear to defend contemplation or
speculation as one rather specific kind of doing among many, to be
commended on the uncertain grounds that it is 'higher', less animal-
like, and unique to man. But these arguments are clearly not
supposed to depend simply on uniqueness; contemplation is chosen
(rather than other unique activities, such as making jokes) because
of its more obvious connection with consciousness, and hence with
happiness:

> None of the other animals can properly be described as happy,
> because they are in no way capable of speculation or
> contemplation. Happiness then covers the same ground as
> contemplation and those who have the greatest power of
> contemplation are the happiest, not accidentally but as an
> essential element of their contemplation. For contemplation is
> itself beyond price.[40]

Contemplation is 'beyond price', not necessarily because there is
something intrinsically better in contemplating than in other kinds
of doing, but because contemplation is the characteristic mode of –
or part of what is meant by – being a conscious and rational creature.
It demarcates the area within which such creatures can be happy.
To the remark 'those who have the greatest power of contemplation
are the happiest' we have, of course, to add 'other things being
equal'; or, we might say, those with the widest consciousness are
most capable of being happy, or capable of being most happy. For
they are those most capable of being in touch with, and enjoying,
various good objects of attention.

This connection of happiness with contemplation, however, sheds
little direct light on the question of *what* should be learned; or at
least it sheds, at this stage, only a single ray, whose illumination is
insufficient for us to see any really useful answer to this question
until we have more fully explored how human beings stand in
relation to learning in general (as we shall do in the next chapter).
For though 'those who have the greatest power of contemplation are
the happiest' (other things being equal), this in itself tells us nothing
about (1) the *content* of their contemplation. The world contains an
infinite number of things that can be viewed and enjoyed; while
some of these may be particularly enjoyable, the demonstration of

this will be empirical and not philosophical: and in any case much will turn on the particular (non-negotiable) tastes, inclinations and make-up of particular individuals. The same points apply, perhaps a little less obviously, to (2) what may be called the *mode* of contemplation. Philosophers often take it for granted that a person's exercise of contemplation must proceed in a certain mode: for instance the mode of asking questions, or trying to solve problems, or achieve certain standards. But (unless these phrases are stretched to the point of disappearance) this is clearly not to be assumed: they do not fit, say, the enjoyment of nature or friendship or even the arts. While there may be a case (see p. 211) for all or most men spending *some* time in the second-order activity of getting clear about what first-order types of contemplation will be best for them and other men – that is, at least partly, in philosophy or in acquiring some general understanding about possible ways of life – nevertheless their actual first-order enjoyments need to be of this kind.

However, the notion of contemplation as *conscious* enjoyment does suggest something, if something fairly obvious, about (3) the *nature* of contemplation. To be happy as a conscious creature, we have argued, I must contemplate and enjoy things at least to some degree distanced from my own self. This means that I have to see these things for what they are; and the more I can do this, while still enjoying them, the more happiness I derive in contemplating. Conversely, 'those who have the greatest power of contemplation' will, in fact and inevitably, spend more time than other men on learning to see and enjoy things as they are: their powers of contemplation need, as it were, more to feed on. Since the contemplation will be more powerful or intense, we can say that the objects of their contemplation are likely to be more *sophisticated*.

It must be stressed again that this is *not* to make the move of identifying, by external criteria, some public activities (philosophy, science, and so on) as 'sophisticated' ('rewarding', 'worth-while') activities in their own right, identifying others (football, washing up, etc.) as 'boring', and then suggesting that the serious or sophisticated man will necessarily choose the former rather than the latter. The point is rather that *whatever* such a man does, he will bring greater powers of contemplation to bear on it and hence, in effect, transform it into a different object of attention.[41] If he plays chess, he will not just mess round with the pieces but see more of the possibilities on the board: if he looks at a building or a view, he will not see it only under a few sentimental or thread-bare descriptions. Even here we have to be careful, for nothing we have said shows that such a man will necessarily spend a lot of *time* on some particular things (any more than it shows what these things are); maybe he will 'dabble' in a great many things, so that his understanding and awareness of them will still be 'superficial' when compared with that of an expert or a specialist. But 'dabble' and 'superficial' here are governed by external or public criteria: the *way in which* the man approaches things, even if he is spending only a little time on them, will show his seriousness and sophistication, whatever public standards he may reach. Thus he will be quick and eager to make sense of them, grasp their essential features, see what is the nature of the delight they offer, and so forth. Rather than saying, what may mislead, that the actual (publicly defined) objects of his contemplation are more sophisticated, we may say that *he sophisticates* whatever he contemplates.

How do these considerations bear on the question of what should be learned? In one way, they do not bear on what *should* be learned at all; the case is rather that *if* a person is in this sense serious or sophisticated then he will, in fact, tend to contemplate (and hence to learn about) things of a more sophisticated nature than other men will. Insofar as he spends the same amount of time on them – and in practice it is, perhaps, not very likely that such a man will wish to spend all his time in 'dabbling' – his chess-game, building, view or whatever will in effect be a different and more rarefied object of attention. To this we may add, for what it is worth, that since we all ought, ideally, to be men of this kind, some sense could be attached to saying that it is (again ideally, and as it were by derivation) these sophisticated things that ought to be or should be learned. But this is not to say much; and clearly we need to look more closely at the whole business of being 'serious'.

In what way do these (admittedly rather high-minded and highly general) arguments have application to the educator? It may be thought that all this is rather like arguing about what people would or should be doing if they were in heaven; and though it may be correct to give an answer in terms of some sort of contemplation (the Beatific Vision, I suppose), the fact remains that we are on earth, and surrounded by all sorts of pressures and particularities.

There are perhaps two main lessons to be learned. We may start by saying that battles between those who want pupils to be happy and those who oppose to this some other ideal are unreal battles. Ultimate grounds for choice reside in the idea of happiness, and nowhere else; to that extent, the truth lies with the former party. This criterion should govern both what sort of education we give, and – a question of at least equal importance – how *much* education we give, to various people: both the content of the enterprise and its extent. But we must rapidly go on to say that the unique way in which, *as educators*, we contribute to happiness should be governed by the unique way in which the particular goods of learning contribute: that is, by providing enjoyable objects of attention which (we hope) will permanently enlarge and enrich our pupils' consciousness. In other words, the educator as such does not dispense just *any* means to the end of happiness that happen to be lying round: indeed he does not (in one sense) dispense any *means* at all. He dispenses a constituent of it. This brings us back to the idea of the defeasibility of educational aims mentioned in part II (p. 109). All sorts of things, in this vale of tears, no doubt have to be learned for purely *ad hoc* or instrumental purposes; and these will, if properly justified, form a right and proper part of the content of particular educational policies. But insofar as the educator as such has scope to angle at all, he is out for bigger fish. He would wish that the instrumental purposes could be taken care of by other instruments, so that he can have more time to dispense the goods which he uniquely offers.

The connection between happiness and awareness is important for the educator in a second way also. Part of the reason why we sometimes feel tempted to oppose the two is an intuition that, unless we establish awareness as an independent value, it is likely to perish; that unless we glamorize it by talking about 'the ideals of scholarship', 'the nobility of knowledge', and so forth, people are likely to remain in brutish ignorance. We feel that learning, or being educated, or enlarging our consciousness by 'facing reality', is a *difficult* thing for human beings, and likely to be resisted unless well advertised. A good deal of what has been written on the subject has, in fact, been not much more than such advertisement.[42]

This intuition is well founded; and it emphasizes the enormous importance of concentrating on methods or approaches which improve *both* happiness *and* awareness. If there are ways in which, or conditions under which, pupils can be happy *in* 'facing reality', then we need to be as clear as possible about what these are. Obviously this is not entirely, perhaps not even primarily, a matter for philosophers; indeed, it is not very clear how far we can expect to get even with empirical generalizations, since in practice we are dealing with innumerable very particular questions ('How can we get Johnny to enjoy reading?', 'How will Mary find happiness in personal relationships?', etc.). But it is perhaps possible at least to set the stage for considering such questions, and I will try to say something about this in the next two chapters.

# Seriousness
# and fantasy

6

We turn now to our second question: what can be said about the general position of human beings in relation to the task of learning or being educated? Our happiness, so far as education is concerned, appears to turn on whether we can enlarge and enrich our consciousness and hence enjoy life more: is such enlargement essentially unproblematic, as it is with the growth of the body by means of food and exercise, or are the difficulties more than just practical and contingent? To put it very generally: are we to assume that everything is more or less *all right* with human beings as learners, so that we can cheerfully go ahead and ask what particular things to be learned might be especially useful or enjoyable? Or are we rather to suppose that there is something peculiarly difficult about the whole business, which needs to be looked at first?

In common with Plato and others, I shall argue for the second position; and before deploying more strictly conceptual arguments, we need to describe in a fairly general way the kind of attitude or mental posture which is inherent in, or lies behind, the acquisition of knowledge and control. At least some aspects of this attitude have received attention from philosophers (Plato's knowledge of the good, Aristotle's *spoudaiotes*, Spinoza's *amor intellectualis*, and so on) and also from psychologists (whose descriptions go under even more exotic titles); but there appears to be no well-established and immediately comprehensible term for it in ordinary English. I choose the word 'serious' partly because it is, at least, a term in common speech; but partly also because it seems to mark a concept on which contemporary philosophers of education rely heavily. Thus, as we have seen, Peters produces for our inspection a kind of conceptual roundabout which starts by pressing (too hard) the words 'educated' and 'educate'; generates thereby a concept that involves not only knowledge, understanding and 'cognitive perspective' but also some degree of 'caring' for various types of understanding and being 'on the inside of' them; and then shows that not only certain basic ethical or practical principles (like justice), but also some engagement in advanced intellectual activities (forms of thought), are in a way presupposed by anyone who 'seriously' asks questions about what to do: being 'serious', he says, involves entering into public discourse, having 'a concern for what is true or false, appropriate or inappropriate, correct or incorrect', and being 'committed to those enquiries which are defined by their serious concern with those aspects of reality which give context to the question.'[1]

Just what sort of weight or content does he, or should we, put into the idea of 'being serious'? One reason why the idea is an elusive one, and why in consequence we need to give an expanded description of it, may be that it penetrates or is taken for granted by all disciplines, but is dealt with specifically by few or none. Thus philosophy or conceptual argument itself often appears, to the layman or 'outsider', curiously self-contained or academic. What he may feel is, not so much that the arguments are wrong, but that (as one teacher put it to me) 'Philosophers' arguments are only any use to people who don't need them.' We could say that only someone who was already 'serious' would understand, let alone be influenced by, these arguments about 'seriousness'; and indeed Peters says that his book 'is only written for those who take seriously the question "What ought I to do?"' Yet (we may also feel) how could he do otherwise? For:

> social situations governed completely by irrational fiat . . . are not situations to which the probing of the philosopher has much relevance. It is no use employing logical arguments with a maniac, a hysterical woman, or an enraged Nazi. But, it is to be hoped, such people are rare in the teaching profession.[2]

This borders on saying something like: either a person is serious (able and willing) enough to follow and be influenced by this (very sophisticated) kind of philosophical argument (sometimes disarmingly described by philosophers as simply 'reflecting on the meaning of words'), or else he's barmy. Of course nobody really wants to say this; and we might more temperately hold that there is a class of people who could be made sufficiently serious to follow the philosophical arguments, which will then make them more serious still, or sophisticate their seriousness, or something like that. But many philosophers seem to think that this initial process–getting people to be (more) serious – is not the concern of philosophy. When they try to say whose concern it is, the attempts do not always carry much conviction. Hare, for instance, says:

> To get people to think morally it is not sufficient to tell them how to do it; it is necessary also to induce in them the wish to do it. And this is not the province of the philosopher. It is more

likely that enlightened politicians, journalists, radio
commentators, preachers, novelists, and all those who have an
influence on public opinion will gradually effect a change for
the better.[3]

I am not sure whether the idea here is that enlightened politicians,
journalists, etc., will improve things (1) by making people more
willing and able to do moral philosophy, which seems unduly
optimistic, or (2) in some other more general, perhaps less strin-
gently rational way (e.g. by stirring up sympathy for various causes),
which seems more plausible – but then where does the philosophy
come in?

People can be – most people are – 'outsiders' in relation to a
particular discipline, such as philosophy, without being 'maniacs' or
'enraged Nazis'; and it would be wiser not to accept the implied
dichotomy that we have either to argue from within our own terms
of reference, or else stop philosophizing altogether and turn to
'politicians, journalists, radio commentators, preachers, novelists'
because these are 'not situations to which the probing of the philosopher has much relevance.' Particularly when we consider the
initiation of pupils into various forms of thought or various types of
rationality, from a developmental or educational point of view, it
is clear that a pupil can have *reasons* (not just 'the wish') for becoming initiated; and we have especially to remember the point that
what the pupil may have reasons for is, not so much particular
*arguments* or *beliefs*, but particular forms of *communication* and *interaction*. It is the forms, the rules and structures, that are 'developmentally' basic, and that may even constitute the notion of 'being
reasonable' in a certain area. Thus the child first learns to talk, to
listen to the opinion of others and to take their desires into account,
and only then forms beliefs which flow from these rules and terms of
reference. He first enters on a form of life in which other people
count and have importance, and then (perhaps) learns or comes to
be conscious of conceptual arguments which show this to be reasonable.

Although the content of 'being serious' will differ in some respects
from one case to another, depending on what one is serious about,
nevertheless there is a lot in common to all cases. I doubt if much
would be gained by squeezing the *word* 'serious'; but if we had to
give a general account of the (or a) concept, I suppose we might say
that we were talking about the ability and/or the will to confront,
attend to, 'hold steady', and act upon certain phenomena in the
'real world', or guidelines to those phenomena: 'logic', 'public
discourse', 'the facts', one's own decisions, principles and interests,

and so forth. Some psychologists refer to this under headings like 'ego-strength' or being 'reality-orientated'. 'Serious', in our sense, is not primarily contrasted with 'joking' or 'trivial'; it is not to mean only 'earnest' or 'with strong feelings' (one can be very earnest about one's fantasies). The theories and behaviour of (say) the Nazis, or some contemporary 'revolutionary' or 'liberationist' groups, are obviously 'serious' in one sense, but not in ours. We have to take them seriously; but we do not have to take them seriously as rational theories or rational behaviour. We take them seriously more as we might take earthquakes seriously.[4]

The coupling of two things seems necessary for seriousness: (1) that there should be enough of the person *in* whatever he is doing – enough weight, so to speak (one might talk here of sincerity, or whole-heartedness, or earnestness): (2) that this weight should not be (as it were) just thrown around, but bestowed on whatever he *is* doing or supposed to be doing – and here one might talk, as Peters does, of 'care', 'respect for standards', the notion of a *techne*, and so on. These features again emerge in the (perhaps paradigmatic) case of language-using. (1) Sometimes a person is 'serious' in what he says, in the sense that *he means* it (or something) all right – he is not just joking or parroting – but he uses words which do not best represent his meaning. We might say here: 'You don't mean *that*', or '*That's* not what you mean'; then perhaps he thinks a bit and uses better words. (2) Sometimes the words *per se* are acceptable, but there is not enough *weight* behind them: the person is saying them because he is expected to, or because he has been taught to (parrotting), or for some other reason. Here we might say '*You don't mean* that', or '*Do you really want to say* that?' (as against 'Do you really want to say *that*?'). It is plausible to connect these with two educational traditions: (1) with a romantic or 'progressive' tradition in which pupils are encouraged to 'be themselves', but allowed to be too autistic in what they say; (2) with a more conservative or imitative tradition in which pupils are supposed to parrot true propositions without 'really meaning' them.

But it is important not to be carried away by the notion that seriousness can only be predicated of people engaged in some *techne* or, as philosophers are fond of saying, 'rule-governed' activity. Certainly only fully rational creatures (not worms, and perhaps not even dogs) can be serious or non-serious in our sense; but this turns, not on the specific notion of norms, rules or standards, but on the more primitive notion of there being *targets* or objects for one's feelings about the world and one's attempts on it. Even to say that one can only be serious if one is *doing* something can mislead; for instance, one can seriously regret one's past, where there is no question (or need be no question) of adopting means to ends. Yet this is still different from being seriously ill: that is a straight *pathos* and no kind of *praxis*. But emotions, wants, wishes, beliefs, attempts, etc., have targets. To put it crudely, seriousness is a matter of how much energy is consciously directed to whatever targets are in question; and this already brings in the notion of conscious as against unconscious direction, about which we shall say more below (p. 176).

For example: if we regard being in love as like catching a plague, to be seriously in love will be analogous to being seriously ill; we might translate 'seriously' by 'gravely' or just 'very much'. But if we ask whether someone is seriously in love *with Flossie*, we can at least wonder whether it is really Flossie, as publicly described, that he is seriously in love with: perhaps it is rather some image or projection in his own mind, whether consciously or unconsciously entertained. One test here might indeed be how he behaves (towards the real Flossie and in other contexts); but just as important, and psychologically prior, will be how he sees and feels about her. The serious man, as we say, 'means business' in the real world; his opposite, however, is not so much the inactive man as the autistic man – perhaps in the extreme case the 'psychopath', by whom – so at least we are told – even the basic categories (space, time, cause and effect) are not properly grasped or used.

The first thing that the serious man does, one might say, is to confront the world and describe it: perhaps two aspects of the same task. He does this before acting upon it and showing the agent-qualities which we more commonly associate with seriousness – consistency, determination and so on. This is why language-using is paradigmatic for seriousness; or rather, not so much a 'model case' (as if 'using words properly' were one *techne* among others), but a general form of activity or confrontation which runs through all specific human activities. Seriousness, and similar basic ideas sometimes marked by 'rationality', 'ego-strength', etc., are fundamentally a matter of stance or posture, of the way in which one *sets* oneself.

In our present state of knowledge (or rather ignorance) about seriousness, perhaps the most immediate practical task for educators is to work out detailed elaborations of how it may emerge *in particular contexts*. Educators too often behave as if they already knew what it was to be serious about such-and-such, and needed only to find out from psychologists what 'motivation' was necessary for their pupils. Rather than asking, for instance, (1) 'What are the "aims" or "objectives" of (say) teaching science?' or 'What do we put into the curriculum under the heading "science"?', along with the question (2) 'What "motivates" children to learn things?', we should ask something more like (3) 'What makes a serious scientist or student of science?' One might say that, under the influence perhaps of certain models or pictures commonly used in social science and experimental psychology, educational theorists have grossly neglected the three tasks most obviously relevant to this area. These tasks, roughly described, are (1) being clear ourselves *what it is* to be serious in various contexts: (2) simply *teaching* or *explaining* this to pupils: and (3) what one might call 'positioning' (I do not say 'motivating') pupils so that they have the best possible chance to *be* serious. In the particular context of serious discussion, for instance, this might mean (1) a full and precise statement of the criteria of seriousness in this context – what counts as 'a good discussion', what rules have to be obeyed or criteria satisfied: (2) the development of pedagogic methods best designed to teach these rules and criteria to pupils: and (3) whatever social or structural arrangements facilitate the proceedings (e.g. perhaps not having too many people present, or arranging the chairs in a circle, or whatever).[5]

There is of course an enormous (perhaps an infinite) number of contexts ('forms of life', rule-governed systems, or whatever it may be most appropriate to say in each case) into which we may want to initiate pupils. In each case, once we are clear about the criteria of seriousness and can explain these criteria, the opening moves may be described as 'structural' or 'conventional'. We put children behind desks in classrooms: position recruits in three ranks on the parade-ground: station crewmen in various parts of the ship: allot places to people in courts of law or debating-chambers, and so on. At the same time we teach them certain linguistic and other conventions (holding up one's hand to ask a question, etc.) which facilitate the operation of whatever we want to go on in the particular context; and these shade off into conventions or 'moves' which actually form part of the operation. Different operations – that is, for the educator, different sorts of learning – obviously demand different contexts and conventions: a truism which would be unnecessary were not there a regrettable fashion for talking in a too general way about 'democratic', 'child-centred', 'authoritarian', etc., 'styles of teaching'.

However, the business of clarifying and 'positioning' only gives us a start (though it is a start that may carry us a long way). Things may still go wrong. On the parade-ground, a soldier may be clumsy or have slow reactions; in the debating-chamber, a speaker may be afflicted with a stammer or lack any natural talent for rhetoric. But in education (or indeed 'intellectual' matters generally, to use the widest term I can think of) we are concerned with the emergence of knowledge, understanding and control from the morass of autistic sensation and emotion; and when things go wrong here, it is nearly always due to non-seriousness. Of course there are competitors. One may go wrong through sheer ignorance; but the man who knows he is ignorant is less likely to get things wrong – he will hedge his bets, tolerate doubt, and so on; and knowing one's own ignorance is again largely a matter of being serious. Another competitor, perhaps, is sheer unintelligence or stupidity. But I doubt whether we have a concept of intelligence[6] which is clearly marked off from other concepts more connected with 'the will' or 'motivation' (and hence with seriousness); indeed we talk of 'behaving stupidly', where a person's IQ (whatever this may be) is not in question. Certainly no empirical tests exist which sever 'ability' and 'motivation' in this area; nor is it easy to sever them even conceptually. We do indeed *say* on different occasions 'He can't' and 'He doesn't want to', but we rarely know when we are right; a hopelessly complicating factor being that his 'inability' (e.g. to learn to read) may itself be the result of some 'motivational' lack at a deeper level, and vice versa.

What sort of enemies (it may be helpful to ask) do we face here? What is it that stands in the way of 'being serious'? It will readily be granted, that, as we noted earlier, earnestness or strong feeling is not a sufficient (perhaps not even always a necessary) condition. Somewhat less obvious, I think, is the point that the actual possession of knowledge or correct belief is also irrelevant. In demanding seriousness of our pupils we demand that they *set* themselves to know: what they actually do know, or will come to know, is not at issue. It is their mental attitude which is at stake. The nature of this attitude is often masked rather than clarified when we talk of people 'knowing' or 'believing'; indeed an inadequate and uncritical concept of belief, in particular, which may even be institutionalized in the use of the words 'belief' and 'believe' in our language, makes us underestimate the extent of non-seriousness and obscures some of its causes.

Consider the 'beliefs' that the result of a mortal combat would prove the truth or falsity of some claim (as in *Richard II*, II, i): that you can run an institution without rules: that human sacrifice is efficacious: that there are angels, fairies, ghouls, demons, etc.: that the world is supported by an elephant standing on a turtle: that 'Because the *Führer* says so' is a sufficient reason for killing Jews. Now all these cases are different from each other; but in all we feel tempted to say 'Do they really *believe* that?' And this is just a way of introducing the important question 'What's really going on in their heads?' In the first example, for instance, are we to say (a) that Richard and Aumerle and the rest really thought that the results of the combat would *prove* – that is, give a good reason for accepting – a particular proposition? They might have thought this, if for instance they seriously held that God or an angel would certainly arrange for the just man to win. Or shall we say (b) that they meant something different by 'prove', rather as we would by 'argument' when we talked of a gunboat being a better argument than a show of words? They might mean simply that the combat would *settle* it (as by tossing a coin).

These particular beliefs, if they are beliefs, may look moderately absurd at first glance. Consider now a much more topical and respectable-looking case. Moralists and educators (among others) ask us to believe that we ought to treat other people as equals, or be concerned with them or allow their wants or interests to weigh as heavily as our own. There are problems about exactly what we are being asked to believe here; but consider one very common reaction, of the form 'Why should I worry about other people?' Now it is at least arguable that if this means 'What rational justification is there?', then we can offer some sort of Kantian answer. It is said (roughly) that anything which we can count as a *justification* must be derived from an impersonal generalization, in which particular terms like 'I', 'here', 'now' etc., do not figure. *My* hunger ought to be satisfied (other things being equal) only because hunger in general ought to be: *I* ought only if *one* ought: and so on. Hence I have no more reason (in the sense of 'justification') to be concerned for my own interests than for other people's.

I do not want here to argue about the validity of this sort of answer, but just to point out that – nine times out of ten, even among fairly sophisticated people – the answer does not fit the question 'Why should I worry?' This is because the 'Why?' is not intended as 'What rational justification is there?' It is often immensely difficult to say just what it is intended as. Sometimes there is a tacit demand (made more overtly in some recent moral philosophy) for a particular kind of justification, in terms of the point or purpose or extrinsic end of morality – roughly, can it be shown to pay? Sometimes it seems to mean 'What incentive do I myself have?', as often when a child says 'Why should I when Daddy doesn't?', or 'How can I be expected to?' or even (with fairly aggressive people) 'Who are *you* to tell me to?' Not infrequently people will say things like 'Of course, if as I do you believe in a loving God who made us brothers', or 'If your heart is filled with the awareness of the dignity of human worth': in other words, if you are already wedded to some such picture (painted in whatever terms, perhaps religious), then all is well. What they want perhaps ought not to be called a *belief* (that other people count) at all: it is more like a fantasy-picture, which is somehow treated as real. Armed with this picture, they then have the incentive ('motivation') and also feel 'justified'.

Whatever may be thought of this particular case or other cases, the notion of believing or 'really believing' something seems far from clear. People can be wedded to utterances or 'pictures'[7] in various ways. Suppose that when children in some family wanted to go for a picnic and it was raining, their nurse invariably said 'It'll clear up soon.' Did she mean 'It'll clear up soon, I hope', or 'It'll clear up soon, I believe', or 'I'm afraid', or 'Possibly, so I'd better cut the sandwiches' (which she usually did)? How could we tell? The question we are asking here is not whether the utterance was of any *use* to other people as an assertion (it may not be), nor whether she meant the utterance sincerely (it may be that she did). The question is rather about *how* she meant it, what she meant it *as*; whether she was wedded to the picture of fine weather in the way one is wedded to a hope, or a fear, or a possibility, or a prediction. What is it to mean something as an assertion: to *believe* something, rather than to entertain a 'picture' in some other way?

Traditionally philosophers have talked here about whether 'the statement' is 'falsifiable'. But this does not answer our question. For it is a question of *how* whatever is said is *meant*: and (1) a person may initially mean something as an assertion or a belief but to be too pig-headed to consider or accept subsequent falsifying evidence: (2) a person may initially mean something as a hope (fear, wish, fantasy, etc.) but still be prepared, subsequently, to consider his actual utterance as subject to evidence and falsification. (Suppose the nurse often said later on, after a day of constant rain, 'Oh, goodness, I was wrong': this does not necessarily show that she *originally* meant 'It'll clear up soon' as a prediction rather than as a hope. In any case there are different ways of being 'wrong'; hopes may be dupes, and fears liars.) There is a connection between belief and evidence, but it is not this connection.

The question is not to be answered by applying some criterion to the utterances themselves. We need to know 'what goes on in a person's head': what sort of mental move he makes. How do we determine this? We might think that this is just a matter of classifying and determining people's 'speech-acts' and begin by asking them 'Nurse, do you mean you think it really will clear up, or do you just hope it will?' 'Oh, yes, dear, I'm sure it will' – and this reply may be, in any normal sense, perfectly sincere. Yet (*pace* some philosophers who believe in 'knowledge without observation') we may think that a person is *not* always the best authority on what goes on in his head. He may think he means something as a belief *but be wrong*.

Without implying that such criteria as the person's own avowal about the nature of his speech-act, his overt behaviour, his willingness to consider evidence and his being prepared to change his mind are irrelevant, one might be tempted to say that a necessary condition for a person's believing p is that his utterance of p is causally derived from evidence. I intend to exclude the cases, numerous among sophisticated people, where the person is aware of evidence, can quote it, and may even be willing to alter his utterance when faced with new evidence, but where his utterance is not the *result* of his attending to evidence in the first place. What we have here are pictures dressed up as beliefs. He was not wedded to the pictures by evidence, but by something else (hope, fear, etc.). His reasons, however good, are rationalizations, because not causally operative. Conversely, a person can believe p even though his reasons are bad ones: provided only that they are reasons, and that it is they (rather than other causes) that he allows to generate his utterance.

If this were not a necessary condition, I do not see how it would be ultimately possible to distinguish between beliefs on the one hand, and hopes, fears, longings, and other emotion-generated pictures on the other. On this view, it is very often an open question whether an assertive utterance is a belief or not; a question which we cannot decide without elaborate methods of assessment, at least in some cases – though others are more simple (it might soon become clear that the nurse never even considered the evidence of weather forecasts, etc.). We should need to know how the person *acquired* his disposition to make utterances; whether his tendency to make it remained unchanged by his perception of relevant evidence would be *one* (only one) check on this.

I am not arguing here that we only use the words 'belief' and 'believe' when we know, or opine, that the person's utterance is evidence-generated. (To determine this in each case would often, as I have just said, require an impossible amount of research.) It seems better to say that we simply *assume* this to be so; or to say that for purposes of human intercourse we have to *take* what look like assertions *as* assertions, at least normally – we do not go further into the matter than that. As Aristotle might put it, we *call* utterances 'beliefs' in a vast number of cases (and perhaps for very various reasons); but we would be willing to consider, if asked, whether they really are so.

What matters is that on this (new) concept of belief, it is very likely that the amount of time children (or adults) spend in acquiring genuine beliefs is fairly small; certainly this is true in areas like morality, politics, religion, art, and personal relationships, where we are not even clear what should count as evidence, and hence cannot be clear when our entertained propositions are generated by evidence or by something else. Nor is this surprising, since a concern for truth and evidence involves much harder work than is involved in any autistic connection with entertained propositions ('believing because we want to believe').

All this is perfectly consistent with our being willing to assert and give reasons for many true propositions – with our 'believing' them, if you like. But as we saw when considering learning, this accidental co-extensiveness of improper mental processes with truth is not satisfactory for the educator. One might put the position, perhaps somewhat extremely, like this: 'We are engaged in trying to impart knowledge and virtues, initiate pupils into modes of thought, and enable them to acquire correct beliefs. But most of our pupils, most of the time, do not want to play this game at all. We may force them to "go through the motions" in an old-fashioned way, or try to arouse their interest by "discovery" methods or "progressive" techniques (hoping in the former case that rote-learning will turn into genuine knowledge, and in the latter that the "interest" will turn into a genuine concern for truth). But the wastage is plainly enormous.'

What is it, then, that our pupils and ourselves are doing, when we are not engaged in acquiring genuine beliefs? It is a striking fact that the examples of 'belief' which we considered earlier were all of *unnecessary* beliefs: or at least, so it appears *prima facie*. Early cosmologists and map-makers gained nothing (we might suppose) by placing known terrain at the centre of the earth, or constructing elaborate stories of elephants and turtles: they could just as well have said 'We don't know.' This bears witness to the fact that human beings do not easily tolerate blanks. There are already powerful mechanisms at work, even before men consider (or appear to consider) what the world is like, which imprint their forms on the world.

This is why it is proper to describe much of what happens as 'fantasy', rather than to use terms like 'wishful thinking', 'prejudice', 'lack of concentration or determination', 'weakness of will', and so forth. Not that these latter are always inappropriate; but it is important to bring out the complexity, as well as the power, of what goes on here. We are not, for the most part, dealing just with 'brute' and unformed desires, fears, hopes, and so on, but with something much more like a connected story, pattern or dream-world which has a life of its own in the mind. Inevitably so: for human desires and emotions involve some degree of conceptualization, and these conceptualizations begin to be interwoven from early infancy onwards. Even non-conceptualized 'imprints', or 'stimulus and response patterns', will inevitably be dressed in some kind of conceptual clothes, involving the notions of (often unconscious) belief and appraisal.[8] A close investigation of even the apparently simplest 'prejudice', or 'attraction', or 'want', soon reveals something of their history and of their place in some fantasy-picture.

So far we have done no more than paint a particular picture of how, as it seems, human beings stand in relation to learning; and we have laid particular stress on the difficulties of their position. This picture has involved more description than argument; and naturally the description may be challenged. I am tempted to say that it would not in fact be challenged by anyone who had himself reflected seriously on his own life, or the lives of others, either with or even without the help of those aids which might fall under titles like 'religion', 'philosophy', 'literature', 'psychology' and so on. But that, of course, is no kind of argument. We need to show, if we can, not just that things are so, but that they must be so: that there is some conceptual or *a priori* inevitability or necessity about it. We need to do this, not only for the trades-unionist reason that the philosopher's business is with conceptual arguments, but because we have to see *why* things must be so in order to grasp what can be done to improve them.

Perhaps our arguments are not too far to seek, and have been missed only because of the systematic error which we have criticized often before – that is, the error of setting up a particular content prematurely. Consider again the movement of thought which begins with the argument that 'worth-while activities' are in themselves more interesting or fascinating than pig-like activities because they provide 'opportunities for skill and discrimination' (see above, p. 136). Our initial objection was that things were 'interesting' or 'fascinating' only in relation to particular people; for most people, simpler activities are more 'interesting' than sophisticated ones. We are now tempted to say: 'Yes, but this just means that these people haven't "come to grasp what there is in these activities";[9] if they did, they would be committed to them and enjoy them', and then we go on to make a conceptual link between being so committed (being 'serious', 'reflective', etc.) and going in for these activities. But this puts us back to square one; for we now want to know how we should determine the extent to which particular individuals ought to go in for this whole 'package deal'. And it seems that all we can do is one of two things; either (1) produce some overall criterion (perhaps 'happiness'), and leave the rest to those whose business it is to discover empirical truths: or (2) to return to obvious contingent arguments (e.g. that all of us need food, health, security, etc., which only the pursuit of 'worth-while activities' – perhaps particularly science – can provide), which are not strictly the philosopher's business.

One reason why this movement of thought looks thin – particularly to non-philosophers, who will remain inclined to accuse philosophers of backing a particular horse ('reason' or 'the intellectual life') – is that it appears to take its stand on conceptual ground which such people might describe as specifically 'intellectual'. This ground is marked out by a particular interpretation of 'seriousness', the use of (public) language, deliberation, asking questions, reflecting, and so on. Thus, after criticizing the 'doctrine of function' as used by Greek and other philosophers, Peters adds: 'Nevertheless . . . it was on the right lines in attempting to justify the good life for man by an argument which appeals to man's use of reason': reason should feature 'as the starting place for some kind of transcendental argument'.[10] Of course it is true that any rational or philosophical argument must 'appeal to man's use of reason', but this is not what he seems to mean. It is rather that (like the Greeks) he supposes that, of the various truths about 'human nature' or 'the mind of man', it is truths specifically connected with *reasoning* (language, etc.) on which philosophers must or ought to base their arguments. But there is no very obvious reason to believe that this supposition is necessary, though it seems widely shared by philosophers. For might there not be other truths about men – perhaps necessary or *a priori* truths, whatever we are to mean by this – which it is the philosopher's job to bring home to us, and which might indeed be more relevant at least to the kind of problems we meet in education, morality, politics and other areas of practical choice?

One set of such truths, at any rate, seems important here. In considering the Socrates-pig problem, we are apt to talk not only as if there were some sharp distinction between pigs, Polynesians, 'the common herd', and 'the level of the necessary appetites' on the one hand, and 'Socrates', 'sophisticated tastes', 'worth-while activities', etc., on the other (whereas in fact there is something more like a range or scale here); but also as if the notion of a human being living entirely at the level of 'the necessary appetites', like a pig, were conceptually possible. But this seems not to be the case. It is not so much that we would not single out entities as 'human beings' unless and until they were language-users (which is not even true), and that the use of language brings some measure of sophistication which allows us to generate conceptual arguments; it is rather that there are certain inexpellable facts about the origin and growth of human beings – I think, of any sentient or rational creature – which make the direct, unmediated, or 'natural' absorption of pleasure or satisfaction an incoherent policy.

These facts are well documented and fairly obvious. Any sentient creature has to be born (or at least to begin), and to grow (or learn, or increase its experience) over a period of time. The objects of the child's initial desires ('love-objects', in the jargon) have to be relinquished as it grows, because they are no longer available, or appropriate, or satisfying. It has to accept substitutes. In order to be able to acquire and enjoy such substitutes, it – or perhaps now we should say, 'he' – has to do two things: first, to develop sufficient rationality actually to obtain the new objects; and second, to be able to see them as sufficiently pleasurable (sufficiently like his original sources of satisfaction) to be worth obtaining. This is hence a doubly difficult task: he has somehow to find, or recreate, as much of his original pleasure as possible, incorporated now in some new object or objects, and this time on his own initiative and in the teeth of a world which is often hostile and largely independent of his own wishes. This process is irreversible, in the sense that (though he may grow tired, relapse, sleep, daydream and in general very often fail, or not even try, to achieve this task) he cannot reasonably adopt a policy of abandoning the real world and recapturing his original sources of pleasure; not only because the sources are no longer available, but also because he is now to some extent 'grown up'. He has incorporated certain norms, reactions and other alterations of the psyche which were necessary for him to survive: and this makes him a different being.

One central point here is perhaps that the *equipment* which the child needs in order to negotiate with the real world is inevitably feeble when compared with the strength of his emotions. Not only is he physically helpless, but he lacks both the 'cognitive' and the 'affective' mental competences. On the one hand, he must learn (via the use of language and different kinds of knowledge) to describe and understand the world: on the other, he must learn to restrain his passions – to 'defer gratification' – so that this understanding can operate. In this learning he fights a constant battle against the immediacy and the uninhibited strength of his desires. He wants everything good and wants it now; but he cannot have it. The 'cannot' here surely represents some sort of conceptual necessity. It is not just that he is bound to see any delay or frustration as intolerable; it is also that he is in a state of mental incoherence, which makes him conceive desires that are impossible to fulfil (for instance, to have his mother wholly inside him).

Since many of the child's emotions will simply be too much for the puny and hard-won ego to handle, particularly if their original objects cannot be achieved easily (or at all), the process usually labelled 'repression' inevitably comes into play. So too will certain distinctions between various levels of the mind, marked (somewhat brutally) by the terms 'conscious' and 'unconscious'. As I have argued elsewhere,[11] we have to accept the existence of unconscious beliefs and emotions, not just of 'imprints' and 'stimuli': here I am suggesting that the existence of a subliminal world not normally available to consciousness is not merely a contingent fact about human beings.

The set of conditions we have described results in two kinds of loss or misfortune. First, and perhaps more obviously, the energy inherent in our desires and emotions will be often *mis-directed*. We shall often see the world, and behave, in ways which we mark by such terms as 'unreasonable', 'irrational' or (in extreme cases) 'insane'. (This is likely to – indeed, it surely must – apply particularly to those aspects of the world which are most closely bound up with our emotions; our perceptions of ourselves, of other people, and of human life as it appears in areas roughly marked by 'morality', 'politics', 'religion', 'literature' and others, are in principle more liable to unreason than our perception of physical objects, and our ability to operate or perform well in these 'affective' areas is more vulnerable than in the more purely 'cognitive' areas.) Second, the energy will be *lost* to the conscious mind, because it is invested in desires and emotions which are repressed or put out of sight by some other means. Much of this energy is, as it were, deadlocked; inevitably so, because the emotions which give it shape will often be in conflict with each other, and this conflict cannot be resolved by (since it is beyond the reach of) conscious control or negotiation. This may create an impression of calm, or at least of inaction, even when such conflicts are conscious or semi-conscious. We sometimes describe extreme cases of individuals in this position as 'insane', 'totally withdrawn', etc.: and the misfortune here is certainly different from the misdirection of emotion, and in a way worse. For here the ego is not functioning at all (hence we do not even call such men unreasonable).

This second type of loss is of great importance for educators, and is connected very obviously with what we said earlier about happiness and the way in which 'awareness' delimits the extent to which a man can be happy. We are accustomed to talk (perhaps for most practical purposes we must talk) as if the area of man's ego or consciousness were pretty well *given*, and we note only or chiefly the mistakes and successes, the virtues and vices, which he displays within those parameters. To use an old simile, it is as if we saw men as islands of various shapes and sizes, and judge them only by what we could see projecting above the water: indeed, meant by 'them' only what was thus visible. But the size of the island is also important. There are indeed occasions when we cannot but recognize this. Teachers feel not only that many of their pupils in schools get things

wrong, or cause trouble, but also that many of them are withdrawn, day-dreaming, in a daze, 'only half there'. That phrase is
exactly right (except that 'half' is unduly optimistic). It is not (only)
that men are irrational: it is also that they are not engaged. We
recognize the immense wastage when we ourselves feel fully engaged
for a time, or when we come across someone who seems more
engaged than we are. Then we talk of him with admiration as
'enthusiastic', 'alive', 'creative', 'energetic', and so on. Most of us,
most of the time, are simply not in that state at all. We feel that we
lack *power*: one reason why powerfulness is a necessary feature of a
god, a hero, or any other external figure whom we construct to
remedy our own impotence. For it is not just 'nature' in the face of
which men feel impotent: or, if we are to say that it is, we must
include human nature.

I have put these points in a highly schematic and generalized
form; the area of enquiry is a vast one, and more closely knit
argument would require a whole book of its own. It would of course
be possible to cast them in a more specific mould and talk (as
psychologists do) of the particular relationships between mother
and child, the inevitable and inevitably painful abandonment of the
mother in favour of other love-objects, the similar abandonment of
infantile pleasures in favour of something more like work, and so on.
I hope to have said enough, however, to show that we are dealing
here with necessary truths and not with empirical generalizations.
If somebody were to suggest that new processes of child-rearing or
new technological devices would change the whole picture, or that
none of this need happen with Martians, I think we should be at a
loss to understand what he might mean. There are logical inevitabilities at work here. It is important to work out these inevitabilities
in more rigorous detail; but perhaps even more important to
appreciate in the first place that they merit philosophical attention.[12]

Even in this highly generalized form these points put the notion of
'being serious' on a somewhat different footing. It is now not so
much that, as language-users, our seriousness logically commits us to
a particular policy and life-style (the 'theoretic' life) which could be
set against other policies and life-styles; rather, the conditions of life
are (inevitably) such that a serious attempt to gain happiness from
the world necessarily involves 'sophisticated' methods. This is of
course consistent with our abandoning the attempt sometimes, often,
or even for most of the time (we tire, 'regress', sleep, get drunk, etc.);
and consistent with our rationally choosing to do this sometimes
rather than always trying to be serious, which we may find either
impossible or dangerously self-defeating. We have these choices to
make; but we now make them from within the knowledge that there

is, as it were, no permanent escape (except death or madness) from things like work, 'sublimation', and the rational search for satisfaction. Briefly: these should now be seen not as following from the notion of already being a rational language-user, still less from a particular 'achievement ethic', but rather from this expanded notion of being human or conscious.

We still do not know how far 'theoretic' activities are satisfactory sources of pleasure in terms of this picture, although we can see from Peters[13] and other writers that one aspect of them, considered in itself, is satisfactory, i.e. they offer plenty of scope and opportunity for sophistication and contact with the real world (though many other activities do this also). What is not so clear is how acceptable they are as substitutes for our original sources of pleasure; the trouble seems to be that they are too sophisticated. One can fairly straightforwardly say to a person 'Look, you can't stay in your pram for ever, you'd better learn how to enjoy working at something', this is so straightforward, indeed, that it sounds odd to say it, because the normal conditions and transactions of life usually (not always) take care of the matter for us and our children, or at least appear to do so. But one cannot so obviously say 'Look, the kinds of childhood pleasures you're having to give up can be recreated for you in mathematics, science, personal knowledge' and so on through the 'forms of thought'.

Nevertheless we have now a different perspective on these activities. We need not present them only as additional and extraneous sources of happiness or self-enlargement (as when we say that a man 'is missing something' if he does not go in for art or literature or whatever); the arguments which result from this line of attack are too fragile and uncertain. We shall rely rather on the fact that the provision of human happiness must necessarily be, in large part, a work of recovery: that is, an attempt to recreate our early infantile pleasures in new objects. For much of the pleasure, like the objects, is necessarily lost (repressed or despaired of): necessarily, because the inevitable harshness of growing up involves a high degree of abandonment, loss, or repression. From this perspective – the point is most obvious in the cases of art and literature – some 'worth-while activities', at least, seem to be determined and valuable attempts to effect such recovery.

In this light the happiness (or even contentment) commonly attributed to Aristotle's 'common herd', or even to the notional Polynesian, may well be specious. In saying of such a person, as we said before, that there may not be 'enough of him' to be (sufficiently) happy, we may mean rather more than is implied by the picture of a narrow consciousness which is, nevertheless, quite happy within its limits. For the part of himself that was repressed, abandoned or lost in childhood does not simply disappear; nor does it merely play the role of a tiresome 'brute' addendum to consciousness – the unconscious is not just something we have to lug around, like a caravan or trailer. It continues to operate, often by setting up conflicts or types of mental paralysis which not only keep the consciousness narrow but cause certain permanent areas of discontent in it. Happiness is (I have argued, p. 145) a descriptive concept, and may be verified; but the more overt signs of discontent, common in most sophisticated people but absent from our notional Polynesians, are by no means the only signs.

Many of us, indeed, are less happy than we suppose; or, rather, we rarely bother to consider in any serious way how happy we are. When we do, we are more forcibly struck by the point that overt symptoms – bouts of pain or anxiety on the one hand, or thrills and pleasures on the other – do not go far to settle the question either way. Indeed large tracts of our lives hardly seem to qualify for the description 'happy' or 'unhappy' at all. The kind of thing that we seem to be missing is not so much some new pleasure or 'interest' or 'activity', but something more fundamental. Sometimes people will say they want to feel more 'real' or more 'positive' or 'engaged': and they may seek an 'answer' in some kind of 'salvationist' approach – perhaps commitment to a religious or other cause. The intuitions here (if not the various 'answers to life') are sound: this is something like the *sort* of way in which worth-while activities have to be worth while. We recognize this when we speak of art and literature as 'profound', 'touching the depths of the human heart', etc. They salvage what we have lost: and some divers go deeper than others.

I want again to stress that these points are not intended to represent a particular outlook on life, *Weltanschauung*, or 'doctrine of man' which could be disproved by reference to empirical facts. We are, indeed, familiar with such outlooks; various authors (Augustine and Freud among many others) have painted more or less gloomy pictures of human existence, and are opposed by the sunnier views of those who seem to believe that there are no inalienable difficulties about being human – that we have only to 'change society', for instance, or to abolish different kinds of 'conditioning', 'indoctrination', and external corruption in general, for everything to be bright and beautiful (Rousseau might be a fair example). The *descriptions* of the former, though they often err in being obscure and mythological ('original sin' hardly explains much), certainly seem nearer the mark; but this is, I think, because they have penetrated nearer to what might be called the essence or conceptual core of what it is to be human – that is, a creature with the potentiality for developing consciousness, and the kind of happiness that belongs to being conscious, from a state of fantasy and autism.

Socrates' dictum that the unexamined life is not worth living might be taken to suggest that certain activities – intellectual enquiry and 'examination' of one's life – are intrinsically valuable or valuable for their own sakes, or *constitute* a worth-while life; and to this it might fairly be objected that such an enquiry would be empty, since *ex hypothesi* there is no better life which the enquiry could determine. It seems clear, however, that this was not how Socrates (or Plato) saw it. In the myth which concludes the *Republic*, for instance, philosophy is plainly needed for extrinsic or instrumental reasons, to gain happiness and avoid the miseries of ignorance:

> Here, my dear Glaucon, is the supreme peril of our human state: and therefore the utmost care should be taken. Let each one of us leave every other kind of knowledge and seek and follow one thing only, if peradventure he may be able to learn and may find someone who will make him able to learn and discern between good and evil, and so to choose always and everywhere the better life as he has opportunity.[14]

Socrates and Plato must in this respect be placed firmly with those religious writers who are thoroughly alive to what might be called the *urgency* of the human condition. (Much of the *Republic*, indeed, is in general tone not unlike some of St Paul's writings: the urgency is even pressed on us by similar metaphors.) An appreciation of this urgency is, in my judgment, the essential first step we have to take if we are to be serious about education – indeed, about life – at all: a step which might, if rather dramatically, be construed on the model of repentance. Unfortunately the next steps are, if anything, even harder to take: it is easy to be over-impressed, or impressed in the wrong sort of way, by our difficulties. At any rate, those who are so impressed will, *pro tanto*, be unimpressed by two well-known reactions to items of educational content. The first is to regard certain subjects – say, the study of ancient Greek history, or French literature, or philosophy – as somehow valuable in themselves. Unsurprisingly this idea is most popular among those who find them absorbing or have a vested interest in pursuing them: many such people purport to see no need of any 'justification' other than that interest. Second, there is a much larger number of people who demand that subjects should be 'useful' or 'relevant': they refer usually to some fairly obvious extrinsic advantage – having a good job, contributing to the national economy, and so on. But if human beings are in the general position described earlier – more or less as in Plato's cave – then both these reactions are naive. As Plato saw, the various subjects and disciplines will have to pass more stringent tests than the test of whether they are 'interesting'. Some subjects (most obviously, science) are demonstrably 'useful' in a straightforwardly utilitarian way: at least they keep us fed and clothed in the cave, which is not nothing. We cannot expect 'usefulness' (or, if you like, the same kind of usefulness) from the humanities, but we are entitled to expect something more from them than a general illumination of consciousness – certainly something more than that they should merely be interesting and seem 'important' to those who practise and teach them. For we are not concerned here with the motives of (for instance) those who pursue philosophy, but with what justification they have for expending their time and abilities (and other people's money) in this way. Do they earn their keep? Of course it is *nice*, particularly for some people, to roam these pastures; and no doubt it does not follow that, if we cannot at once find some justification for them, we ought immediately to disband them and send them down the mines – goodness knows our society is utilitarian enough, and perhaps they earn their keep just by being representatives of 'non-utilitarian values' (whatever this may mean). All this and more can be said; but the need for justification remains. In the last resort, philosophy is either just a pleasant and absorbing pastime that enriches the mind, or else it *matters*. Either the plays of Shakespeare are just good fun (for sophisticated people), or else they are *needed*. This contrast will not prevent us from *also* wanting to defend 'enriched minds' and 'good fun' as independent values; but it is a contrast just the same. We shall return to this point below (pp. 194 ff.).

If this is how things are, what can the educator do about it? There are, I think, three reactions or sets of reactions which these considerations characteristically provoke, and which are worth classifying despite the dangers of oversimplification. Very roughly, (1) we may deny that this is the business of *education* at all: we may admit the problems, but classify them under some other heading, as perhaps 'religion' or 'mental health'; (2) we may accept that men can learn or can be educated to become more serious, but regard fantasy purely as an enemy, demanding its repression and the turning of the pupil's attention to some *external* source of goodness or power; (3) we may try the more direct approach of treating the pupil's fantasy and seriousness as part of the *subject-matter* of education: regarding fantasy as at least potentially an ally, and hoping to improve the pupil's self-knowledge and self-control.

The first option gains plausibility only at the cost of a pre-emptive idea of education. If we narrow this idea so that it includes only what might (roughly) be marked by such terms as 'culture', 'the intellect', or 'intellectual sophistication', then of course we shall have to classify *other* kinds of learning, however important, under other headings. Whatever needs to be learned for our soul's salvation, for instance, will now come under 'religion'; and we shall engage in muddled arguments about how far it is desirable for good Christians to be – in this pre-empted sense – educated. Or if we can learn from a psychotherapist to be happier and less neurotic, this will now be classified as a matter of 'mental health'; and we shall now contrast – disastrously, as I see it – 'psychotherapy' with education, and make this a matter for doctors and not teachers.[15] We may also, more or less consciously, unduly restrict the idea of education in other ways. Reactions expressed by 'But you can't *teach* seriousness', or 'But this isn't the sort of thing that can be done in *schools*', suggest various such restrictions. Perhaps 'teach' is not or not always the word we should want to use; and perhaps schools, as many of them in fact are, could not do the job effectively. But that goes no way to show that seriousness cannot be learned, or that schools could not be made into effective institutions for such learning. These objections would have seemed grotesque to Plato, as they must seem grotesque to anyone who wishes to consider what it is important for men to learn: for we cannot even reflect on the options if some of them are disqualified by pre-emptive definition.

Rather more extremely, one may deny that this is the business of education not on the grounds that it is the business of some other enterprise, but on the grounds that it can be the business of none. We often talk as if seriousness were non-negotiable; understandably, for in many contexts we have to take whatever seriousness anyone has as given, and get on with what we are doing. 'Nature' is characteristically used as the title for non-negotiable features of human beings, though we may also talk of 'temperament', 'endowment', and so forth. Nobody of course denies that 'nature' affects our chances of being serious; but if we thought that seriousness was *wholly* a matter of natural or non-negotiable endowment, we should be talking not about seriousness but about something else. For in speaking of seriousness we are pointing to whatever is common to all the cases of being serious about, or confronting, or paying attention to, particular objects: just as 'consciousness' or 'awareness' has to be consciousness or awareness of *something*, and hence necessarily involves learning – though natural endowments and physical causes can accelerate or retard the enterprise. Seriousness and non-seriousness only have application above the animal level: insofar as a person's behaviour is governed entirely by physical causes, he is neither serious nor non-serious. We are here in the realm of intentional behaviour: of reasons, appraisals and conceptualized goals. The fact that a large part of this realm is below our normal level of consciousness makes no difference; or rather, the difference resides primarily in the need to become more conscious of this part if our learning is to be effective.

A much more plausible line of argument involves doubting whether any *direct* approach in education to seriousness and fantasy would pay dividends. The standard objections are similar to those that one might raise to, for instance, special courses on 'critical thinking': roughly, that one has to 'think critically' (or 'be serious') *about* something – physics, mathematics, personal relationships, or whatever – and that therefore all one ought to or perhaps can do is to teach people how to engage rationally in these areas of under-standing. For instance, if we want to turn out people whose view of the physical world will be serious rather than dominated by anthro-pocentric or other fantasies, surely what we should do is simply to *teach them science*: would anything much be gained by examining whatever fantasies impeded the development of science in the past? One might even say, is not *just this* (i.e. teaching them science) the way to get them to overcome their fantasies about the physical world? Again, the way to overcome racial prejudice, it might be argued, is simply to present people with the facts and first-hand experience of what members of other races are actually like, to show them the reality: why should we need to investigate fantasies about Jews and negroes, which may only flourish in the absence of knowledge? Fill in the interstices and fantasy will have no room.

I am inclined to think that this line of argument appeals most to those who conceive of education primarily or exclusively in terms of the acquisition of propositional knowledge (the learning of subjects or forms of thought). Even on this conception, however, the argu-ment appears doubtful, and its force to depend very much on the particular case. It seems clear that some areas of understanding, and some people, are more (or at least more obviously) liable to fantasy than others: thus, it is hard to think of what fantasies stand or stood in the way of mathematical progress,[16] easy to quote examples of fantasy impeding the proper pursuit of science and history, and easier still to make this claim in the areas of morality and religion. In default of any proper research, however (which would be very hard to conduct), it is not absurd to adopt some sort of general view; and the view I am taking here, of course, is that the picture sketched above is a naive one, even in respect of particular subjects, disciplines, forms of thought, or kinds of propositional knowledge. If one had to argue for this further, one would naturally quote examples (like the popularity of astrology) to show how skin-deep, in fact, is the grasp of (in this case) 'scientific method'; it is easy to turn out people who 'go through the motions' of rational understanding, but mere practice and habituation to certain styles of thought – though this achieves something, and often a lot – is insufficient. We need stronger defences. On this view, the *compulsive* quality of most fantasy has to be emphasized: it was not just chance, ignorance, or a piece of playfulness, for instance, that made us believe that man was the centre of the universe and now makes us victims of astrologers and many other kinds of charlatan.

In this respect the apparent domination and acceptance of 'science' (to continue with this example) may be misleading at least for the educator; it is quite possible to run a *society* on science rather than witchcraft without very many of the *individuals* in that society having any real commitment to science. Such a set-up may keep the wheels of industry turning, but shows little advance in *education*. It would be interesting to try and see how much would be gained, or how much time wasted, by teaching science with the typical fantasies of pre-scientific ages (or the outlooks typical of young children in early stages of development) very much in mind. This sort of programme might, for instance, have defended supposedly 'educated' Germans in the 1930s from believing (if that is the right word) all the nonsense about 'Aryan blood'; whereas their ordinary scientific education did not do so. Certainly in these extreme cases it seems clear that the crux does not lie simply in habituation to rational procedures, but rather in the remarkable vulnerability even of habituated people when confronted with new cases that spark off fantasies; and it is difficult to see how to reduce this vulnerability without a more direct approach to fantasy.

In any case, we may argue that it is a mistake to take for granted, or to demand, a content of *this* kind for education. The demand is, in effect, for particular Xs which come in the category of 'subjects', 'topics', 'forms of thought', or 'intellectual disciplines': not in the category of virtues, or qualities, or states of mind. It is, I think, a peculiarly modern attitude, or at least one which is more likely to flourish when the satisfaction of aims in the second category – what might be broadly called 'moral education' or 'education in virtue' – is either (as now) largely despaired of, or else assumed to be the business of some other institution than the school: perhaps the church, or the Party, or the family. But this, as we saw earlier, identifies education only with what goes on in institutions called educational: a fatal error. We might prefer to argue the other way round: to say that the primary job of educational institutions was to ensure that the pupils learned to be serious, and regard the learning of subject-matter (mathematics, Latin, woodwork and so on) as of secondary importance, to be conducted in whatever ways and by whatever institutions were most convenient. I do not, of course, want to argue in that way, because what other things pupils learn is in fact important. But these things derive their importance from or at least by reference to, the notion of seriousness.

The second option requires somewhat fuller illustration. Those who are struck, as Plato was, by the immense strength of fantasy or irrational passion in general are apt to react by casting fantasy in the role of an enemy. This reaction is strongly reinforced if there is a deep fear – I do not say an unjustified fear – of certain evils which it may bring: in particular those associated with the ideas of disorder, unpredictable change, and anarchy, whether in the individual or in society. To counter these, we set up an external and unchanging world whose contents, if sufficiently attended to, may enable us to find safety or salvation. We are either to turn our backs on the world of fantasy, or to keep it under iron control; and we shall see those parts of life in which its force emerges – including art, literature and music – primarily as dangerous.

It is extremely difficult to do justice to this reaction even in a general way (and I shall not attempt the task of doing justice to Plato himself); since it contains, of course, much that is obviously true. Indeed, insofar as men can be simply *given* certain goods, it is entirely appropriate. In many areas of practical living – and one would be a fool to forget this – we may reasonably be content chiefly to preserve ourselves from dangerous error. Thus certain types of things may be achieved even in morality, as in other fields, by habit, 'will-power', obedience, the imitation of heroes, gods, etc.: a man could, I think, be just *told* in a fairly straightforward way to attend to some specific moral principles, and just *given* some such 'motivation' to act on them. This would enable him to avoid beating his wife or cheating his friends, though it would not enable him to love her or forgive them – unless, again, 'love' and 'forgive' are being used in a dehumanized sense. We may thus produce passable, perhaps in a sense even virtuous, people: no mean achievement.

There are, however, certain goods which cannot be given in this way: and the goods gained directly by learning – that is, knowledge and control – are in this class. Since these are (as we saw earlier) constituent of happiness, it seems mistaken for any educator to disregard them in favour of types of learning which are designed, in effect, simply to avoid trouble. Not that avoiding trouble, or getting the right things done, is unimportant: but the rational and 'auto- nomous' *doing* of the right things is equally important, so long as men are to remain men and not become robots or ants. For behind the idea of 'doing' lies the whole territory of intentions, reasons, appreci- ation, and that connection of our minds with the world which constitutes seriousness. If our chief concern is to get the right things done, our chief virtue will be obedience. One may learn to obey, however, not just in order to avoid making mistakes, but for the more positive purpose of coming to see for ourselves what is right or true.

The dangers of treating fantasy as an enemy emerge very clearly in Plato's views on aesthetics. If we did not know from external sources that he was only too sharply aware of the nature and power of poetry (among other arts), we should feel tempted to say that (in the *Republic* at least) he had no clear understanding of art *qua* art at all, or that he disregarded the whole area of purely *aesthetic* merit: certainly that he disregards the educational benefits of art for fear of its moral and political effects. They emerge also in the *Symposium*: if the result of this immensely charming book is to make one believe that what one should love is not people, but the Form of Beauty, something has gone badly wrong. A real person wants, and needs, to be loved for what he is (warts and all); this is something we know perfectly well when we are not dazzled. But they are almost equally apparent in his moral theory itself. He has to believe, for his purposes, both that the Form of the Good has some sort of solid existence independently of the desires of men – that it is *given* – and that the perception of it will motivate conduct; and this is, in effect, to deny or at least to distrust the substance of human wants and wishes.

The logical difficulties of such a moral theory have been clearly pointed out by other writers.[17] Here I want to make the more general point that Plato, along with others who react to the human condition in this way, fails to distinguish between the aspect in which fantasy has to be welcomed, and the aspect in which it has to be rejected. It has, of course, to be rejected *qua* irrational: that is, the desires, and the stories which connect desires in some kind of pattern, have to be brought up against the world as it actually is. This task is largely a matter of having a firm conscious grasp on what the original object and nature of the desires were, so that their targets can be changed in the light of that knowledge; one might say, a historical enquiry, as against the quasi-mathematical procedures by which Plato hoped to persuade us to leave 'the world of sights and sounds', the particular, behind us in our ascent towards the good.

There is indeed a sense in which we do, in fact, have to leave the world of childhood behind. The *objects* of our desires can be changed, though with great difficulty: very often we have to settle for our desires retaining at least a permanent shape (as one might say), even if we can become aware of more realities that may fit that shape. But what we cannot leave behind is the raw material, the *energy* or prescriptive force which resides in the desires. The point is that it resides nowhere else. This is not to deny that we can be moved by external considerations: but what makes the external considerations effective is that we see them as fulfilling, or echoing, or in some way *meeting* our desires. If they did not, they would be just so many meaningless *things*: as music is just so much noise to the uninitiated – that is, to those who can make no connection between their own desires and the sounds they hear.

Plato and his followers (who include many adherents of orthodox monotheism) must ultimately either deny the force, as they deny the reality, of human desires as they appear in each individual's early case-history: or else import something like a diabolical power to account for them. Either we interpret (as indeed was done in pre-Freudian eras) the child's passions as rather half-hearted attempts upon the world, lacking in force what they plainly lack in rationality: or else we accept their force, and ascribe them to the operations of Satan. This latter alternative at least paints a more consistent picture; but by extrapolating and hypostatizing goodness and badness in this way we gain nothing except a certain element of melodrama. The psychic energy remains where it was, and where it always must be: inside people. Such energy can be unlocked and redirected; but it cannot be produced to order, or magically reinforced from some external power-bestowing source. Not, again, that external things cannot encourage, calm, illuminate and inspire us: but we can take out of them only what we put in, and it is precisely how to get people to put enough in – how to get them to be serious – that we are discussing.

What is essentially the same reaction as Plato's comes out even more clearly in a contemporary author, Murdoch,[18] who gives an extremely accurate and effective description of the operation of fantasy. But her main positive thesis (as opposed to her admirable descriptions[19]) seems to incorporate the mistake of supposing that we can solve our problems (and hence presumably our pupils') in relation to fantasy by turning our gaze elsewhere – towards the Good (or God, or Reality, or whatever). It is a striking combination of facts that (a) many people interested in education agree that the general aim here is of immense importance, but (b) there is what looks like a very determined, if largely unconscious, resistance to doing anything about achieving it. Most contemporary practical projects under the heading of 'moral education', for instance, are not concerned with fantasy and the emotions, but with general discussion of controversial, often political problems (war, pollution, 'society', etc.): problems which, by having no clear solutions and being fairly far removed from any immediate concern of the individual pupil, cause no trouble or heart-aches. For the rest, the picture is still that pupils must be 'fed' from the outside: by the 'atmosphere' of the school, 'good examples', the practice of religion or other practices designed to 'build character', or (in some progressive quarters) various 'encounter-', 'therapy-', or drama-groups which for the most part are determinedly anti-cerebral. Not very many determined, hard-nosed and strictly analytical attempts are made to teach pupils about their own and other people's inner feelings.

Murdoch's thesis seems to bear the same latent contradiction. On the one hand she describes very convincingly the immense difficulty of seeing clearly, together with the projections, illusions, deceptions, and other devices of the self; there is an 'almost irresistible human tendency to seek consolation in fantasy', and 'Success in fact is rare.'[20] The natural conclusion to this would be to seek for causes and find techniques to remedy them: as she seems to say, 'Are there any techniques for the purification and reorientation of an energy which is naturally selfish?'[21] But what we are told to do, in fact, is to look *away* from the causes in the self, to attend to the Good outside. We are not given much argument for this, except 'It is an attachment to what lies outside the fantasy mechanism, and not a scrutiny of the mechanism itself, that liberates. Close scrutiny of the mechanism often merely strengthens its power.'[22]

This could be parodied as being rather like saying: 'If we're ill, don't let's study medicine, that merely makes us concentrate on our ailments; let's focus our gaze on supremely healthy people, or Health itself.' Unfairly parodied: but there is certainly a curious misconception, as well as a reasonable mistrust, of techniques which do focus on the self. Christian confession and self-examination are (oddly) not considered; but what she calls 'psychoanalysis' comes in for some predictably rough treatment. 'Why should some unspecified psychoanalyst be the measure of all things? Psychoanalysis is a muddled embryonic science' and so on[23] – as if any competent practising therapist regarded himself as 'the measure of all things' or indeed as a *scientist* at all in any relevant sense. Respectable psychotherapists, of whatever 'school' (many are of none), aim to do no more than assist the patient in precisely the task which Murdoch describes. The advantages they have for doing so are of a commonsense nature: a social context (the consulting room), a special role (the benevolent but detached 'neutral' other person), and special training (their own analysis and experience), all of which minimize the dangers of reinforcing (as against exploring and recognizing) the patient's fantasies. What we are talking about is a form of *education*.

The central point is that without some such techniques of exploration – and it is foolish to be put off by words like 'psychoanalysis', or its unfortunate but now thoroughly dated accretion of 'reductionist', 'scientific' or even 'clinical' imagery – we are left with nothing which, in respect of this problem, could be described as education. This is not to say, of course, that pupils cannot be strengthened, inspired, etc., by attending to what is outside their own minds (just as the body is by food); nor that pupils cannot be educated in other modes (the arts and sciences) by attending in this way (just as the body can by exercise). But if the presupposition is, as it must be, that we and our pupils are in some fundamental way ill, 'fallen', fantasy-ridden, or whatever, then any direct educational method – or, at least, any method that proceeds by improvement of the understanding in relation to the subject-matter – must take something like the form of psychotherapy. This involves (among other things) long, hard and above all *detailed* work. There are no short cuts.

We must avoid supposing, then, that fantasy is only relevant to anything that can properly be called 'education' as something to be firmly set aside in favour of belief: as an enemy. For not only does fantasy provide a great deal of motive power for becoming educated, but also the structure and quality of the fantasy is in various ways relevant to the kind of education the person will acquire. It is not just that some desire, as expressed in fantasy, is a useful piece of temporary 'motivation' towards education: e.g. I picture myself as a great healer, hence decide to become a doctor, hence am 'motivated' to learn medicine. The implication here is that the fantasy, having done its work, can be set aside in favour of some 'intrinsic' as against 'extrinsic' motivation.[24] There is a fairly sharply drawn difference, the story goes, between someone who is not really interested in (say) science or medicine in itself but just wants to acquire this knowledge for some external end – to become famous as a doctor – and someone who becomes genuinely interested in the subject. Of course we do distinguish in this way. But then we come across cases of people who we should have sworn were interested in something 'for itself', but who suddenly give the whole thing up for no very obvious reason: rather like someone who loses his faith. Does this mean that we should have sworn wrongly – is the criterion of 'being interested in something for its own sake' to be that *nothing* 'external' must check the person's interest? Or should we rather say that interest in X, while it may be more or less genuinely an interest in X *qua* X (rather than in some false picture of X), must be sustained by some desire or fantasy, perhaps unconscious?

Surely we should say the latter. Things, even interesting things which we see to be and find interesting, are not sources of motivation in themselves; they have to attract us, and to continue to attract us.

They may attract us as means to one sort of an end (science as a means to becoming a doctor and making money) or as a means to another sort (science as a means of expressing and/or sublimating our infantile curiosity about our own bodies, or whatever). We can say, if we like, that the former is an 'extrinsic' end, and deny that the means–end picture fits the latter case at all. But is it so simple? If it is true that we study science in order to gain some inner advantage – say, satisfied sexual curiosity – then why not call that a means–end relationship just as much as the other? And does not this 'inner'– 'external' distinction break down anyway – since money is only an advantage if it can buy things, and things only if they give us some 'inner' satisfaction? Certain things are indeed more publicly visible, and/or more universally felt as advantages: money, power, status, health, etc. We can call these 'standard interests' or 'external ends' if we want to. But this perhaps reflects only our state of psychological knowledge, or even our particular ('utilitarian'?) culture: not an absolute distinction.

There is a clear sense in which almost all our conscious motives, including whatever drives us to be guided by evidence and to be concerned for truth, are derivative. We find pleasure in certain subjects, art-forms, enquiries and so on because they symbolize something for us. One does not need to accept very specific Freudian stories about this (interest in the earth and geography equals interest in the mother's body, etc.). But we have to see the notion of an interest in something 'for its own sake' as in a way naive. We are not and could not be born being interested in things like geometry and history; and there is not some magical, pleasure-bestowing aura about them that wafts the spirit of enjoyment into our souls as soon as we know something about them. This is, if you like, no more than the truism that there is something in our case-histories which makes different enterprises pleasurable for different people. But to try to uproot all this from the past, by talking as if there were some feeling called 'love of truth' which springs fully armed like Athene from the head of Zeus, is to deny this truism. (The Greeks who wanted to enhance Athene's status tried to make just such a denial.)

Often we do not know, not even if we are expert neo-Freudians, why certain pupils get pleasurably attached to certain enterprises or subjects; certainly we cannot yet predict this in advance. But we have to allow for it. The reason why it is particularly important for the educator to allow for this, rather than for other types of motivation (e.g. the desire to get a better job, the desire to avoid punishment, etc.), is that this kind is *more* intimately connected with the enterprises themselves than other kinds are (if you like, more 'intrinsic'). Suppose, whether it is true or not, that the passion for maps and plans and terrain, curiously more common in our society among males than females, has its origins in a desire for exploration of the mother's body; well, this is as near as we can (logically) get to the 'motivational aspects' of an interest in geography 'for its own sake'. This is the inevitable material out of which our interest is made and sophisticated. If education involves getting pupils to have some sort of *abiding* care or concern for these enterprises, then this kind of motivation will clearly be more important to us than other kinds.

This suggests that what we might call the *image* of the enterprise is very important: not only the logical types of questions posed in the various forms of thought, but the symbols involved with the subject-matter. This is clear in games: the popularity of chess, or even Monopoly, is partly dependent on the symbols and tokens used. The *glamour* of the subject counts. However, we want it to count not as an auxiliary ('extrinsic') addition, but as something which sustains and renders magnetic the subject itself; thus the glamour of learning Greek is not displayed by presenting pupils with pictures of a gleaming Parthenon, but (if at all) by presenting them with the complexities and (for some) enticing involvements of the Greek language itself. Similarly it is one thing to find literature or music attractive *per se*: quite another to be interested in the 'socially' relevant novel, or the latest pop tunes. Educators are not clear about what glamour there may be in subjects or forms of thought: this is partly because we have not looked at them very closely (being largely distracted by romantic fantasies of our own), and partly because we do not know enough psychology. But it would bear thinking about.

One implication for educational practice is clear. We shall plainly have to give these images a chance to work: we shall have to present pupils with the various enterprises in the right sort of way if they are to have a chance of responding to them and attaching their unconscious feelings to them. It ought to be possible to give most pupils some idea of *what it is like to* learn various Xs at quite a young age. I do not say that it is possible to get them to *know* very much about these Xs: but that is not the point. Thereafter a strong if not necessarily overwhelming argument exists for allowing pupils to pursue those enterprises to which they are genuinely attached. For the importance of this kind of motivation (if they are to be educated, rather than just told a few facts or made socially viable) is so great that it should override most of what is said about 'specialization', 'the curriculum' and so on.[25]

But this is merely one instance of the way in which these general considerations about seriousness and fantasy bear on practical education. If we take these considerations seriously at all and wish to explore our third option (that of trying to deal with the difficulties of human beings *qua* learners in a more direct way), we have to reflect more widely on what sort of posture or attitude educators should in practice adopt. General terms like 'posture' or 'attitude' are appropriate at this stage, to prevent us from talking too quickly about specific 'aims', 'content', 'context', 'methods', 'motivation', 'preconditions' and the like – words constantly used by philosophers of education and educationalists in general, but the meanings of which are extremely unclear. We have especially to reflect on those *concepts* which seem important; for these will largely determine our attitude and render it effective. In particular, I shall argue (ch. 7), we need the idea or ideas marked by 'love'.

Before concluding, however, I ought perhaps to make it clear that I am not here attempting any general 'theory of motivation'. I am not sure, indeed, whether such a thing is logically possible, or what it would look like. If it were possible, it would certainly have to include much that has been said by psychologists (1) about the 'intrinsic' types of motivation (commonly referred to under titles like 'mastery' or 'competence'), and (2) about the social factors involved (parental and peer-group attitudes, for instance) and their relation to the individual's self-esteem. I do in fact believe that all or most of these are best understood against the kind of psychic background I have tried, too briefly, to sketch: that is, the idea of the child as a *conceptualizing* agent who is not just 'motivated' in some brute way, but who sees things *sub specie boni alicuius* and whose emotions and motives make sense only in terms of the ideas, fantasies and other pictures that structure his conscious and unconscious mind. On these basic or primal features, contingent social conditions and other such factors work in many different (and in some respects important) ways: but the fundamental material is given, and often receives a shape well before any such contingent factors come into play.

Be that as it may (and one major problem is to determine how far we are dealing with conceptual, and how far with empirical, truths in this area): I have stressed this aspect of the matter because it is certainly *one* centrally important aspect, which has received too little attention both from philosophers and from educators. The same holds, remarkably enough, for the (even more obvious and basic) notion of love, which is closely connected with the picture I have tried to present, and to which we shall now turn.

# 7   Love and morality

In this final chapter we face our third question, the question of whether we can establish any specific aims as priorities in practical education. Although most of what I shall say about this follows from what we have already noticed in earlier chapters, different parts or aspects of it can be classified under two headings, in a way that it may be helpful to make clear in advance.

There is, first, the task of generating what seems to be required by the form of the enterprise – that is, by any kind of education whatever the content may be: namely, as we have seen, the task of making some rather more *direct* attempt to increase our pupils' seriousness. I have given reasons for regarding this task as crucially important; and although it is extremely difficult to specify with any exactitude *how* it is to be achieved (for one thing, many of the questions are empirical), I shall try to show that it requires both a certain kind of context and a certain kind of content. Second, and here taking for granted whatever seriousness we *can* generate, there seems to be one particular area of life which we particularly want pupils to be serious *about*. 'Morality', if taken in a sufficiently broad sense, is as good a name for this area as any; I shall describe the area in more detail, and give reasons for its unique importance. These two priorities are not logically on a par with each other: the first enters into the second, and much that we say about the first will also apply to the second. Nevertheless, the distinction may be useful.

We have already seen the conceptual connection between seriousness and happiness; and the connection appears even closer if we bring in the idea of love, which may be used to re-describe or thicken out our overall justification both for the general enterprise of education, and for particular items of educational content. At first sight, this idea may seem to do no more than restate points already made here and elsewhere. Thus loving something is very like, or perhaps the same as, Peters' 'caring' for it, or 'being on the inside' of it, or being 'committed' to it. Love involves both seeing things straight and taking pleasure in them, thus bridging the gap between heedless 'play' and unpleasurable 'toil' (to use one author's vocabulary[1]). Add pleasure to seriousness in respect of the same object of attention, and we can bring in all the terms like 'appreciate', 'enjoy for its own sake', and so on. But this condition, or state of mind, has to be seen as justifiable in a stronger sense, and not only in relation to education or items of educational content. It is not, or not only, that a life of 'love' or 'cherishing' is on the whole the best for human beings, or the noblest ideal, or the wisest policy for keeping us humane and civilized, or the only way to avoid the extremisms of uncaring enjoyment and joyless toil.[2] The point is rather that the apparent alternatives are the alternatives of fantasy, and ultimately display conceptual incoherence. 'Love' describes the only possible mode in which sentient beings, who have of necessity to sublimate their initial desires, can successfully – that is, both pleasurably and realistically – relate to the world. In this light, the term may act as a criterion, or indeed a description, of 'happiness'.

The word 'love' will make many of us think at once of loving or being in love with a *person*; and the *reciprocity* of personal love fills an important gap in the kind of justification usually advanced by philosophers. Whether in the light of some criterion like 'happiness' or in some other light, one may fairly object to the one-sidedness of question-forms supposed to be basic, such as 'What ought I to do?', 'Why do this rather than that?', or 'What sort of activities should I engage in?' The forms imply that the emphasis must fall only or chiefly on *my doing* something, rather than having things done to or for me. Even push-pin has it in common with poetry that both are forms of doing something. The man in the street would more naturally make his point not by contrasting one kind of activity with another, but by contrasting the absorption or ingestion of pleasure (food, drink, etc.) with various kinds of striving or achievement. There is a long philosophical tradition which gives an absolute priority to the choosing or reasoning agent; even though, developmentally speaking, human beings start their lives in a more passive or receptive role, so that one might reasonably suppose that questions of the form 'What do I get out of it?' or 'What's in it for me?' are just as basic. With love, this point is less easy to miss; the lover wants to be loved back. This is not a matter of the social convenience, as one might call it, of A liking B to gain B's ends and B liking A to gain A's; nor of the adult rationality implied by such terms as 'respect for persons'. It is better described as a paradigm case of a basic and inevitable conception – the idea of giving and receiving pleasure from a being like oneself – having hope of permanent fulfilment in the real world. This is not, of course, to deny a certain reciprocity in the love of other objects; it is more or less 'rewarding' to love art, or mathematics, or old furniture, or cats – indeed, to love anything. But the reciprocity here is obviously different, and on many counts perhaps less satisfactory.

Without the idea of love the notion of happiness, which we used above (p. 143), may appear naive. If terms like 'caring' and 'appreciating' play down the importance of pleasure and of 'getting something out of it', so too terms like 'happiness' and 'pleasure' may miss something of the quality of love-objects, the *kind* of thing we 'get out of' them. For, in the case of sentient and (inevitably) repressed creatures, these objects will be largely symbolic; and they will have the magnetism and distinctive sweetness of symbolic objects, which is importantly different from the 'natural' sweetness of chocolate. 'Love' is sufficiently near 'in love' to remind us, at least, of the Greek *eros*. It is the objects of this love, or this sort of love, that we have to marry up with the real world. As we have seen, it is inevitably something of a struggle to make such marriages; but it is the only coherent policy for human beings.

In this light the notion of love does, I think, expand or sophisticate the criterion of success that we need, when as educators we face questions about what sort of (and how much) education to give to various pupils. For it now appears naive to regard these questions as calling for some admixture or balancing of two dissociated 'values' – 'seriousness' or the 'theoretic' life on the one hand, and the 'natural' pleasures or enjoyment on the other. For pure 'seriousness' or 'toil' would ultimately have no point without the pleasure which is one aspect of love; and equally, purely 'natural' enjoyment is not possible for human beings, at least above the level of mere sensation – some degree of conceptualization and sublimation always creeps in. The two aspects of love are separable only in theory. Hence it would be absurd to represent our answers as compromises; as if pupils required a dollop of 'seriousness' and a dollop of 'pleasure', to be mixed up anyhow; or as if it were possible to have *too much* of either ingredient. We ought rather to ask, in each particular case, 'What can this person be brought to love?' Provided that we keep in mind the conceptual inevitabilities that form the background of human love, this question is perhaps some improvement on 'What will make this person happy?'

This background may also prevent us from raising and answering too quickly the dangerous question 'What things are most worth loving?' (analogous to 'What things most make for happiness?' or 'What activities are most worth while?'). For this is like asking 'If we could bring up people who really were able to love, who constantly made a successful marriage between their fantasies and the real world, and who were not liable to projection, denial, self-deception and the other devices which at present cripple us – if we could do this, as now we cannot, what would such people turn their attention to?' To this there are only two sensible answers. First, we do not (usually) know: and second, it does not (much) matter. Here perhaps the model case of loving a person may again help us. A man who cannot relate to and love a woman, for example, is not helped by answering the question 'What sorts of women are most worth loving?' He is helped by being made more able to love. If and when he becomes able, we may still not be able to predict what sort of woman he would choose; and, in one important way at least, it does not matter whom he chooses – or, if you like, his ability to love (which includes the prudence and understanding involved in the 'seriousness' of love) will choose the right woman for him. Both from the strictly philosophical and – perhaps more clearly – from the educator's point of view, it is better to concentrate on improving the capacities for choice by improving the ability to love than to offer set answers about the 'best sort of life' or the 'most worth-while activities'. Perhaps all we can do – but it is a lot – is to try to understand people a bit better, and offer or present to them such love-objects as our present understanding suggests may suit them: these two moves in themselves being part of the process of increasing their ability to love.

This is not, of course, to deny *sense* to the idea that some things (people, activities, works of art, etc.) are more 'worth loving' than others. But, first, it is to point to the danger of *starting* with this idea; consider how much we rely on mothers *not* asking which children – or even which of their own children – are 'most worth loving'. Here the notion of everything being equally lovable (as it appears, for instance, in Christian or Buddhist writing) is not as silly as it may sound. Second, it is to suggest that, if we must find arguments for this being more worthy of love than that, little is gained by overall assertions to the effect that the former is 'less boring' or gives more 'rich opportunities' than the latter. For a great deal depends on whether this or that *fits* the conscious and unconscious character-istics of the person who loves; and not only may this vary from one person to another, but also a person good at loving may (so to speak) extract much from a 'boring' object that a person bad at loving cannot extract even from a 'rich' one – and here the infinity-in-a-grain-of-sand, eternity-in-an-hour idea that everything is interesting is not silly either.

1 First, then, and taking up from where we left off in the last chapter, what has to be done if we are to make a more direct and determined effort to deal with fantasy, increase seriousness, and

improve the basic capacity to love? We have already seen that this basic capacity or ability may – indeed, that it must – be acquired by learning. Loving X is like being serious about X in that it involves a clear understanding of what X actually is, and some kind of attachment – a pleasurable attachment, if it is love rather than just seriousness – to X as thus understood. In discussing seriousness, we suggested that to describe the difficulties of understanding various Xs merely, or even chiefly, as a lack of *information* was naive. The position is rather that we are blinded by, or blind ourselves with, fantasy and egocentric feeling in general; and I have tried to show why this is inevitable for human beings (pp. 175 ff.). It follows, then, that we can only come to love by developing understanding: that is, by learning. Nor is it only that we can: we must, since understanding is not something which can be simply *given* to us, or which somebody else can do for us. It further follows that the relevant kind of understanding is primarily – I do not say wholly – the understanding of ourselves; because, again, the main problem is not that we do not see enough of the outside world, but rather that we see it wrong.

Here, however, we seem to face a paradox: if our pupils (to put it briefly) are to learn how to love, must they not already be able to love – or at least to be serious about – whatever that learning may involve? How can one learn to be serious, if one is not already serious enough to do the learning? This is not, of course, a vicious circle, provided that we have *some* capacity to love or some seriousness to begin with; and fortunately all or nearly all human beings are in this position (one might even count this as a necessary condition for being human). We are suggesting only that whatever seriousness and powers of paying attention they do actually possess should be to some extent redeployed: that they should pay more attention to these qualities in themselves, and perhaps less attention to things outside.

But the apparent paradox is not without interest. It is worth noting, first, that the initial development of any seriousness or capacity to love at all remains, indeed, extremely mysterious, despite the best efforts of psychologists. If we knew more about this, we might be able to do more for education by improving the child's early experiences than by anything we could later. We should, as it were, have much more basic capital to work with, instead of the meagre amount that we now have in later childhood and adult life. Indeed, it is tolerably clear that most of what we can do later on will necessarily be a matter of *recouping* losses sustained earlier. Second, and for connected reasons, it is often very unclear just *where* a person's seriousness and love may lie: at what points he is in pleasurable contact with the real world, and what points he is distorting the world or deceiving himself. (Many of us put up a very good pretence of seriousness and love in relation to all sorts of things.) We want to know just what there is in each pupil which is solid enough to build on. Until we can answer some of these questions, what we do will inevitably be a very hit-and-miss affair.

There is also a third point which emerges from the paradox, and which has to be accepted. Something must *constitute* 'learning how to love': there must be some content to the process, something which we want the pupils to pay attention to and take seriously. We have to accept the fact that teaching people to love or be serious in *general* must involve their loving (or at least being serious about) certain *particular* things: that is, those things which we judge will increase the general capacity. But it is extremely difficult to state with any clarity or precision just what these particular things are: partly for lack of empirical knowledge, but partly also because it is hard to draw here those distinctions which we use in clearer cases (as for instance between 'methods' and 'content').

We shall find it better to begin by considering the essential background for any kind of learning in a more general way. Here the notion of personal love again seems crucially important. Human infants and children build up their selves, their preferred pleasures and their activities in the context of other *people* – their parents or parent-figures. This seems to be a conceptual point, not just a contingent one: a child could not become fully human except in such a context. Just as the child is initiated into human language by other humans, so other humans are necessary both as the foci and as the mediating agencies for the child's desires and conceptions.[3] That just *is* the child's world; and it would have to be like that for any entity which had any hope of growing up to be sentient or rational. There is a certain logical primacy about people both as love-objects and as the mediators of love.

This world is also primarily or basically a physical one. By 'basically' I do not of course mean that loving a person can be reduced or translated into physical terms: nor that the physical aspects are from all points of view the most important: nor even (though this may be true) that they form a model or paradigm for other aspects of love. I refer to the necessary truths that people are physical entities, and that growing creatures (children) inevitably begin by confronting people as such entities; so that the rest of the child's experience will necessarily be built on or out of – or at least take its points of departure from – these physical aspects. (It is for this reason that specific stories about the mother's breast, the child's body and so on are worth taking seriously: whether or not any particular story is thought to be correct.)

There is an important connection here with the notion of *belonging*, which is bound up with loving and being loved. In considering seriousness, we noted one feature of loving or taking an interest in something 'for its own sake' – namely, that the thing is seen clearly for what it is, uncorrupted by our own projections or illusions. But there is another feature especially relevant to educators and all those whose jobs involve personal or parental relationships. To be loved for one's own sake need not suggest to us a picture whereby some of one's attributes count as part of 'oneself' (intelligence, kindness) and others do not (birth, wealth), so that one is loved 'for oneself' when the former qualities are loved and not when the latter are. Apart from the difficulties in deciding whether certain attributes are to count as 'inside' or 'outside' (what about one's appearance or physique, for instance?), we are clear that we do not want to be loved for *any* of our *attributes*.[4] Unsurprisingly and inevitably, in view of our experience as children, we want to be loved by the other as belonging to him or her, whatever our attributes may be or may come to be. Parents love their children because they are theirs; if you like, because they are extensions of themselves.

This sense of belonging (for which 'possessiveness' is too loaded a word and 'concern' too vague) is what enables the child to steer his way through the passionate and uncertain world of childhood towards the maturity of himself being able to love in the same way: and, again unsurprisingly, it is what enables the patient under psychotherapy to do the same. Whether they choose to concern themselves with it or not, teachers work against a similar background; and their ability to feel and show that their pupils 'belong' is hence of crucial importance, not only in itself but as a necessary precondition for other aspects of education. (Obviously relevant notions here include such things as physical warmth and contact, the exchange of food and drink, the importance of what one might call 'cosiness' in topological arrangements, and so on: precisely those things, perhaps, which are conspicuous by their absence in a great many schools today.)

Whether or not a large part of happiness will *consist* in what are (rather odiously) called 'personal relationships' is not now in question; though one might not unreasonably be suspicious of the person who claimed to be happy without taking some deep delight in other people, if only for the reasons Aristotle advanced.[5] The point here is, more simply, that the ability to love something (anything) is required for happiness of any kind; and that, because of the (inexpellable) facts which govern our growth or upbringing as people, this learning will necessarily involve 'personal relationships'. We need a mediating person who will not only introduce us to possible love-objects, but help us to shake free of the fantasies and distortions of perception which prevent us from viewing those objects in the right way. We cannot negotiate all this by ourselves: if we could, we would not be human beings but angels.[6] It is not only that we are unlikely to see ourselves clearly except via the insight and perception of another person, but that the process of overcoming fantasy in favour of reality is psychologically (not just intellectually) difficult. We are trying to replace a whole world, which very powerful motives have forced us to adopt hitherto, with another which may be ultimately better, but which (if only because it is strange) will certainly be alarming. To do this requires not only hard work and patience: it also requires courage. Hence we need somebody on our side, somebody who loves us and will help us to find the necessary strength.

Here again it would be possible to describe things in a certain kind of language, that of the psychiatric or psychotherapeutic encounter. We could talk of 'resistances', 'the transference', and so on; and point out that the psychotherapist has to act not only as a source of information and insight (much of that the patient could get from text-books), but also as somebody who is concerned for the patient in at least a semi-parental fashion. But this is just one case – perhaps an unusually clear one – of a general principle. We might equally well consider parental love, or the language and practices of certain religions. It is not for nothing that most believers are asked to consider themselves as *children* of God: that self-analysis and the confessional are religious practices: and that Christians are supposed to love Christ 'because he first loved us'. (There is a wealth of meaning in that 'because'.) Indeed most effective religions, or other such outlooks, gain their force from reproducing or generalizing on a large scale – in the grand manner, so to speak – those principles which affect each of us in his individual case-history as a human being.

If – though even the idea may be somewhat corrupting – we think of love as a form of 'motivation', it is not hard to see why the mediation of the loving parent (teacher, educator) is essential. Here Peters' model of 'initiation into public forms' or 'worth-while activities' is appropriate. It is not so much that the initiator stands as a shining example to be admired and imitated by the pupils; for unless they have some other kind of contact with him, they will (a) hardly know what he is a shining example of, or what mode of activity they are to imitate, and (b) have no particular incentive for following the example. The kind of contact or imitation required is some form of shared enjoyment, and the classic case is the parent *playing* with the child (this is one reason, perhaps the most important,

why games-playing may be educationally important as a paradigm).
The child is 'motivated', not just by the 'intrinsic' pleasure of the
activity (which would not be apparent to him unless mediated by
the parent), nor just by some 'extrinsic' parental pressure (admiration, fear, etc.), but because the parent *enjoys the activity with him.*

In order for this to work, the child has to see the parent (teacher,
etc.) as loving him and as having good things to dispense to him
personally (idiosyncratically). Without the conscious or unconscious
thought 'You are my child and belong to me, and this is a good
thing I'd like to give to you and share with you', some shadow of
corruption enters the activity; and it is then that we would most
naturally find ourselves talking of some 'motivation' dredged up for
a particular 'task'. The corruption may take many forms: hero-
worship, anxiety to please, or the more obvious kinds of reward and
punishment. By contrast, the activity is viewed in its own right and
becomes its own reward – in a sense, becomes part of the child –
only insofar as it is incorporated into the child via the parent's love;
very much, to quote the psychoanalysts, as the child's attitude to
food will partly depend on his infantile experiences at the mother's
breast. In education such sharing and giving is necessarily metaphorical; but the metaphor is important.

This aspect of love goes further than those attitudes discussed by
philosophers under such headings as 'respect' and 'friendship' or even
'sympathy' and 'benevolence'. If we compare, for instance, the
vivid accounts in Plato[7] of the educational power of love with what
modern authors put under the (already over-clinical) heading of
'personal relationships', we can hardly avoid feeling that something
has been omitted. Such authors characteristically raise two basic
difficulties. First, there is the fear that love will interfere with the
particular duties and 'role-relationships' which teachers and pupils
have to each other: love may be a useful addition, as it were, but
involves dangers of favouritism. This emerges clearly in:

> within the sphere of teachers' and pupils' duties, affection can
> add extra motivation for doing what in any case ought to be
> done and thus far is a good thing. But undue affection, if felt
> for some and not others, can make teachers or pupils *partial.*[8]

Second, there is the connected notion that 'affection cannot be
produced at will' ('such attractions are particularized and cannot be
commanded', 'friendship, as distinct from the friendly behaviour we
have just been discussing, is not something that can be produced to
order', and so on).[9]

Both objections fail; ultimately for the same reason, which may
appear most easily in an example. Suppose I am a housemaster in

charge of a large group of children. Then it is clear that I may do the job badly because I have favourites, and because I find some children hard to love; but it is equally clear that, if I did not see myself primarily in something like a parental position to them and them as my 'family', I should not be seriously attempting the job at all. So I should work away, with my colleagues or my psychiatrist or with the pupils themselves, at trying to overcome my deficiencies: at trying to love them all. Depending on my intellect and temperament, I might find it easier or harder to do well at this task – loving – than at satisfying those demands commonly supposed to be more 'under the control of the will': respect, friendly behaviour, justice, and so on.

The mistake is to classify love as a *pathos* rather than a *praxis*, as if it were like being struck by lightning or lumbago; and then to consider other *praxeis* only under watered-down headings like 'friendship' or 'respect'. Thus Hirst and Peters say of the teacher and his pupils: 'There is no requirement, for instance, that he should like or love all of them', so that we are immediately up in arms, feeling perhaps that teachers ought to love all their pupils: but they immediately continue: 'in so far as love denotes an a-rational attraction and is distinct from respecting them as persons'.[10] But we do not want either of these alternatives.

Nor, again, do we want the interpretation sometimes put on notions marked by 'charity', 'benevolence', 'agape' and so on: that is, an impersonal feeling of good will. We want the feeling to be personal ('directed to the idiosyncratic self'). Of course this places practical limits on love, since we cannot (in this sense) love people whom we do not know; but it is a *praxis* that can be indefinitely extended. It is not absurd that Christ should have commanded that we love one another in this sense; we obey the command chiefly by trying to *see* the other person in a favourable light, and also by trusting him, understanding him, sharing with him, putting ourselves in his shoes, and so on. At the least, it would be a sign of a serious attempt to love if one acknowledged failure in particular cases, and tried to negotiate it: I mean, for instance, of the housemaster (father, husband, etc.) *admitted* to various attractions or repulsions, and tried to improve the situation by some kind of discussion or inter-action with the pupils concerned. 'You get on my nerves and I get on yours', if it is intended to lead to 'Let's try to improve things between us', can be a genuine, if embryonic, expression of love: 'I like you and you like me' is, as it stands, no more than *égoisme à deux*.

We also feel, perhaps, a more justifiable fear of institutionalizing opportunities for love in the wrong way. Certainly we have to beware of the determinedly vague, over-contrived, and often grotesque contexts that are fashionable nowadays; but this is no excuse for not taking the task seriously and giving *some* adequate shape to it. Our ideas here are sometimes incoherent or positively contradictory: thus Hirst and Peters say that the value of personal relationships 'certainly does not require, for instance, that they should be ringed round with a halo and put on the curriculum! The point is, surely, that they arise more or less spontaneously in the context of communal activities'[11] – which suggests that we do not have to organize them all. On the other hand 'a degree of emotional involvement with people of a more intimate sort is necessary before people can discover much of importance both about themselves and about others'[12] – and obviously if this is to go on between teachers and pupils in any significant way, it has to be organized or catered for. Some institutions, for instance, simply do not allow *space* (or time) for such involvement; and few even consider it seriously as an educational aim.

It is true that we may too easily be tempted to list certain items of content, or certain methods and techniques, in a way which disconnects them from the background. If we ask 'What is it, specifically, that parents do when they so arrange things that their children learn to love?', it would not be absurd to answer that, in one sense, they may not 'do' anything specific – they just love their children. The love they have for them runs through all the activities which they enjoy together: the children learn to trust the parents, and to enjoy what the parents share with them. Whatever the parents themselves naturally enjoy and value for its own sake will be an adequate 'content', and the sharing an adequate 'method'; indeed if the parents insincerely pretended to a particular interest, the love would necessarily be lacking. What the children gain here is not so much special types of knowledge and understanding, but a general attitude or outlook; they come to feel, in the light of what their parents do for and with them, that the world is lovable, and that they can love it. But we have still to distinguish here between spontaneity and genuineness. It would be odd if parents who genuinely loved and cared for their children did not often act spontaneously with them; but it would be equally odd if they did not also make regular provisions and plans with them and for them – indeed, we should then suspect that they did not really care for them at all. Nor need our suspicions be more aroused if some of those plans are geared to a more direct approach to the task of learning to love.

The difficulty that we feel here is partly caused (and partly reflected) by the present lack, at least in 'pluralist' societies, of any widely accepted or traditional arrangements of this kind, and the consequent problem of describing such arrangements without the impression of artificiality; a difficulty which is largely absent if a particular social group happens to share some fairly clear and distinctive ideal or religion. A Christian or Communist school, for instance, would naturally consider and practise the task of learning to love in the setting of a particular language and environment; there would be talk of God or the Party, the Bible or Marx: and then there would flow from this, in an entirely natural way, certain specific practices – religious assemblies, Party meetings for self-criticism, the confessional, prayer groups, and so forth. It would then seem strange if some at least of these were *not* 'ringed round with a halo and put on the curriculum'. On the other hand, the isolated mention of practices under such titles as 'psychotherapy', 'group dynamics', 'counselling' and so forth, and the use of such general terms as 'techniques', 'social skills', and even 'methods', can hardly fail to suggest something far too contrived, *ad hoc*, and (in a debased sense) 'utilitarian'.

This difficulty is, at root, the same as that which we encountered above (p. 196) and which we shall meet again later when considering 'morality' (p. 219). We find it immensely hard to achieve any kind of psychological security – one might say, any feeling that either the outer world or our own inner world is 'solid' or 'real' – except by putting our money on some highly *particularized* ideal or outlook: in effect, by adding to those worlds another world which has its own separate language, values and ontology. This may, though it need not, take the form of some overt ideology, or religion, or other kind of 'ism'; but the crucial question is how far we are prepared to bet on *ourselves* rather than on some illusion or projection which appears to do most of the work for us. General terms like 'reasonable', 'sane', 'serious', and even 'loving' are apt to sound bloodless; but if we can feel as secure with them as we now feel with our partisan terminology – 'God', 'the Party', 'liberation', or whatever – the apparent difficulty of working out particular methods and practices will largely disappear.

There is a constant pull from these partisan positions; hence in considering particular methods or items of content, our first duty is to avoid doctrinaire adherence to some *one* particular method or subject-matter. As with moral education, one would naturally think in terms of a whole range or dimension of methods and techniques, with the more 'abstract' or 'academic' at one end and the more 'real' or 'lifelike' at the other. Thus (purely for the sake of example) it seems reasonable to suggest that a fairly hard-headed intellectual study of the emotions themselves would be profitable, particularly if conjoined with and related to the actual feeling and expression of these emotions in a more natural context. Somewhere in between we might locate such things as the study of literature, discussion, role-playing, the use of films, and video-tape, drama, and various kinds of 'therapy groups'. I have discussed all this more fully elsewhere;[13] here I am only anxious to show that the subject-matter does indeed exist. The trouble is, in fact, that it is too vast and heterogeneous for us to handle effectively at present; we need a much more effective taxonomy of its various aspects, which would enable us to pronounce more judiciously on what particular objectives are achieved by what particular methods.

It may be helpful (if only to avoid one common misconception) to suggest another range or dimension, marking one end by some term like 'enlightenment' and the other by 'habit-forming' or 'training'. For there are certain features of love, as of seriousness, which are amenable to training – often of a fairly tough-minded and impersonal kind. Some people, perhaps misled by a sentimentalist notion of love, talk as if the ways of learning to love were exhaustively described by such terms as 'sympathy', 'concern', 'enlightenment', 'empathy', 'non-directive guidance' and so forth. But this is clearly wrong. There are certain *rules* which one who loves, or is trying to learn to love, will obey. Many of these have to do with paying attention: for instance, listening carefully to what other people say. One can be trained to do this, just as one can be trained in other ways to be honest about what one feels and careful about what one says. Habits may be formed which will keep at bay, if only temporarily, the pressures of internal fantasy or the more obvious pressures of the external world (the peer-group, 'fashion', 'authority', and so on). Thoughtfulness and self-discipline in reflection and action may be induced by constant practice or even by a form of conditioning.

This is not to deny, however, that – so far as this particular objective is concerned – such training and habit-forming are best seen as facilitating the task of learning to love, not as logically central to it. For the core of seriousness and loving, as we saw above (p. 190), involves the person's own desires; we have to *use* and *direct* these, together with the prescriptivity for action that is inherent in them, rather than simply train them. This does not make the training less important; without it, the person would often not know *how to address* the task of learning to love. But unless the person himself, at some stage (I do not say at the initial stage), comes to value the training and habits that are conducive to love, they become hollow: almost certainly, since he does not see them as *his* but as imposed on him, he will resent them; and this at once sets up a conflict of desires which militates against the success of the whole enterprise. We face here a problem with no determinate solution: to put it in a rather technical way, the problem of how to preserve prescriptivity along with rationality (see pp. 230 ff.).

In this task we have, indeed, a 'subject-matter', which might be described under various titles ('the emotions', 'our unconscious feelings', 'personal knowledge', 'psychology', and so forth); but it is important to conceive of what we do wholly in terms of those expectations which the word 'subject' is likely to arouse in us and our pupils. Thus Peters quite rightly says that subjects 'such as literature, history, geography, branches of psychology and social science, human biology, classics and games' might be thought to contribute importantly to 'interpersonal understanding' and hence to 'mental health', but that 'there is no research which shows that the humanities do in fact have any influence of this sort'; adding 'But neither is there much evidence to suggest that they are often taught with the development of interpersonal understanding as one of their main objectives.'[14] We are bound to grant, as the phrase 'interpersonal understanding' suggests, that pupils should know some facts about themselves and other people; and (perhaps even more important) that they should be familiar with proper or relevant processes of acquiring such facts. But the crux is whether these facts and methodologies are *used* outside the classroom; and this involves the development of powers of the mind which are not necessarily developed by the subjects themselves (though they may be). We may want to know whether this or that subject increases certain qualities in the pupil that could be described as 'serious-ness'; but it is difficult to see how a 'subject' as such can be a plausible candidate. Nor is it sufficient to talk of 'the way in which the subject is taught'. We are naturally driven to think of it in a different sort of way.

The whole business is much more a matter of getting the pupils genuinely involved in certain kinds of interaction (the partial analogy of a game is useful here); and there is something to be said about the supreme importance of some of these kinds. It is clear that we cannot properly investigate and understand our own feelings (nor those of others) except with the help of other people, and by paying attention both to what we and others *say*, and the (non-verbal) expressions of what we and they feel. We have, then, a rough model of a basic context and content (whatever variations of it we may adopt) in which the importance of *paying attention* and *describing* is paramount. I do not deny the importance of other aspects: for instance, of gaining some general or *theoretical* grasp of the emotions from academic study, or (at the other end of the scale) of actually coming to *have* certain feelings – that is, of allowing them to enter one's consciousness. But a very large part of the job is a matter of *interpreting* the data: identifying and making sense of the raw material of emotion which is, as it were, sloshing around in ourselves and others in an inchoate and unformulated way. It seems clear that we already have available a number of techniques and methods for getting pupils involved in this process, and for improving their competence in such matters; rather than discuss them at greater length, I will refer the reader to some of the literature.[15]

Having said all this, I do not for a moment deny that (at least in the present state of our knowledge) it will still be very much a matter of trial and error. What still seems to count in this business is the way in which familiarity with certain people, or certain contexts, or certain subjects, may (or may not) change one's life. It is easy to say this, but extremely difficult even to specify possibly relevant factors. Consider the Socratic dialogues: we should be hard put to it to assess the comparative importance of (a) the nature of the 'philosophy' itself, (b) the personality of Socrates, (c) the social context of the operation, and (d) the manner of teaching and learning. This is an example of a situation where something of genuine educational importance happens, at least to some people (a situation still very rare, of a type which most educational systems do not even try to cater for); and even here a Cephalus will go away laughing to the sacrifices, a Thrasymachus will become angry and sulk, a Critias will bide his time and turn murderous. *Behind* the facts, the methodologies, and the 'subjects' lies this largely unexplored emotional hinterland.

How much of what we do, then, should in fact be given (whether in schools or universities or outside them) impressive titles like 'philosophy' or 'psychotherapy' is perhaps ultimately important only because certain public standards and procedures, which act as defences against autistic fantasy, are attached to such titles. But at certain stages even these defences are inadequate, and offer an escapism of their own. It is impossible, I think, to lay down rules about this: there are times when we can identify cases of a person just 'going through the motions' or the ritual of the activity, opposite cases of a person throwing public standards to the winds, and (rare) cases when something real seems to happen. Equally difficult is to distinguish between the aspect of muddle or bewitchment that is apparent to the philosopher as it emerges in language, and the aspect that appears to the psychotherapist as it emerges in grosser behaviour or symptoms. But these are the paradigm situations in which men try – as in a way they always try – to pull themselves up by their own bootstraps, so to speak: situations in which the avowed aim is to reflect rationally, not only upon the world, but upon their own irrationality in looking at the world and describing it and responding to it. What I have tried to bring out can only be, at best, a sort of philosophical prelude to much more detailed conceptual and empirical work on the structural and other arrangements necessary for schools and other educational institutions.

2 Second, there is the question of what things we want our pupils to love in particular: what we especially want them to learn, pay attention to, be serious about, and if possible to take pleasure in. This is, of course, the question with which educational writers usually begin; but our delay in answering it will, I hope, now seem at least partially justified. For I have claimed, in effect, that if only we can succeed in producing people who have the basic capacity, more than half the battle will be won. Once again: it is not so much that we are focusing our vision on the wrong objects, but that there is something wrong with our vision. One might be tempted to say that, given a reasonable amount of clear-sightedness, the pupils themselves will soon know what it is important for them to look at. But that is certainly going too far; for one thing, even if our pupils eventually do turn out in that way, they will rightly blame us if we have not directed their attention, during their less serious nonage, to the appropriate objects. Moreover, we are still left – whether as pupils or teachers – with the question of what things a serious and loving person would, in fact, devote particular attention to.

There are also fairly obvious reasons why the educator cannot restrict his concern to developing the capacity alone; for one important way in which the capacity to love must be developed is, precisely, by loving something. To take a parallel: in order to keep our bodies in trim we need not only to make sure that they receive enough vitamins and calories, and are free from some inner disease, but also to exercise them, which usually involves some kind of learning. We learn to run, or play golf, or climb mountains, or whatever. It is not necessary to think that there is something good *per se* in particular forms of exercise; though it may be that different people find a special pleasure in one or another form, and that those forms which are in some sense most demanding may afford more opportunities for such pleasure. The point is rather that exercise of some kind is necessary both for enjoying our bodies and for keeping them healthy. In much the same way, it is not (and could never be) enough simply to bring up children who are capable of love, by ensuring that they do not suffer from some inner disease or deficiency of the mind: they have also *to love*, to exercise their minds in that mode. Otherwise they receive no actual benefit or pleasure from the ability to love; and without the exercise the ability may wither or become distorted.

The question is susceptible of a tolerably clear answer; but we have to keep two distinctions in mind. First, we must distinguish between reasons which relate to a man's own happiness on the one hand, and those which relate to the general happiness on the other. Naturally this raises a further question about how we are to distinguish between those contexts in which we are entitled to use the first set of reasons, and those in which we must use the second; but I shall postpone discussion of this, claiming only that there will be *some* contexts of each kind. Second, we may use some sort of distinction between items of content which are to be valued and argued for 'intrinsically' ('for their own sakes'), and those which are to be 'extrinsically' justified or regarded at least partly as means to some end. The interaction between these two distinctions is one of the difficulties of our topic: the other is the difficulty of specifying a particular content which is of paramount importance without being thrown back, or thrown back too quickly, on the general idea and importance of seriousness.

We might begin simply by considering the individual's own happiness in relation to the learning of various Xs for their own sake. In one sense, there will be no determinate answer to our question here. As we have already argued, we have no solid grounds for assuming that the *same* sets of Xs – the same objects of appreciation and enjoyment, or the same love-objects – suit all individuals. It is true, and important, that there are certain traditions which can be seen as encapsulating the past experience of human beings (or perhaps just some kinds of human beings) in this area: certain institutionalizations, as it were, of what many men at many times and in many places have directed their seriousness towards. But these are of very different kinds: they comprise not only traditional subjects of study (mathematics, philosophy, art and so on), but also various games and hobbies that have stood the test of time (chess, gardening), different kinds of activities which might be classified under 'personal relationships' (marriage, parenthood), and a number of activities which are hard to classify under any heading ('travel', for instance, is a popular and well-institutionalized activity, but it is not at all easy to see what goods it aims at). Without these traditions and institutions, of course, education could not function at all: there would simply *be* no Xs, or no easily visible Xs, which pupils could be presented with, or into which they could be initiated. But that hardly helps us to decide *between* these Xs for individual pupils: not, at least, until we have some idea of the general direction of the pupils' inclinations.

It is easy to say that we need to introduce the pupil to as wide a range as possible of topics, subjects, disciplines and forms of thought:

to other Xs which come under the heading of 'virtues' or 'excellences'; and also to those Xs which are not institutionalized under those two sets of categories and cut across them. But, as I have argued elsewhere,[16] this gives us no determinate suggestions, even if we stay within the category of subjects or forms of thought; for everything turns on what criteria we use for 'a thing to be learned'. For instance, if we allow pupils to specialize in X and give up Y, we do not have to say that we have narrowed our range; for someone who *specializes* in X, as against doing the subject superficially, learns a new and different thing from someone who does not – he has now been introduced to both $X_1$ and $X_2$, and why should this be 'narrower' than X and Y? Again, while it is clearly useful to categorize forms of thought and virtues according to strictly logical criteria, it does not at all follow that these categories will also divide up our (almost infinite number of) Xs in terms of what sorts of things different pupils are likely to love or take seriously: that is a matter of psychology, not of logic.

One conclusion we might draw from this is that, rather than attempting the impossible task of introducing our pupils to *every* X, we should spend at least some time on enabling the pupils themselves to perceive this variety and heterogeneity of Xs in a more general way, and to understand something of the criteria by which the Xs may be classified. Parts of this might, in effect, involve introducing them to some kind or aspect of philosophy; and there are, of course, other and weightier reasons for introducing them to philosophy in general (briefly, because philosophical or conceptual competence is an essential part of the serious man's equipment, and one potentially effective defence against fantasy). Here my point is simply that any general insight into the different sorts of things that can be learned is plainly desirable.

But apart from this, we can only offer each pupil a *particular* content in the hope that it will suit his natural desires: in the hope that he will find it *easy* to love. To do this efficiently would depend on a much greater grasp of unconscious desire than we now possess; nevertheless, an imaginative teacher who knows a pupil well can often guess rightly about what content will suit him. This is not necessarily a matter of what is *immediately* 'stimulating' or 'attractive' to him, but of what will (perhaps only after a good deal of toil) give him a love-object which actually fits his nature. The way in which this may help him to love is tolerably clear: besides giving him at least one thing to love, it also gives him a taste of *what it is* to love something, a model experience on which he may build, and which he may be able to extend to different objects.

There is an obvious but somewhat more hopeful point to be

added. Insofar as the pupil does actually come to love something, he will want and need whatever content (knowledge of subjects and forms of thought, virtues, skills, etc.) is necessary to express his love. Thus if he turns out to become genuinely attached to (say) boat-building, he will want to learn whatever mathematics, etc., is needed for that business. Moreover, the knowledge which he acquires because of his initial attachment will enlarge and to some degree change the nature of the attachment. 'Boat-building' comes to mean something wider, and something different, when he has learned the mathematics. The direction of change cannot be easily predicted, however, because we cannot easily know just what it is *about* boat-building that forms the unconscious basis of the attachment. Perhaps he will be led from making canoes into the more abstract realms of mathematics and science: or into a study of different kinds of materials – wood, fibre-glass, and so on: or towards different kinds of boats – sailing boats, dinghies, tea clippers and hydrofoils: or towards geography and the voyages of discovery in the fifteenth century: or almost anywhere.

None of this suggests, of course, either (a) that pupils should themselves *decide what* content they are to have, and that we should allow them to chop and change such content when they feel like it, or (b) that pupils should *decide how much* learning or education they should have. Those questions are different, and turn on whether the educators are in sufficiently close communication with the pupils – whether, in fact, they know the pupils and love them well enough – to be able to make better decisions than the pupils can. Clearly this ought to be true of any respectable educational system; but as it is obviously not true of many institutions (even many families), the questions must be left open. For it is, I think, virtually impossible to generalize, at least in the present state of our knowledge: sometimes a pupil's strong initial attraction to some X may seem to be evidence for supposing that the X is in fact suitable, but sometimes the initial glamour wears off. (This is rather like asking whether people are any better off making their own marriages than having them made for them: an equally open question.)

So much, rather obviously, for the Xs which the pupil is to enjoy in themselves, and for his own benefit. The rest of our discussion consists essentially in pursuing two thoughts, which would naturally enter the mind of any serious pupil (or the educator who is deciding on his behalf). The first of these is that there will be *some* things which he needs to learn for 'extrinsic' reasons, in order for him to be happy: and the second, which is a good deal more complicated, is that the happiness of other people must also come into the picture.

At a certain point, as we shall see, the first of these thoughts merges with the second.

In talking about what a man needs to learn for extrinsic reasons, we need not refer only to his particular position in a certain society at a certain time: that is too fluctuating an idea for us to be able to say anything very useful about it. We cannot generalize about *ad hoc* pressures of this kind, just because they are *ad hoc*. We may say, however, that the serious and well-educated man would be best placed to recognize these pressures, evaluate them, and engage in whatever learning was required to meet them: and that is not unimportant, since failure actually to meet such pressures is just as likely (probably much more likely) to be due to these difficulties – which only more seriousness can overcome – than to other causes. This would again suggest a general educational content of a kind similar to that just described: that is, one which enabled the pupil at least to *recognize* those different expertises, forms of knowledge, and characteristic pressures on society which he might, if only for *ad hoc* purposes, have to take seriously. But this, I think, is as far as we can go in that direction.

Equally we may mention, but cannot profitably elaborate on, those Xs which relate to very obvious practical goods, important though they certainly are: for instance, whatever pupils need to learn in order to maintain their own health and safety. Most of these are more easy to generalize about than, for instance, what kind of skills a man needs if he is to be employable in a particular society; partly because the human body is a rather more *constant* factor than a rapidly changing technology, and partly because everyone has more or less the *same* body (whereas not everyone needs to undergo the same vocational training). Nor, again, is there much profit in trying to determine other less clear-cut 'standard interests' of human beings, to satisfy which certain Xs would have to be learned. It is easy to think of examples: for instance, most people are concerned with some kind of sexual relationship and financial security, so that it would pay them to devote attention to whatever Xs are extrinsically necessary for these; perhaps they should learn to improve their physical appearance, or something about practical economics. But apart from the fact that not *everybody* has these interests (certainly they are not of equal *weight* for everybody), the trouble is once more that the means of satisfying them fluctuate too much to allow of any permanently valid items of content. Educational courses on how to dress or how to invest one's money are not to be sneezed at; but as these examples suggest, the answers may vary from one year to the next. Here too we might say that if we can get people to be serious in the first place and help them to recognize the general *categories* of 'standard interests', the individuals themselves would want and be able to learn whatever items were at the time relevant to the categories, without our needing to make those items a matter of educational priority.

Nor, finally, need we have only in mind those items of content which can be seen as necessary for the learning of other things: for instance learning to read. Many of these, in fact, are part of (or closely related to) the idea of seriousness itself; and for that reason alone we cannot deny their importance. Other items, more concerned with basic knowledge, competence, or skill, are not a matter of attitude or mental posture: they are more like pieces of equipment which the serious man will want to collect. Hence we can fairly argue, once more, that either (1) these items come under the heading of seriousness, and have been (although inadequately) dealt with already, or (2) they are such *obviously* necessary tools that any even minimally serious person would see the need for them.

I do not suggest that such items as those mentioned in the last few paragraphs are unimportant. But there are difficulties in specifying them in any way which gives them permanent importance for all men, while sufficiently disconnecting them from the general idea of seriousness and at the same time justifying them on purely extrinsic grounds. Reading is perhaps a candidate; we could say, with some plausibility, that *whatever* a man will come to be serious about he will find it a pre-eminently useful or even a necessary tool. Yet there are still weaknesses here: either the man could get on well enough by using other signs and media (tape recorders, television, a sign-language and so on); or else we extend the concept marked by 'reading' to cover virtually any kind of sign-interpretation. In the former case reading is dispensable; in the latter, virtually inevitable – for how could there be a rational person who did *not* interpret signs, or a serious person who did *not* regard this as important? Similar arguments would apply, fairly obviously, to other things, such as elementary mathematics. There are, in fact, remarkably few items which can be claimed as strictly necessary in this sort of way; either the items are not closely enough connected with human nature, in which case they are at least in principle dispensable, or else the connection with seriousness is too close – that is, they come near to *constituting* what the serious man is like.

What needs to be pursued is a rather different kind of extrinsic consideration. We have to ask in what general respects, or departments of life, our lack of seriousness is likely to cause damage or let us down; in what areas this lack most militates against happiness. Here it is virtually impossible to proceed without bringing in the idea of the general or collective happiness of human beings. One reason is precisely that we are trying to say something about priorities in education for human beings in general; another, that anyone who had achieved an adequate degree of seriousness and capacity to love would recognize and accept the existence and claims of other people in the world. I do not here wish to become deeply involved in an ongoing philosophical discussion about (to put it very roughly) whether the crucial step for this latter is the Humean step of developing some kind of sympathy or feeling-attachment to other men, or the Kantian one of perceiving and acting upon certain principles of reason enshrined in moral language. Whatever the truth may be here, one thing at least seems clear. Faced with the choice of producing a new generation and society of individuals who *did* recognize and accept (at least in some degree) the claims of others and the importance of their happiness, as against a generation of individuals who did not, no reasonable man could prefer the latter; because, of course, the former policy would maximize the happiness of most or all individuals of that generation and society in a way that the latter stands absolutely no chance of doing. Whatever may be the position for individual adults in particular cases, any discussion of general policy for the future must take this into account. We could, of course (though with some difficulty), conceive of a man who had absolutely *no* concern for anyone's happiness except his own; but even if such a man could not be convicted of unreason (as, in my judgment, he could), it is hard to see how he could have much interest in education – and certainly he could not have grounds for interest in the kind of collective educational debate in which we are now engaged; that is, a debate about what *there is reason* for regarding as particularly important for men, in general and collectively, to learn.[17]

I shall return to one of the points at issue here below (p. 230): meanwhile, can we give some rough description of a particular area or department of life which seems to have the extrinsic importance we are looking for? At first sight, the suggestion that some one sort of knowledge or control is in *general* more important than another may seem absurd as it stands, for at least two interconnected reasons. First, we shall want to say that the importance of particular kinds or chunks of knowledge will be relative to particular situations. In many, perhaps still most, societies the most 'important' kinds of knowledge seem to be concerned with survival (health and hygiene, agriculture, elementary technology); in other societies we can afford luxuries like literature and sociology. Second, and more radically, it is very difficult to conceive of any satisfactory human life which did not depend on causal interconnections between many kinds of knowledge. We cannot do much in the way of personal understanding if we are starving; we have to know some elementary agriculture not to starve; we have to have some social co-operation if we are to practise agriculture securely and effectively; we have to have some personal knowledge and understanding in order to co-operate. So what could be *meant* by saying that one sort of knowledge was 'more important' than another?

However, while the urgency of particular needs is indeed largely context-dependent, there are some things we can say about our particular context. We live in an age when it is hardly plausible to hold that our major ills derive primarily from lack of expertise in the world of physical objects, or lack of intelligence and cleverness. Even for meeting material needs (food, health, and the avoidance of many natural disasters) the know-how and expertise are generally *available*; so too, at least in principle, are the resources. The problem seems to lie rather in the area of moral and political development. Granted that particular social groups may have other more urgent priorities: nevertheless, if we take mankind as a whole, not many people would deny that the major obstacles to our happiness derive from our inability, or unwillingness, to deploy techniques and resources already at our command. When we consider those specific evils which are man-made (war, over-population, crime, etc.), the point is obvious; we are, collectively at least, in a fair way to be masters of our natural environment, but we have yet to go far in understanding and mastering ourselves. And if we look beyond material needs – for the existence of mental illness, loneliness and plenty of other things shows clearly enough that material prosperity is far from a sufficient condition for happiness – the point becomes more obvious still. We do not, of course, want to drop those expertises that are indispensable to our material welfare, like medicine and science; but that is not the front on which we most urgently need to advance.

To put this another way: we might say that we know how to handle certain problems or questions, but not others. In some departments of life we are (as it were) solidly, securely and collectively 'in business', whereas in others we are uncertain, floundering, and in a state of (armed or unarmed) conflict. Thus, whatever our particular disagreements or particular areas of ignorance, we know *how to* conduct such enterprises as science, history, mathematics and various practical *technai*: well enough, at least, to keep our heads above water. But in the areas vaguely labelled 'morality', 'politics', 'religion', 'personal relationships', 'the emotions' and so on, it is plain that we are not in this happy position. We have no common methodology, no sensible and agreed ways of proceeding; hence, unsurprisingly, we differ in our particular substantive opinions and in our overt behaviour.

I have suggested above (p. 184) (and I shall not attempt to argue more fully for it here) that there are *a priori* or conceptual, not just contingent, reasons why we are peculiarly deficient in this sphere. The reasons are connected with the difficulty of emerging from 'the world of sights and sounds', itself connected with the obvious fact that our sense-perceptions are less liable to fantasy than are our perceptions of emotion. The scientist or practical technician who engages in the world of physical objects has an easier time, in this way at least, than the rest of us; and it is not accidental that the emergence of a rational scientific method has antedated the emergence of a rational moral methodology. Again, one could hardly even imagine a child developing moral and emotional competence before some competence in dealing with the objects of sense-perception; his initial world, as we have seen, is basically and necessarily a physical one, and it is not surprising that children learn a great deal about objects before they know much about people or how people feel.

One of our difficulties in dealing with this department of life is, as so often, taxonomic. We have such *words* as 'moral', 'political', 'religious', and so on, but we do not have agreement on the delimitations of whatever enterprises these words are to mark; and this causes (or is caused by, or anyway correlates with) the standing temptation to define them in terms of a particular content – if not the actual moral (religious, political) beliefs of some society, then at least the way in which that society may construe the delimitations of the enterprises. Thus if 'religious education' avoids the risk of being taken as equivalent to Christian education, it may suffer the slightly more sophisticated fate of being taken as equivalent to education in the 'higher' ('advanced', monotheistic, or in some other way accredited) religions. Not only particular beliefs, but also particular delimitations, may be fairly called 'partisan' in this sort of way.

These two moves can be clearly seen as erroneous, if only because they distort normal usage in the interests of prejudice; thus whatever 'religion' may mean, it is plainly not exhausted by the notions of either 'Christianity' or 'the higher religions'. But there is a third obstacle which is at once less obvious and less easy to surmount. In this general area, which we have so far tried to describe nontendentiously by using a wide variety of conjoined terms ('moral', 'political', 'religious', 'emotional', etc.,) all individuals and societies will, of course, have principles of behaviour, predominant emotions, basic beliefs, and sets of values which encapsulate what they take to be of most importance in life, and dictate what they actually do and feel (or at least what they think ought to be done and felt). Now it

will surely be these overriding and prescriptive 'values', if that term
is suitably general, which the educator at least will be chiefly
interested in: the values which, as it were, actually make his pupils
tick. But – and this is the taxonomic difficulty – different individuals
and societies, even at a high level of sophistication, will give different
names even to this enterprise. Some classical Greek philosophers
brought it under the general heading of *politikē*, a wider term than
our 'politics': religious cultures would naturally construe it as a
matter of *religious* education: some people nowadays might use the
term 'ideological': for others, the word 'moral' may seem the most
natural one to use.

These classifications are hard to fault on linguistic grounds, just
because there is not much linguistic agreement about them; but the
obvious danger lies in the implication, which any such title-heading
may carry, that our 'values' must take on what might be called a
particular *shape*. For the terms 'moral', 'political', 'ideological', and
– still more clearly – 'religious' are not *wholly* blank; as they or their
counterparts appear in particular languages and at particular
times, they carry with them conceptual trappings which are not
easily shed. Thus, even if (with some modern theologians) we extend
the term 'religion' so widely that almost anyone's values could be
described, in this loose sense, as 'religious', nevertheless some
questionable implications are likely to remain – for instance, that
men do have or ought to have some kind of large-scale and coherent
'outlook on life', perhaps of a vaguely 'spiritual' kind. Similarly,
unless 'ideology' is stretched to the point of vacuity, the term is likely
to imply that a man's values must be clad in the particular clothes
of some coherent creed or 'ism'. Thus, even if we wish to deal with
our pupils' overriding values *as such*, the mere entitlement of this
educational enterprise as 'education in X' (where X is 'morality',
'ideology', or whatever) may mislead; because, for many people, the
general shape of X may already be delimited by other criteria.

Nevertheless, it is convenient to use *some* title for this enterprise;
and though there are competitors ('values' is perhaps the most
obvious), I shall use the term 'moral'. As will now be clear, this is
not to deny either (1) that there are other ranges of meaning that the
term may also mark, or (2) that it would be extremely desirable to
have agreed markers both for this general area and for various
sub-areas or sub-departments which we might want to distinguish
within it. But we have not yet reached this position. Moreover,
while the proper delimitation of these enterprises is clearly very
important, nothing much may be gained by clinging closely to the
*word* 'moral'; it may be too versatile a term for ordinary usage to
lead us at once to an obviously correct answer. We may have to

mark out this and other areas on strategic rather than linguistic grounds. Be that as it may: in this broad or architectonic use of 'moral', as I have tried to clarify elsewhere,[18] we should be talking (very roughly) of those values, principles, or states of affairs which a man takes to be of overriding importance in his thinking, feeling, and practical behaviour (whether or not these are encapsulated in forms and backed by reasons which one might by other criteria want to call 'religious', 'political', 'aesthetic', and so on); in particular, though not exclusively, those which significantly affect the happiness of other men besides himself. Moral education, in this sense, is to be distinguished from other kinds of education in that there are principles of reason, concepts, attitudes, abilities, skills and other attributes which are relevant to this subject-matter (though not, in all cases, relevant to it alone).

It is perhaps worth noting a rather more general point of methodology here. The notions of seriousness and love, as priorities in practical education, emerged from *not* taking up too quickly any particular options on what Xs were to be learned: essentially, from trying to gain as much ground as possible from the form, rather than from some specific content, of education. So too in this particular department. To take sides with some particular ideology or set of values is precisely *not* to solve – not even to try and solve – the educational problem; and we have seen throughout this book the various ways in which it merely makes things worse for educational theory and practice. We have to ask, not 'What values are right?', but 'What is the form of the enterprise by which we and our pupils can come to perceive and live up to whatever values reason may demand of us?' It is not possible to make any significant progress in this (or any other) department of education until we have some grasp of this form.

One might ask how, if at all, education in this enormously broad area is to be distinguished from education designed to promote seriousness and the capacity to love in general. There is, as I granted at the beginning of this section (p. 210), a considerable amount of overlap; indeed we may see morality as a (rather large) sub-set of the set of enterprises which we want our pupils to be serious about, and one to which the general quality of seriousness is especially important. But it is only *one*: clearly a man may perform very well in this area (even defined thus broadly), and very badly in others. Nevertheless, it is clear enough that part of the importance of morality derives from its architectonic position: that is, there is a sense in which it stands behind or above the other enterprises or *technai*, and determines how they are to be used. The force of this point does not, I think, rely on any linguistic fiat that 'morality' is to be used in this way. A man might construe 'morality' much more narrowly, in such a way that it would be at least possible for him to think that morality did not matter much,[19] for instance, he might use it to mean (very roughly) 'utilitarian morality', and believe that human suffering was unimportant so long as there were enough glamorous heroes, or beautiful women, or exciting works of art in the world. He might not think – though in such cases one might doubt whether he was really *thinking* or reasoning rather than rationalizing some compulsion or fantasy (see p. 148) – that the particular goods dispensed by this (narrow) conception of morality had much value: let people suffer (kill, lie, break contracts and so forth) so long as heroism and beauty flourish. But there will still be some need to ensure that heroism and beauty (or whatever our 'ultimate values' are) *do* flourish: some architectonic enterprise whose job it is to make the necessary arrangements and see that they are adhered to.

It would be wrong, however, to see morality merely as a device (even an architectonic device) for avoiding harm and allowing various goods to flourish. For though it must have a point or object of roughly this kind, some of the goods are such that they cannot be dispensed by architectonic or any other kind of experts. This is not because the idea of expertise or 'right answers' in morality is inconceivable, but because of what morality itself involves; and it is the conjunction of these two points which gives morality its unique status. Thus morality has in common (1) with some other areas – notably, as we have seen (p. 124), aesthetic appreciation – that a man's own *feelings* are very much involved, so that (if for no other reason) nobody else can conduct a man's morality for him; at the same time, it has in common (2) with such enterprises as mathematics and science that it is related, in a fairly direct way, to the production of external goods of an important kind. We pick morality out of these two categories partly because it is the only candidate which figures in both. For it is not absurd to argue (1) that it would not very much *matter* if men were not seriously educated in aesthetics – no doubt a lot would be lost, and no doubt there are important connections between art and morality itself, but at least failure to appreciate works of art is unlikely to result in global war; (2) while the goods produced by the more purely 'cognitive' enterprises (in particular science) are important, it is not necessary that *all* of us should go in for these: for this purpose, we can perfectly well organize other people to do our science for us, which we cannot do in morality.

This is, of course, a rough-and-ready line of argument, the weakest point of which may be thought to lie in (2): could we not, in fact, produce the goods – the end-products, we might call them – of morality without educating everybody (or even very many people) in it? As I have said above,[20] we cannot dispute this on the grounds that the idea of moral expertise is inconceivable; and one might, in fact, believe that for some moral issues of a large-scale or global kind – political questions, perhaps – it would be much better to identify teams of such experts and trust them with power, rather than engage in what are called 'democratic' procedures. In principle, Plato was right about this. One might even be prepared to argue that, compared with the chaos and insecurity of most industrialized societies today, many or even most people might be happier and better off under something more like a feudal system or a benevolent despotism; and the obvious dangers of such a system are not a knock-down argument against it – perhaps the dangers can be avoided, and perhaps sensible people might themselves come to see the advantages, and freely contract to live within it.

There are in fact three answers to this objection. First, if people *are* actually going to accept such a system, they will have to be sufficiently educated at least to *recognize* moral expertise when they see it. Otherwise they will not be able to identify the relevant experts, and will have no reason to obey them. This itself demands quite a high level of moral education: at the least, a firm intellectual grasp, and prescriptive acceptance, of the appropriate methodology. They must have a clear idea of how to do the subject, as it were, and sincerely believe that it should be done in that way, even if not all of them are very good at it: otherwise they will not know whom to trust as being better equipped than themselves. One could, I suppose, imagine a successful *coup* on the part of a minority who simply imposed their expertise on the rest of us; but this would, I think, itself run into insuperable moral objections – quite apart from the contingent unlikelihood of any such *coup* being *permanently* successful.

Second, it is misleading to describe *all* of the external end-products as 'large-scale', 'global' or 'political'. One reason why it is inconceivable that moral experts should run all of our lives is simply that there are too many end-products to be supervised; there are so many decisions to be made that some end-products, at least, will have to be at the mercy of individuals. It would be difficult even to conceive of a situation in which *every* moral decision – that is, in effect, every decision relevant to a man's relationship as a person to other men – was taken by some authority, and not by the individuals concerned: if only because there is no method by which the number or variety of such decisions can be limited in advance. The authorities might try (again as in Plato) so to fossilize human life that change is impossible; but this cannot be done, even in principle, so long as that life remains human and not ant-like. The system can never be entirely closed.

Third, though some of the goods of morality – or, more easily, avoidance of certain evils – may be seen as end-products, this is not true of all or even most of them. If, again, we are to describe anything that could be called human life at all, we have to make considerable allowance for relationships that cannot, in principle, be dictated. A moral expert might tell me whom to marry or what job to do; but, as we have seen, he cannot (logically) relate to my wife or my colleagues *for* me. He can tell me how to behave towards them; but only I can love them, forgive them, enjoy their company, and so forth. This is as much as to say that these goods cannot properly be called 'end-products' at all; they are inherent in the relationships of one man to another, as they are not inherent in the interaction of social roles and the bestowal of impersonal services. These are also among those particularly important goods which we discussed above (pp. 158 ff.): those connected with the loving enjoyment of the world, and hence with happiness, not those which may be necessary as means to that end.

There remains still plenty of room for argument about how far and over what areas we should allow the notional 'moral experts' to govern our lives. But this is, in essence, an argument about how to compare those particular goods which we can be given with those which we have to achieve or enjoy for ourselves; and there is no determinate procedure for settling this question. We can, of course, try to get much clearer about the nature of the goods in question, and to be much more honest and perceptive about our own and other people's particular dispositions; but thereafter we can only refer each case to the criterion of happiness. It is above all important not to be in the grip of some particular ideology: thus in many quarters nowadays there is a fashion for particular social regimes and personality-types (often marked by such terms as 'liberal', 'autonomous' and 'democratic') – a fashion which is very evident in educational theory, and which has been partly responsible for changing many important aspects of educational practice over comparatively few decades. But these are, indeed, 'substantive' positions, to argue successfully for which we should need much more empirical evidence than we actually have. What sort of regime – either in social groups or in the individual psyche – actually *suits* people will, in any case, largely depend on the group or the person in question: no overall thesis is likely to be plausible. Part of the trouble here, I think, is a fairly obvious muddle between the ideas (1) that all people should be allowed to enjoy (or suffer) whatever regimes they contract or opt for, and not be prevented by *force majeure* even if such prevention is 'in their own best interests', and (2) that certain particular ('liberal') regimes or life-styles *are* actually in the best interests of all people.

There remain two important questions for the educator which require a brief discussion: first, a question about what (in a very general way) the *aims* of education are in this area; and second, a question about the *possibility* of educating enough people to an adequate standard (whatever this may mean). These questions are of course interconnected; and they overlap – though they are not co-extensive – with a number of problems in moral philosophy and the philosophy of mind. We shall not here consider these latter in any detail; partly because there is already more than enough literature about them, but chiefly because they must not be allowed to obscure (even if they often enlighten) the nature of those demands which the *educator* is called upon to meet, and which it is the peculiar task of the philosophy of *education* to emphasize.

As we noticed in chapter 4, any effective classification of areas or departments of life – what might broadly be called 'enterprises' – involves both 'cognitive' and 'affective' elements or attributes: both certain types of knowledge, and certain virtues or powers of the mind. To be initiated into these areas is to gain those attributes which each area requires; and every major area can be seen, in fact, to require quite a wide and complex variety. What constitutes a good or properly educated scientist, architect, historian, musician, etc., cannot be construed solely in terms of a number of Xs to be learned, if these Xs describe only specific beliefs and behaviour-patterns; for these will not adequately represent the enterprise or form of life for what it is. 'A good scientist' cannot be wholly cashed out in terms of such 'brute' Xs as that he believes the earth to be round, or that he does not knock over test-tubes in the laboratory: he has rather to think and feel in the way that the enterprise of science demands.

We are bound also to feel some pressure from the idea (also discussed in chapter 4) that some of these Xs, at least, should have *permanent* validity: and this alone would make us hesitate before construing the relevant Xs solely in terms of a specific set of beliefs or behaviour-patterns, for the obvious reason that these may become obsolete as we continue to make progress in the enterprises. In other words, we want our pupils to have some grasp of what we might roughly distinguish as the form (rather than the content) of each enterprise, if only because the content is more fragile. In the case of the area marked by 'morality' ('religion', 'politics', 'ideals', etc.) this pressure is particularly strong; we cannot feel much confidence about any large area of specific content in these departments – not, at least, in advance of a proper understanding of how the departments should be run. We cannot reasonably take, as a basis or starting-point, any particular and detailed substantive position, creed, ideology, or partisan doctrine: if only because history is littered with these, and most of them are covered in blood. But if there are features or characteristics relevant to all men at all times, and able to be learned, which can be seen as logically required by anyone entering these departments of life (and nobody can avoid entering some of them), then the learning of these will have enormous value. If we can become clear about, and teach people, *how to conduct* these enterprises, that will be worth much more than rapidly changing and intellectually uncertain attempts to teach them specific and particular beliefs and behaviour-patterns – changing and uncertain, precisely because not flowing from a properly founded methodology.

Though the idea goes back to Socrates, the last decade or so has seen a large quantity of literature devoted to 'moral education' ('values education', 'character education,' 'education in virtue', etc.) in this sense: I mean, a sense whereby something other is aimed at than just the inculcation of specific and contestable beliefs and attitudes. There is, of course, a great deal that can be (and has been) said about exactly what, in that case, our objectives should be[21] (and even more about how we are to achieve them[22]) which need not be repeated here. But the important thing is that we should accept the *possibility* of the task; and there is still a good deal of (admittedly rather nebulous) resistance to the idea of being able to educate people in this area without connecting such education wholly to what are sometimes called 'specific' or 'substantive' moral attitudes or beliefs.

It is not always easy to determine just what lies behind this resistance, but a brief example may at least help to clarify some possible misundertandings:

> what on earth is 'success in the moral area' if it is not allowed
> to be identified with *becoming morally good*? Yet [*sc.* on the
> theory being criticized] we are debarred from so identifying it,
> since if we did so we should be taking up specific moral
> attitudes: to reveal this is dangerously to indoctrinate our
> pupils.[23]

This (very common) view arises, I should guess, from a movement of thought which starts from the correct ideas (1) that morality is not just a theoretical or 'cognitive' matter, but involves some actual commitment, or 'affective' disposition (not just knowledge, skills and abilities, but also dispositions and attitudes) and (2) that (partly for this reason) morality is not just a practical art or *techne*, but governs a man's life and behaviour in a much more general way, so that we cannot talk without some absurdity about being 'good at' morality, as if it were such a *techne*. For these reasons one might indeed be willing to identify 'success in the moral area' with 'becoming morally good', so long as the latter phrase is handled with circumspection. The danger arises when the meaning of 'morally good' is cashed out wholly or primarily in terms of some specific set of moral values, rather than in terms of those qualities which the enterprise of morality itself makes necessary for anyone who takes it seriously. This is not, of course, to deny that there are correct moral attitudes, sound moral principles, or demonstrable moral truths (just as there are in science or any other department); it is to claim only that what makes them correct, sound, or demonstrable must relate to some logically prior methodology or set of rational procedures, on which education in this department ought to be based.

Similarly the connected idea (3) that teachers and other educators ought sometimes to be 'taking up specific moral attitudes' is not *per se* in dispute – indeed, if they are to function as people within the school and other communities they could hardly help doing this, and would not need to 'reveal' it. The establishment of an educationally desirable moral tradition or set of practices in the school requires such attitudes, for all sorts of reasons. But the notion of what is educationally desirable, in morality as elsewhere, cannot be wholly construed in that light. An art or English teacher, for instance, will have particular views, and behave in a particular way, about painting or literature: he will furnish his rooms, and perhaps the school, with a specific selection of paintings or books – in this way both declaring his own views and setting an example of what is (he hopes) worth looking at or reading. But if he did not also – partly with the help of the specific background, but partly and necessarily also in a more general way – try to get his pupils to judge and act more perceptively and reasonably for themselves in the general area of art or literature, we should rightly feel that he was not doing his job. The pupils need to know, not just *what* judgments to make, but *how* to make such judgments.

What is lacking here is the idea of morality as an enterprise in its own right, with its own set of procedures, principles of reason, skills, abilities, attitudes and what might be generally called the necessary 'pieces of equipment'.[24] Just as one can identify, at least in principle, a serious and competent scientist (educator, artist, politician), so one can identify a serious and competent moral agent: that is, somebody who takes the enterprise seriously and abides by its rules. The rules and equipment that govern or constitute the enterprise are not, of course, the *specific* beliefs and actions that emerge from it: just as the rules and equipment governing the successful practice of science or musical composition are not to be identified with the particular scientific theories or the particular symphonies that emerge. What constitutes a good performer in any area is not defined by, though naturally it is connected with, particular end-products. That is why we can accept, in this sense, the phrase 'morally good' (i.e. a person who is serious and competent in the area of morality) without having to base the notions of seriousness or competence on specific moral values. Indeed, to make this move would lead at once to trouble; for if two 'specific moral values' conflict, we must presumably think that there is *some* kind of competence or application of seriousness which would in principle enable us to resolve the conflict: either that, or such conflicts are at some level irresolvable and beyond the scope of reason.

Our last question is about whether we can in fact educate everyone (or a majority of people) to an adequate standard in the moral sphere. I do not deny that there are problems about this; but they are not intractable, and not primarily philosophical. Hare says rather alarmingly:

> We have, armed with a clear understanding of the concepts, to think out the principles for ourselves, and see which of them we can accept. This is the most important part of what Plato wanted his guardians to do. The crucial question is whether those who are able to do it are few or many, and what is to be done with those who are not able.[25]

But the palliatives are fairly obvious if we are really prepared to accept that there is a rational methodology, set of procedures and 'necessary equipment' for morality as for other departments or forms of life. First, it will not be a simple question of being 'able' or 'not able', but a question of greater or less ability. Moreover, since the range of equipment required for the morally educated person is very wide, there need be no question of some single across-the-board ability; different people may – indeed, certainly will – rate differently at different things, possessing some pieces of equipment but not others, or being more or less near to such possession. Second, it is not clear that 'ability' is the whole story, or even most of it; if there are moral idiots, their deficiencies are likely to be due as much to lack of seriousness (will, motivation) as to lack of innate talent. The purely 'cognitive' aspects of moral education – the required concepts, knowledge, and procedures – do not, in fact, demand much intelligence or intellectual sophistication; though the person needs a good deal of seriousness if these aspects are to operate effectively and be translated into action.

Of course, this still leaves the core of the problem untouched, since whatever the reasons may be for bad performance there will still be bad performers; whether we are to say that they cannot or that they will not learn, they still exist. We have this problem with people who perform very badly in other areas – science, literature, art, mathematics, and so forth; and we solve it, or deal with it as best we can, by methods which are perfectly well known to us. We have a *tradition* of science (literary criticism, etc.) which is established in our society, and in its educational institutions; and the tradition is clear enough, and sufficiently well established, for most people at least to recognize its existence. It has accredited representatives to whom the ignorant and incompetent may turn when necessary: books are written, at various levels of sophistication, which will explain all that is needed: and, above all, children are educated in this tradition. By 'tradition' here I mean not only a general acceptance in the community that a certain set of intellectual procedures is appropriate, but also that the growing child is surrounded by people who *act* on those procedures. The same is true of other departments: what helps the child to behave rationally in regard to the physical world is not only the 'scientific method' professionally deployed by scientists, but the fact that something of that method – the general orientation of which it is a sophisticated product – has penetrated the community as a whole. The child does not normally see his parents casting spells or looking into crystal balls.

If a general tradition of this kind did exist (as, perhaps, it does and has in small pockets of humanity), that would be precisely because we had matured sufficiently to behave in that way without an intolerably high level of conflict; the acknowledgment and institutionalization of moral expertise are themselves dependent on a general increase in seriousness and love, so that there may appear to be a vicious circle here of the kind noted above (p. 198). But there are two points which may give some grounds for optimism. First, as has just been said, there does not seem to be anything of great *intellectual* difficulty about the general 'methodology' (as I have called it) of morality. I grant (1) that there are still plenty of philosophical problems to be discussed, (2) that some moral issues, at least, are intellectually complicated, and (3) that the particular 'pieces of equipment' – for instance, being aware of one's own and other people's feelings – require a good deal of intellectual sophistication for their full development. But compared with the sophisticated and complex knowledge and conceptual grasp that we expect of the average pupil learning, say, mathematics or science, the basic outline of rational moral thinking is fairly straightforward. This may, of course, be taken to show only that there are greater difficulties elsewhere, in the 'affective' elements; but these are not intellectual difficulties, and at least we need not imagine that there will be many people to whom the world of moral thinking is a complete mystery, in the way that many people are obliged to see the worlds of nuclear physics and the calculus as mysterious.

Second, it seems possible that, *if* and *when* the methodology is generally recognized as appropriate, people might have enough seriousness to institutionalize it in some way even if they do not have enough seriousness to practise it properly in their own lives. It is, or can be, a saving grace for human beings that they are prepared to establish and endorse procedures and institutions which represent, as it were, their better selves or their saner moments: we accept courts of law even if we do not always behave legally, and accept the authority of a dictionary even if we do not always speak in accordance with it. Given the intellectual conviction that the methodology is more or less sound, not all that much seriousness is required to institutionalize it. Again, I do not deny that our fantasies will do their best to prevent even the intellectual conviction; but there is at least some possibility for progress and (so to speak) self-education along these lines.

Naturally I do not suggest that the tradition, as I have called it, should be established as unalterable and immune from criticism; nor could anyone who accepted the (partial) parallel with other departments of thought and action suppose it. We initiate our children into what we now take to be the most reasonable and justifiable ways of answering questions about the physical world, under the title of 'science'; but that does not inhibit the work of top-level scientists and philosophers of science, work which may make us change our minds about what we had taken as true and give us a clearer or deeper understanding of what science is. Nor, again, is it necessary to suggest that bad performers should be quickly written off as hopeless cases, bullied into accepting the tradition, or totally neglected. This too is not how we should behave in parallel situations. We should do the best we can for each case, perhaps allotting more time and resources to the most difficult cases; and we should use only such compulsion, by way of making the pupil at least attend to what (in our judgment) he ought to learn, as we thought legitimate and effective. This is more or less like the learning of other subjects, with perhaps the important difference that the learning of morality is more closely bound up with the ideas of prescriptivity and seriousness: so that we may require a good deal more patience, methods of teaching and influence which cut more deeply into the pupils' minds and hearts, and in general more attention and resources devoted to the task, than we might feel inclined to bestow on other areas.

This does not mean that we can avoid the existence of scientific, moral, or any other kind of idiots; but it does mean that we can recognize them as such, and make sure that they do not masquerade as *savants*.[26] Of course if there are a great many idiots and very few *savants*, or if (as is in fact the case) the vast majority of people are generally muddled about the whole business, then we cannot solve the problem: but that is to say, in effect, that the tradition is not yet established. We are, I think, actually now in this critical position: it is a toss-up whether we shall come to see what sort of tradition we need and thence come to establish it, or whether we shall regress to some kind of intellectual (and probably practical) anarchy or totalitarianism. I would not like to lay any bets on this.

We have considered particular items of educational content under the heading first of the individual's happiness, and then of the general happiness; and a question remains about the comparative weight to be given to each. *Prima facie* there seems no reason – that is, no justification – for my preferring my own happiness to that of another, or of men in general: and this might suggest that what we said under the first heading was largely a waste of time. For if I take the happiness of others seriously, is there really any justification for my using time (space, resources, etc.) in learning things which may only be of value to myself? Certainly my own needs and desires count along with those of other men; but, unless I am myself in a peculiarly under-privileged position, do not other men have greater needs which I should be trying to meet? There is nothing wrong with learning the fiddle in itself: but Rome may be burning.

We must not, in my judgment, try to evade this by reneging on the general point that my own happiness is not to be preferred to that of others. Of course objections can be (and have been) raised to this point. *Can* a man (it might be asked) be seriously expected to give exactly the same logical weight to his own happiness ('projects', etc.) as to other peoples'? Would this not reduce him to a sort of utilitarian calculating machine? If everyone in fact did this all the time would there in fact be any first-order individual desires for the calculus to work on? And what would such a man's motives be?[27] But sometimes, at least, we see people (think of the loving mother of a large family) who are able and willing to abandon their own projects for the benefit of others and spend a lot of time in such planning, where it is plainly grotesque to see them as without integrity or as calculating machines (she gets her integrity from *loving* them); normally we praise this, and try to encourage it under headings like 'justice' or 'benevolence'.

Certainly human beings are not and cannot be infinitely flexible. The ideal, often associated with utilitarianism, that our actions should be governed solely by some sort of universal benevolence together with a rational calculation of good and harm, remains and must remain only an ideal. However, we condemn men not only for lack of integrity and firm commitment ('These are my moral principles; but if you don't like them, I have others'), but also for inflexibility ('That's just the sort of person I am'). We do not expect, nor always want, them to abandon the way in which their feelings are set; but we do expect and want them to change – most commonly to extend the range of – their feelings. For instance, if a man is loyal and loving in relation to a particular group (his family, or tribe, or whatever) we do not wish simply to dismantle these feelings, and replace them with a wishy-washy 'benevolence'; but we do want the love and loyalty to be extended, to include (at least) *more* people, if not the whole world. Most or all of us do, in fact, display insufficient seriousness in our adherence to this principle. It may be, in some cases, that we are simply unaware of the needs and sufferings of other men (perhaps far removed from us); but even in these cases we should say that such unawareness was usually the sign of an inadequate moral imagination – that if we really cared for other men, we would take the trouble to find out how things were with them. We should not think much of a corn baron who only helped those whom he could actually *see* dying of starvation outside his own house. But then how far are we to go? Are we – that is, those of us whose needs are not desperate – to spend *all* our time in the service of others?

Various things may be said at this point: all are true, but none seems to offer an adequate reply. First, some of what I may learn under the first heading – that is, purely for my own enjoyment and happiness – may also happen to be useful in meeting the needs of others: but then only *those* cases will be justified. Second, one may reasonably subscribe to a system which decentralizes, as it were, the various tasks of meeting our needs; it may be agreed that it is up to me to look after my own finances (wife, children, country, etc.) and up to you to look after yours. But not many people would rationally contract for, or prescribe for themselves and others, a system so *laissez-faire* as to permit such grave evils as actually exist. Third, it may be said that I need *some* egocentric enjoyment (free time, a reasonable standard of living, etc.) in order to perform adequately on those (other) occasions when I *do* minister to the needs of others;

but this argument does not seem to justify anything like as much scope for self-enjoyment as most of us characteristically allow ourselves.

Nevertheless, it is this third line of argument which offers the most hope, by bringing us into a largely unexplored area of moral philosophy which has close connections with the idea of seriousness discussed earlier (p. 163). As well as questions of the form 'What ought one (anyone) to do?' or 'What is the right thing to do?', which may seem tacitly to assume that individuals are infinitely flexible, there are also questions of a different kind about what some particular individual ought to do, *being the kind of person that he is*; and we do not answer these questions if we say simply that he ought not to be that sort of person. In practice – that is, for particular individuals at particular times – not everything can be negotiated by the direct or immediate control of the will: not, at least, without loss. I may give up smoking, but only at the cost of bad temper and anxiety. Anyone can say that I ought to be the sort of person who neither smokes nor is bad-tempered and anxious; but that is no help in making the choice.

Naturally we have a standing duty to increase our seriousness and love: that is, to turn ourselves into the right sort of (altruistic) people; and it is not, of course, to be denied that there are many occasions where we can enforce correct choices of an altruistic kind upon ourselves not only without loss, but even to our ultimate benefit. But if our seriousness and our love are too small for such choices to flow naturally from our feelings, some degree of conflict is necessarily inherent in them. Quite apart from the fact that the interests of other people often demand loving feelings (the mere altruistic *action* may be positively counter-productive), such conflicts build up a kind of unconscious resentment which may well cause more damage, often in unseen ways, to others than a reasonable amount of straightforward selfishness causes. It is really a question of how hard in any particular case, one ought to *try*; and we have to accept the fact that the instant perfection of the will is, even when possible, not always desirable. In practice, the proper level of altruism (as with any other 'ego-ideal') for individuals is indeterminate. This applies particularly to the young child, who himself needs to be loved before he can build up a self capable of loving another; the point goes back to what we said earlier about preserving the force or prescriptivity of desire along with rationality. It is always an *open* question when to apply pressure and when to allow nature its own way.

To say that it is an open question, however, is not to renege on the general principles of altruism. No doubt whatever things may be marked by 'whole-heartedness', 'spontaneity', 'living according to one's nature', or even perhaps 'integrity' ('feeling all of a piece') are only possible without too much conflict or repression; but the general happiness must be the only criterion for deciding how much conflict or repression to allow, and in what particular cases; and by that criterion each man, other things being equal, counts for one and no more than one. It is too easy (at least for those of us who are not addicted to conflict or repression) to magnify these goods into alternative ethical systems of a romantic or existential kind; whereas what we ought to say is only that they are, indeed, goods which we ought to take into account, and may sometimes give precedence to. This problem, then, can have no determinate solution. To be human is to face a dichotomy which applies to many areas of life and can be described in various ways. We may oppose Kantian to Humean types of motivation: reason and duty to the natural sympathies and affections: convention to authenticity: law and order to freedom: the super-ego to the id: seriousness to animal pleasure. But we cannot sensibly take one side or the other; our job is to negotiate between the two, and our powers of negotiation can only, in the last resort, be augmented by the (inevitably slow) growth of love. There are no easy ways out, no short cuts, and no sudden conversions. All this we have to *learn*; and that, ultimately, is why education is important.

# Notes

## Introduction: Philosophy and education

1 Wilson (1975, part 2).
2 Ibid., chs. 2 and 3.
3 Peters (1973), p. 2; see, however, also p. 3 in the same volume.

## Part I Education

*Chapter 1 The words and the enterprise*

1 For what seems to be a different view of the importance of this task, see Warnock (1977): particularly the Introduction.
2 Cf. Warnock (1977), pp. 11 ff.; for instance, 'There is no mysterious unanalysable essence either of education or of football for which we must search' (p. 13). But this is an Aunt Sally: not many professional philosophers today believe that there must always be such essences.
3 On this see Wilson (1977), ch. 5.
4 Cf. Kenny (1963), ch. 8.
5 We seem sometimes to count education as part of upbringing, particularly with children; but we may also disconnect the two, as in the case of adult education, or as when we might say that a child's nurture is the business of his parents, but his education the business of his tutor. In any case, it seems clear that as we now use the terms 'education' and 'educate' they are restricted by the idea of human learning.
6 There are two grammatical constructions which may follow 'educate', and one which may not. We may use:
(a) A final construction, with the force of 'They educated him in order that he . . .':
(b) A consecutive construction, with the force of 'They educated him in such a way that he . . .'.
These would both be represented by *ut* and the subjunctive in Latin, and both are possible in English; but neither are normally represented by 'educate to'.
(c) A prolative construction, with the force of 'They educated him to . . .' (where Latin would use the infinitive), like 'compelled to . . .' or 'taught to . . .', is not possible.

7 'Training teachers' has a proleptic force ('training people *to be*
teachers') which 'educating teachers' does not have; the latter is
equivalent rather to 'educating people who happen to be teachers.'

8 The best guide is Hare (1972a), pp. 55 ff.

9 See Leviticus, XI, 17.

10 Hartnett and Naish (1976), pp. 74 ff.

11 This seems to be widely believed, but not widely argued for at length:
see, however, Hartnett and Naish (1976), pp. 73 ff. The origin of the
phrase is an article by Gallie (Proceedings of the Aristotelian Society,
vol. LVI, 1955–6), which I find far from clear.

12 Ibid.

## Chapter 2 Mistakes and methodology

1 O'Connor (1968), p. 5.

2 Frankena in Lucas (1969), p. 288.

3 *Republic*, 336 ff.

4 In Lucas (1969), p. 112.

5 Warnock (1975a).

6 Nor am I clear whether the reviewer is really much concerned with
definition: 'teaching people to understand and to contribute to the
culture which they inherit' does not seem a very good shot. (Must
they really *contribute*? Must all, or some, or indeed any of what is
learned come under the description of *culture*? Must it be the culture
which *they* inherit – what about other culture?)

7 *Laws*, 643–4: translation by T. J. Saunders (1953), p. 73, slightly
emended. (Saunders rightly uses 'education' for *paideia*: for *trophē* he
uses 'training', which is surely a mistake. Both the context and the
usual meaning of *trophē* suggest rather 'upbringing'.)

8 *Republic*, 414 ff.

9 Cf. in the *Republic*, the fairly brusque introduction of *paideia* (376e),
immediately followed by the advocacy of censorship: the overriding
concern with 'true education' (*tō onti pepaideumenoi*, 416b: *tēs orthēs
paideias*, 416c): and the undifferentiated conjunction of *paideia*,
*paideusis*, *trophē* and other terms in 423e ff. This is sad and surprising, in
the author who first showed us the importance of viewing *technai* and
other enterprises in their own right. Hare says (1970, p. 15) that 'it
would not be much of an exaggeration to say that for him philosophy
*was* the philosophy of education.' That is, indeed, just the trouble:
philosophers tend to think either that the philosophy of education is
everything, or that it is nothing.

10 Peters (1966), p. 29.

11 Ibid., p. 45.

12 Ibid., p. 71.

13 The fact is that the ground covered by 'methods' is very uncertain.
We normally include systems of rewards and punishments as a fair
part of an answer to some such question as 'How did they teach you
Latin?', and a burned child learns to dread the fire partly by being
burned. If on the other hand we stipulate that nothing is to count as a

method of learning except the internal process of understanding, grasping, coming, to see, etc., then it is hard to see how any moral objection could conceivably arise.

14 Peters (1966), p. 31.
15 Hirst and Peters (1970), p. 25.
16 Ibid., p. 40.
17 Wilson (1977), ch. 7.
18 Hirst and Peters (1970), p. 40.
19 Ibid., p. 33.
20 Ibid., p. 11.
21 Downie *et al.* (1974), p. 11.
22 Ibid., p. 173.
23 Ibid., p. 13.
24 Ibid., pp. 13–14.
25 Ibid., p. 12.
26 Ibid., p. 42.
27 Ibid., p. 57.
28 Ibid., p. 71.
29 Ibid., p. 70.
30 Ibid., p. 70.
31 Ibid., pp. 88–9.
32 Hirst and Peters (1970), p. 29.
33 Peters (1966), p. 144.
34 Ibid., p. 15.
35 More recently, however, 'They are hesitant about saying that conceptual issues can be clearly distinguished from empirical ones: they contemplate with equanimity the possibility that there may be moral facts; some of them even welcome the return of metaphysics' (Peters, 1973, p. 2).
36 Woods (1972), p. 31.
37 See Wilson (1977, ch. 4), for a further account.
38 Or rather, as one would more naturally say, *come to appreciate*.
39 Though, of course, philosophers could issue imperatives like 'Don't think that . . .' (*sc.* because it's conceptually incoherent, or contradictory, or whatever).
40 Wilson (1975, 1977).
41 Peters (1966), ch. V.
42 Downie *et al.* (1974), pp. 48–9.
43 See Wilson (1971), pp. 206 ff.
44 I am not sure what words to use here: 'prudence', at least as a virtue word, may be thought to involve more than the ability and willingness to defer gratification. But it certainly does involve that.

**Part II Learning**

*Chapter 3 The implications of learning*

1 Hirst and Peters (1970), p. 75.
2 Kenny (1963), pp. 172 ff.

3 It might be argued that there is a separate sense of 'learn', roughly equivalent simply to 'be informed' or 'be told', and hence not tied to truth: so that we could, in this sense, say 'He learned that p' when we think that p is false. The position here is not immediately clear, and the same problem arises for some other terms in other languages. (Thus although in Latin one cannot *cognoscere* what is false, it is not clear that *certior fieri* – literally 'to become more certain', but commonly translated 'to be informed' or 'to learn' – follows the same rule.) The answer must depend on whether a man would retract the term on discovering that the information was false. In my judgment, we would so retract the word 'learn' in contemporary English.

4 Kenny (1963), p. 177.

5 Hamlyn in Peters (1973), p. 180.

6 Vesey (1967), p. 63. I am nevertheless much indebted to this article.

7 *Aeneid* XII, 435–6 (*disco*): *Iliad* VI, 444–6 (*manthano*).

8 These uses are so obviously astray that they need no detailed quotation or criticism here; see, however, Hamlyn in Peters (1973), pp. 178 ff. with references.

9 For a fuller discussion see Wilson (1971), pp. 121 ff.; Bennett (1964); and Kenny (1975), pp. 99 ff.

10 Some may prefer to say that 'learn' (and other terms in the same boat) has the same sense or meaning in both cases, but different criteria of application. But I do not think that such epistemological disputes, no doubt important in some fields, are relevant here. It is certainly entirely natural to say, and we can be content for our purposes with saying, that the word 'means something different'.

11 Downie *et al.* (1974), pp. 37 ff.

12 See Wilson (1977), ch. 6.

13 Ibid., chs. 1–4.

14 Ibid., chs. 3 and 4.

## Chapter 4 *What there is to learn*

1 Bloom (1956).

2 See Wilson (1973) for an attempt on the area of moral education.

3 *Aeneid* XI, 435.

4 This I take to be the point of eliciting conceptual truths. It is not just that anything we would *call* a person must, logically, have (say) something we would *call* emotions; it is also that, *because of* this conceptual or logical point, those existing entities which we *do* call people must in practice have those things which we *do* call emotions. (Similarly because of the logical truth that a puppy is a young dog, the child who is correctly told that he is getting an actual puppy for Christmas can know that he is getting an actual young dog, so that he knows what to expect and can take practical action on this basis.) The nature of logical or conceptual truths – what makes them true – is one thing: their practical use or value for us, if we are given some empirical facts to work with, is another.

5  Hirst in Dearden *et al.* (1972), pp. 405 ff.
6  Hirst and Peters (1970), pp. 64–5.
7  Dearden (1968), pp. 64 ff.: see also Pring and Sockett in Peters (1973).
8  Hirst (1967), p. 51.
9  Hirst (1971), p. 13.
10  Peters (1966), part II.
11  Wilson (1971), pp. 251 ff.; 1973, pp. 1 ff.
12  Hirst in Dearden *et al.* (1972), p. 406.
13  All this has of course given rise to an immense amount of
    philosophical literature. Good contemporary guides are Harré and
    Secord (1972) and Ryan (1973). (The gentlemen-prefer-blondes
    example is not just flippant: see Wilson (1971), pp. 121 ff.)
14  Or perhaps not just possible but in some sense inevitable or necessary
    for all rational creatures: that is, there may be conceptual links
    between being such a creature (language-using, living in space-time,
    etc.) and *some* knowledge in *all* the forms.
15  Dearden (1968), pp. 64–5.
16  Austin (1962), p. 72.
17  Macintyre (1964), p. 121.
18  Ibid.
19  Hirst (1974), p. 92.
20  Ibid.
21  See, e.g., what Strawson (1974, pp. 178 ff.) has to say about
    aesthetics.
22  Hirst (1974), p. 96.
23  See Hirst and Peters (1970), pp. 49–52; Dearden *et al.* (1972), pp. 466
    ff.; Wilson (1971), part 2.
24  Peters (1966), pp. 46 ff.
25  Hirst and Peters (1970), pp. 54–5.
26  Ibid., pp. 61–2.
27  Here appears the tension between two ideas about the 'forms of
    thought': (a) as the only *possible* 'modes of experience', so that *all*
    intelligent activity (chess, reading, driving a car) must (logically) fit
    into them somewhere: and (b) as different *genres* of 'the knowledge
    that we do now have'.
28  Peters in Dearden *et al.* (1972), p. 519.
29  Ibid.
30  Hirst and Peters (1970), p. 57.
31  Ibid., p. 40.

## Part III Education and human nature

*Chapter 5 Happiness and learning*

1  Peters (1966), ch. V.
2  Ibid., p. 157.
3  Ibid., p. 156.
4  Ibid., p. 157.

5 Ibid., p. 160.
6 Ibid., p. 163.
7 Ibid., p. 163: cf. *Love's Labour's Lost*, I. i. 55 ff.
8 Peters (1966), p. 161.
9 Ibid., p. 156.
10 Ibid., p. 152.
11 Ibid., p. 156.
12 Ibid.
13 Ibid., p. 157.
14 Further analysis of them will be found in Downie (1974), chs. 3 and 4.
15 Similarly with Hirst (1974, p. 42): 'To ask for the justification of any form of activity is significant only if one is in fact committed already to seeking rational knowledge. To ask for a justification of the pursuit of rational knowledge itself therefore pre-supposes some form of commitment to what one is seeking to justify.' Some form of commitment, yes: but what form, and how much?
16 Peters (1966), p. 157.
17 E.g. Bambrough (1956), Hare (1972b, pp. 4 ff.) and many others. I disagree (Wilson (1977, ch. 7)). Barrow (1975) seems along the right lines here.
18 E.g. Warnock (1971), ch. 3: Williams (1973): Smart and Williams (1973). For a good recent discussion of happiness in relation to education, see Barrow (1975), with references.
19 The remarks which follow are an emended and abbreviated version of Wilson (1968).
20 *Fortunatus* and *felix*, and (in a slightly different way) *beatus*, represent the endowments of fate or fortune which give you a better chance to be happy (*laetus*), and may give you particular moments of joy or pleasure (*gaudium*).
21 More or less pleased: hence 'happy' has a comparative and a superlative.
22 'I'm so happy when I'm with her' says the lover. He is not lying, but we see him anxious, timid, perhaps in tears. We are right and he is wrong. 'He's not happy, he only thinks he is' is not nonsense.
23 *Pace* von Wright (1971, p. 100), to whose discussion I am nevertheless much indebted.
24 Hare (1963, pp. 126–9) points out (rightly) that I need not call happy a man who 'gets what he likes and does not dislike anything that he gets', but ascribes this (wrongly) to the possibility that the man 'has desires, likes, and dislikes which I very much dislike the thought of myself having' (p. 128). (He distinguishes this (p. 127) from the case where I lack the imagination to put myself in the man's shoes. In the latter case I can't imagine it; but in the former I can't stomach it.) Hare wants to deny that we can 'content ourselves with merely recording how he appraises his life from his point of view.' Certainly this must be denied, but only because we are not infallible judges of our mental states. The basic point is that many cases of happiness or unhappiness are not obviously connected with wants, desires, likes,

dislikes, etc., at all. (Kenny (1973, pp. 60–1) flirts with the same idea: 'we might be reluctant to call a man happy whose only concern was to procure heroin, even if he was in a position to obtain regular and safe supplies.')

25 Macintyre (1967), p. 236.

26 C. Taylor (1973) puts the relevant points here very clearly. See also Quinton (1973), pp. 366–74.

27 See particularly Hampshire (1972) and Williams in Smart and Williams (1973).

28 Williams (1973, pp. 89 ff.) quotes outlooks like those of Luther and D. H. Lawrence as concerned with things like 'penitent suffering' and 'authenticity' rather than happiness. But insofar as these are to be seen as rational or recommendable outlooks (rather than verbalized desires or fantasies), it is difficult not to make some connection: e.g. one might say that a man who did not see and shudder at the horrors of sin, or did not find and prove his 'deepest impulse', was only half-awake – that 'he' might be happy, but that there was not enough of 'him' to be happy enough.

But the important point is that we need much more interpretation of what such moralists really mean. Certainly we have available, in superabundance, what they *say* (and what they do); but without much more detailed investigation we cannot assume either (a) that they offer us anything that could seriously be described as a set of *beliefs*, or (b) that we know what these beliefs actually are. One does not have to be a professional psychiatrist to appreciate that expressions of belief cannot always be taken at face value.

29 Hampshire (1972), pp. 31–2.

30 Cf. Williams (1973), pp. 116–17.

31 Kenny (1973), p. 61. This is a very common idea: cf. Downie *et al.* (1974, p. 78) 'he may find a lively discussion in the office merely irritating, because so many questions are begged and terms undefined; or he may find the office reproductions of popular art tasteless and sentimental.'

32 One difficulty, for people in our culture, is to put these points with suitable neutrality. Thus one might say that you have to 'take fishing/marriage seriously', 'make a job of it', 'work at it', and so on. Then we are accused (often justly) of thinking that the only way of taking things seriously, the only way of attending to them, of being in touch with the realities, is the 'protestant-ethic' way. It is to be like toil, not like play. We need perhaps some revisions or at least clarifications of language in order to describe neutrally. See Passmore (1970), ch. 15.

33 White elephants aren't whiter than white mice. Are they stronger? Yes, if 'stronger' is used absolutely: no, if we imply 'for their size' or some similar *pro tanto* clause. 'Happy' is or can be like the absolute use of 'strong', not like 'white'.

34 This is why we should have doubts about calling a man 'happy' who was constantly given sensations of pleasure from electrodes wired to

his brain; a point missed by Smart in Smart and Williams (1973, pp. 18 ff.). Of course if the electrodes were subtle enough to give him enjoyment of just those 'objects of attention' which, say, a Beethoven symphony gives us, all would be well; but we already have Beethoven symphonies, and ears, for this purpose.

35 Aristotle (1953), 1099a. What Aristotle meant by *eudaimon* and *eudaimonia*, normally translated 'happy' and 'happiness', is much discussed: see Kenny (1973), with references. I do not myself think that this translation is right, either for Aristotle or for classical Greek in general. *Eudaimon* means literally 'having the right sort of daimon (fate, fortune, presiding genius)': it is like the Latin *felix*, *fortunatus*, or *beatus* in referring to a man's position in the world, not to his state of mind: see above, pp. 143 ff. There is, I think, no commonly used noun or adjective in classical Greek which corresponds to our 'happiness' and 'happy': normally some part of the verb *hedesthai* (to be pleased) is used. This may relate to some of the difficulties in Aristotle; but it does not affect the present argument.

36 Aristotle (1953), 1177a.

37 Ibid.

38 Aristotle (1953), 1178b.

39 Peters (1966), p. 153.

40 Aristotle (1953), 1178.

41 Peters himself sees this very clearly: see, e.g., Peters (1966), pp. 151 ff., and Peters (1973), pp. 262 ff.

42 This is rather severe if applied to, for instance, A. E. Housman's introductory lecture (1933), which contains a variety of embryonic arguments presented with great force, if not worked out in great detail, and many sound intuitions. But it amounts in the end to the (highly persuasive) advocacy of a particular 'self-justifying' ideal, which will appeal mainly to those who (like Housman) fail to find much happiness elsewhere: in his own words, it is 'too much the language of a salesman crying his own wares.'

## Chapter 6 Seriousness and fantasy

1 Peters (1966), p. 116.

2 Ibid., p. 125.

3 Hare (1963), p. 224. In this connection it is interesting to compare Hare's own account (1972b, pp. 32 ff.) of how he clarified the mind of an 18-year-old Swiss boy who, having read Camus and others, thought that 'nothing matters'. (Even 'thought' may already misdescribe the situation, but Hare goes further and says: 'It was this proposition of the truth of which our friend had become convinced.') If the boy recovered his senses and 'ate a hearty breakfast the next day' (p. 47), this is likely to be more because of the benevolent and clear-headed attention that went with the philosophy – even perhaps some background of trust and esteem already established – than because of the philosophy itself.

4 At least, so I myself think. But when to take things seriously as rational offerings, and when to take them seriously as merely 'brute' psychological or other phenomena, seems to be one of the most important questions in education: indeed, in all one's dealings with other people. When ought one to answer as to another rational being, and when does one say such things as 'Look, dear, aren't you really just worried about so-and-so?' – or perhaps you just smile, or put an arm round the person, or change the subject? The latter move may seem patronizing and arrogant; but the former is often irrelevant and a waste of time. Of course there's no determinate answer to such a question; but it's useful to be clearly aware of the alternatives. (Perhaps sometimes one should just say or do *nothing*.)

5 For an outline sketch of this practical task ('teaching discussion'), see Wilson (1972b), part 2. But a great deal more remains to be done: what is striking – in view of the importance commonly attached to 'discussion' by educators, one might say shocking – is that so little has been done already. Peters (1966, p. 165) very well says 'it is rare to find people who really listen to what other people say' – an apparently simple competence to transmit to our pupils, but there is little or no adequate research on how to do it.

6 Wilson (1972a), pp. 59 ff.

7 Wittgenstein (1956), pp. 6 ff.

8 See Wilson (1971), ch. 9; Kenny (1975), pp. 99 ff.

9 Peters (1966), p. 146.

10 Ibid., p. 153.

11 Wilson (1971), pp. 121 ff.

12 Peters well says (1966, p. 233) of the 'insights' of 'thinkers such as Piaget, Freud, Marx, and Sartre' that 'they might incorporate important truths expressed in too concrete and particularised a form.' But I am not sure that he has necessary truths in mind: immediately afterwards he says that 'Freud's notorious Oedipus complex might incorporate an important *generalization*', and that 'his *theory* of unconscious sexual wishes might be subsumed under a wider *theory* of passivity' (my italics), which suggests some sort of empirical operation. The point is that 'thinkers' of this kind often show us important conceptual or *necessary* truths, even when they aren't professional philosophers.

13 See ibid., ch. VI.

14 *Republic* 618 (Jowett's translation).

15 See Wilson in Dearden *et al.* (1972), pp. 85 ff.

16 Those of the Pythagoreans might be a fair example.

17 See particularly Hare (1970), pp. 18 ff.

18 Murdoch (1970).

19 Much of these I would wish only to echo – perhaps particularly the importance of the concept of attention (her example of M. and D., ibid., pp. 17 ff. and elsewhere): the common elements in the rejection of fantasy in art and the *technai*, as well as in morality (ibid., pp. 59, 65 and elsewhere): the notion of 'knowledge of the good' borrowed

from Plato (*passim*). Some of what she says reads like a rather more high-minded, discursive and exciting version of Peters' notion of 'being serious' or 'initiated'. See also Peters' reference to 'knowledge of the good' in Dearden *et al*. (1972), p. 17.

20 Murdoch (1970), p. 64.
21 Ibid., p. 54.
22 Ibid., p. 67.
23 Ibid., p. 26.
24 Peters follows the psychologists in making a good deal of this distinction, wobbly though it is in more than one way: see Peters (1966), pp. 61–2, and cf. Wilson (1972a), pp. 94 ff.
25 See Mary Warnock in Peters (1973), pp. 112 ff.; cf. Wilson (1977), chs. 6 and 7.

## Chapter 7 Love and morality

1 Passmore (1970), ch. 14.
2 Ibid., chs. 14 and 15: the best philosophical account of love that I know of, though the author does not present his points as matters of conceptual necessity.
3 Cf. Hamlyn in Peters (1973), pp. 183 ff. and Hamlyn (1978).
4 Cf. Downie *et al*. (1974), pp. 158 ff.
5 Aristotle (1953), 1169b ff.
6 These notions emerge very clearly in many religions: e.g. Christ as mediating and interceding; ourselves as 'fallen' and in need of 'salvation', 'grace', 'deliverance from the law', and so forth. We need to retain these ideas without any projective fantasy that may attach to them.
7 Particularly in the *Symposium*.
8 Downie *et al*. (1974), p. 160.
9 Ibid., pp. 158 ff.
10 Hirst and Peters (1970), p. 99.
11 Ibid., p. 103.
12 Ibid., p. 104.
13 Wilson (1971), p. 241; (1972b).
14 In Dearden *et al*. (1972), p. 518.
15 See references in Wilson (1972b).
16 Wilson (1977), ch. 6.
17 I touch here on a central problem in moral philosophy, still much discussed: but cannot enlarge on it. In general I follow Hare particularly in Lewis (1976); cf. Wilson (1971), pp. 217 ff.; see also Richards (1971). For opposing views see Williams (1973), Williams in Lewis (1976), and Quinton (1973); also Foot (1972). Cf. Warnock (1971), pp. 162 ff.
18 Wilson (1971), pp. 251 ff., with references.
19 Warnock (1971), pp. 152 ff.
20 P. 138, with references.
21 Wilson (1971; 1973).

22 Wilson (1972b), with references.

23 Mary Warnock (1975a). Cf. for further discussion M. Taylor (1975, pp. 103–22).

24 Certain fears and misconceptions seem remarkably persistent, particularly (a) that we may be dispensing only the views of 'one powerful school of moral philosophy', 'a kind of rational utilitarianism'; (b) that we may fail to give 'moral commitment' (as against moral reasoning) the importance which it obviously has; (c) that we may fail to use the force of the moral example set by teachers and others; (d) that putting *any* features of moral education into timetabled periods may involve us in (a)–(c) above. These are all found in Warnock (1977, pp. 131 ff.). I attempted to clear up the muddles in Wilson (1972b, part 4; 1973).

25 Hare (1970), p. 30.

26 As I have tried to show elsewhere (Wilson, 1977, ch. 7), it follows from the fact that morality is within the scope of reason that some people must be better at it (or at different aspects of it) than others. There are, in principle (and often to be identified in practice) *savants*, 'experts', 'authorities' or whatever we may want to call those who possess more and better moral equipment than the rest of us. This, to my mind rather obvious, conclusion is often passionately resisted. Mary Warnock (1977, pp. 169–70) says:

> People who are amateurs but who are capable, as everyone is, of forming value judgements, are perfectly entitled . . . to demand that education shall go the way they want . . . it is not necessary that only one person, or one kind of person should (ultimately) wield the power.

But (a) of course everyone is capable of *making* value judgments: yet some people are worse at it than others (morons, Nazis, psychopaths and others are just extreme examples): (b) it might be right to entitle people with equal power in educational and moral matters, but it might also be sensible for many people, so entitled, to delegate much of that power to those who can wield it more reasonably.

27 Cf. Williams in Smart and Williams (1973), pp. 108 ff.; Lewis (1976), pp. 306 ff.; Williams (1973).

# Bibliography

ARISTOTLE (1953), *Nicomachean Ethics*, translated by J. K. Thomson, Penguin, Harmondsworth.

AUSTIN, J. L. (1962), *How to Do Things with Words*, Oxford University Press, London.

BAMBROUGH, J. R. (1956), 'Plato's Political Analogies', in Laslett, P. (ed.), *Philosophy, Politics and Society*, Blackwell, Oxford.

BARROW, R. (1975), *Plato, Utilitarianism and Education*, Routledge & Kegan Paul, London.

BENNETT, J. (1964), *Rationality*, Routledge & Kegan Paul, London.

BLOOM, B. S. (1956), *Taxonomy of Educational Objectives*, Longman, London.

COLLIER, G. (ed.) (1974), *Values and Moral Development in Higher Education*, Croom Helm, London.

DEARDEN, R. F. (1968), *The Philosophy of Primary Education*, Routledge & Kegan Paul, London.

DEARDEN, R. F., HIRST, P. H. and PETERS, R. S. (eds) (1972), *Education and the Development of Reason*, Routledge & Kegan Paul, London.

DOWNIE, R. S. *et al.* (1974), *Education and Personal Relationships*, Methuen, London.

FOOT, P. (1972), 'Reasons for Action and Desires', Proceedings of the Aristotelian Society, Supp. vol. XLVI.

HAMLYN, D. W. (1978), *Experience and the Growth of Understanding*, Routledge & Kegan Paul, London.

HAMPSHIRE, S. (1972), *Morality and Pessimism*, Cambridge University Press, London.

HARE, R. M. (1963), *Freedom and Reason*, Oxford University Press, London.

HARE, R. M. (1970), General Introduction to *The Dialogues of Plato*, Sphere, London.

HARE, R. M. (1972a), *Essays on the Moral Concepts*, Macmillan, London.

HARE, R. M. (1972b), *Applications of Moral Philosophy*, Macmillan, London.

HARRÉ, R. and SECORD, P. (1972), *The Explanation of Social Behaviour*, Blackwell, Oxford.

HARTNETT, A. and NAISH, M. (1976), *Theory and the Practice of Education*, Heinemann, London.

HIRST, P. H. (1967), 'Logical and Psychological Aspects of Teaching', in R. S. Peters (ed.), *The Concept of Education*, Routledge & Kegan Paul, London.

HIRST, P. H. (1971), 'Literature, Criticism and the Forms of Knowledge', in

*Educational Philosophy and Theory*, vol. 3, no. 1, Routledge & Kegan Paul, London.

HIRST, P. H. (1974), *Knowledge and the Curriculum*, Routledge & Kegan Paul, London.

HIRST, P. H. and PETERS, R. S. (1970), *The Logic of Education*, Routledge & Kegan Paul, London.

KENNY, A. (1963), *Action, Emotion and Will*, Routledge & Kegan Paul, London.

KENNY, A. (1973), *Anatomy of the Soul*, Blackwell, Oxford.

KENNY, A. (1975), *Will, Freedom and Power*, Blackwell, Oxford.

LEWIS, H. D. (ed.) (1976), *Contemporary British Philosophy*, Allen & Unwin, London.

LUCAS, C. J. (1969), *What is Philosophy of Education?*, Collier–Macmillan, London.

MACINTYRE, A. (1964), 'Is Understanding Religion Compatible with Believing?', in J. Hick (ed.), *Faith and the Philosophers*, Macmillan, London.

MACINTYRE, A. (1967), *A Short History of Ethics*, Routledge & Kegan Paul, London.

MURDOCH, I. (1970), *The Sovereignty of Good*, Routledge & Kegan Paul, London.

NYBERG, D. (ed.) (1975), *The Philosophy of Open Education*, Routledge & Kegan Paul, London.

O'CONNOR, D. J. (1968), *An Introduction to the Philosophy of Education*, Routledge & Kegan Paul, London.

PASSMORE, J. (1970), *The Perfectability of Man*, Duckworth, London.

PETERS, R. S. (1966), *Ethics and Education*, Allen & Unwin, London.

PETERS, R. S. (ed.) (1967), *The Concept of Education*, Routledge & Kegan Paul, London.

PETERS, R. S. (ed.) (1973), *The Philosophy of Education*, Oxford University Press, London.

PLATO (1953), *Laws*, translated by T. J. Saunders, Penguin, Harmondsworth.

QUINTON, A. (1973), *The Nature of Things*, Routledge & Kegan Paul, London.

RICHARDS, D. A. J. (1971), *A Theory of Reasons for Action*, Cambridge University Press.

RYAN, A. (ed.) (1973), *The Philosophy of Social Explanation*, Oxford University Press, London.

SMART, J. J. C. and WILLIAMS, B. (1973), *Utilitarianism, For and Against*, Oxford University Press, London.

STRAWSON, P. F. (1974), *Freedom and Resentment and Other Essays*, Methuen, London.

TAYLOR, C. (1973), 'Neutrality in Political Science', in A. Ryan (ed.), *The Philosophy of Social Explanation*, Oxford University Press, London.

TAYLOR, M. (ed.) (1975), *Progress and Problems in Moral Education*, NFER, Slough.

VESEY, G. (1967), 'Conditioning and Learning', in R. S. Peters (ed.), *The Concept of Education*, Routledge & Kegan Paul, London.

VON WRIGHT, G. H. (1971), *Explanation and Understanding*, Routledge & Kegan Paul, London.

## Bibliography

WARNOCK, G. J. (1971), *The Object of Morality*, Methuen, London.

WARNOCK, M. (1975a), Review of *The Philosophy of Open Education* (edited by D. Nyberg, Routledge & Kegan Paul, 1975) in *Times Educational Supplement*, 28 November.

WARNOCK, M. (1975b), Review of *Values and Moral Development in Higher Education* (edited by G. Collier, Croom Helm, London, 1974) in *Times Literary Supplement*, 18 April.

WARNOCK, M. (1977), *Schools of Thought*, Faber, London.

WILLIAMS, B. (1973), *Morality*, Penguin, Harmondsworth.

WILSON, J. (1968), 'Happiness', *Analysis*, vol. 29, no. 1, October.

WILSON, J. (1971), *Education in Religion and the Emotions*, Heinemann, London.

WILSON, J. (1972a), *Philosophy and Educational Research*, NFER, Slough.

WILSON, J. (1972b), *Practical Methods of Moral Education*, Heinemann, London.

WILSON, J. (1973), *The Assessment of Morality*, NFER, Slough.

WILSON, J. (1975), *Educational Theory and the Preparation of Teachers*, NFER, Slough.

WILSON, J. (1977), *Philosophy and Practical Education*, Routledge & Kegan Paul, London.

WINCH, P. (1972), *Ethics and Action*, Routledge & Kegan Paul, London.

WITTGENSTEIN, L. (1956), *Lectures and Conversations*, Blackwell, Oxford.

WOODS, R. G. (1972), *Education and its Disciplines*, University of London Press.

# Index